From Christendom
to Americanism and Beyond

The Long, Jagged Trail to a Postmodern Void

Thomas Storck

From Christendom to Americanism and Beyond

The Long, Jagged Trail to a Postmodern Void

⊕

Foreword by
Joseph Pearce

 Angelico Press

First published
by Angelico Press, 2015

For information, address:
Angelico Press
4709 Briar Knoll Dr.
Kettering, OH 45429
angelicopress.com

978-1-62138-144-0

Cover design: Michael Schrauzer

CONTENTS

Foreword

by
Joseph Pearce

THOMAS STORCK is a well-connected man. Indeed, there are very few men who are *better* connected. I do not mean that he is well connected in the sense in which the world normally thinks of being connected. He does not have legions of powerful friends walking and stalking the corridors of power who can make things happen for him. On the contrary, he has so few friends in such places that this timely and important book will certainly not make *The New York Times* Bestseller List, nor is it likely that the wisdom it contains will enlighten the darkened minds of that highly prejudiced journal.

Mr. Storck is well connected in a much better and more important sense. He knows and makes the connections between those branches of knowledge that have been severed from each other by the modern world's radical disconnectedness with the wholeness of things. He makes these connections and connects himself and his understanding of things to this wholeness. Finally, as this volume and Mr. Storck's other writings testify, he connects us to this wholeness, helping us to become the well-connected people that we need to be.

First and foremost, he connects the lesser sciences of philosophy, history, politics, and economics to the queen of sciences, theology. He knows that to separate *theos* from *logos*, God from meaning, is the beginning of the dis-integration of knowledge into disconnected and atomized "disciplines," each of which is effectively excommunicated from the others.

In philosophy, the humanism of the Renaissance, divorcing itself from the scholasticism that connected Man with his Creator, has led inexorably to the anthropocentrism that is the blight of our self-centered culture. In politics, such humanism has led to the cynical *realpolitik* of Machiavelli and the justification of Machiavellian self-interest over Christian concepts of social and political justice.

The separation of *theos* and *logos* has also led to the divorce of physics from metaphysics, separating what was once known as natural philoso-

1

phy from all other aspects of the love of wisdom, thereby ensuring the decay of science into scientism.

Mr. Storck connects these radical problems, rooted in the story of man's divorce from God, to the historical developments that led to the economic, social, political, and cultural problems facing our world today. In doing so, he reminds us of others who have endeavored to do likewise. We think perhaps of the works of Christopher Dawson or R.H. Tawney, or of Chesterton's *The Everlasting Man*, written as a charitable response and riposte to H.G. Wells's superciliously "progressive" *Outline of History*, or of Hilaire Belloc's own response to Wells, less charitable but nonetheless effective, in his *Companion to Mr Wells's 'Outline of History'*. Apart from his war of words with Wells, Belloc also wrote panoramic studies of history, such as *The Servile State, Survivals and New Arrivals*, and *The Great Heresies*, each of which illustrated that ideas have consequences and, more specifically, that bad ideas have bad consequences.

Like his illustrious forebears, Mr. Storck illustrates that one's philosophical presuppositions will invariably and inevitably color one's understanding of the "outline of history." He understands the beliefs of the past and why people acted as they did; he sees *why* things happened, as well as *when* and *how* they happened. Such a vision of the past contrasts starkly with the "progressive" view of history now in the ascendant, which regards the beliefs of the past as primitive and superstitious and therefore unworthy of serious consideration. This chronological snobbery blinds the secular historian to the ideas that motivated the actions of the past, thereby preventing modernity's understanding of history from rising above the *when* and *how*. In stark and much-needed contrast, Mr. Storck shows that the *when* and *how* are determined by the *why*.

Once again, Mr. Storck emerges as a worthy heir of Hilaire Belloc. "In history we must abandon the defensive," Belloc had written in 1924, "...We must make our opponents understand not only that they are wrong in their philosophy, nor only ill-informed in their judgement of cause and effect, but out of touch with the past: which is ours."[1]

Like Belloc, Chesterton, and Dawson, Mr. Storck insists that the history of Western civilization can only be comprehended if we see it as *Christendom*—as the cultural and political manifestation of the fruits of the Faith, and for this reason he shows that the history of modernity

---

1. Hilaire Belloc, Preface to Dom Hugh G. Bevenot, OSB, *Pagan and Christian Rule* (London: Longmans, Green & Co, 1924), ix.

can only be comprehended if we see it as an anthropocentric rebellion against Christendom and the Christocentrism that informed it.

As in *Survivals and New Arrivals* and *The Great Heresies*, in which Belloc maps the war of ideas that forged the history of the modern world, Mr. Storck illustrates in the present volume how the historian can emerge as a prophet, not only teaching us about the past but also warning us of the abyss we shall face if the ill-fated path we have been following is not abandoned. Like Belloc, Thomas Storck is not merely an historian but also a prophet. He must be heard and heeded.

Introduction

THIS BOOK is not a history of the last few centuries. Neither is it a history of the Church nor an intellectual history of Europe or the United States. Rather its aim is to be a guide to understanding that history, to understanding the last several hundred years, particularly the way ideas about the social order have changed and the immense implications of those changed ideas for modern thinking about politics, about economics, about art, and in fact, about nearly every other aspect of human life—and, by implication, about what might be the proper response of Catholics to these changes.

It might seem that when we look at the history of any particular time or place, the task is simply to note down what happened and then to try to make sense of it. But even what we should note down will often not be obvious if we do not already have some framework for interpretation. The past abounds in facts, but which are important and why? Should we view the nineteenth century as a record of increasing freedom or of increasing dechristianization? as the triumph of the Industrial Revolution or the destruction of traditional ways of life? Depending on which historical process we think primary or important, we shall probably highlight certain events and ignore others. And which we think primary and important will depend on our own first principles. A non-Christian historian who sees any form of Christian faith as an unfortunate survival of mythological thinking will probably pay attention to the diminishing place of Christianity in the public life of Europe, chiefly in the context of the triumphs of natural science and of philosophies that set themselves against all religious belief. A Catholic, on the other hand, even when looking at the same facts or events, will not only understand them differently, but will also have a different organizing principle for recounting and evaluating them. This book is intended to help the reader place the events of the past several centuries into a Catholic context, to understand them relative to the Church's unique place in human history, which is ultimately founded on the unique place of the Incarnation in history—the actual coming of God upon earth for the salvation of mankind and the Church's subsequent mission to evangelize all of human life, to shape cultures, not merely to provide religious solace and foster private piety and morality.

Until recently in the West we divided the past into B.C. and A.D. Now, of course, the fashion is to use the terms B.C.E. and C.E., and for a non-Christian this is entirely understandable. But Catholics, one presumes, will continue to recognize that the earlier terms expressed the truth that Our Lord's Incarnation really was the turning point of human history, indeed of the entire cosmos. Too often, though, Catholics have implicitly accepted an historical narrative that belies this supposed recognition of the centrality of the Incarnation. To see, for example, the last few centuries primarily as a succession of triumphs in the cause of human freedom or as a record of technological betterment and the conquest of nature, or to regard the regime established by the American Revolution as the New Order of the Ages and a departure from all past history, is to look at history not in the light of the Incarnation and its effects, but according to some other organizing principle. If we think of history as the march of freedom or of material progress, then it matters little if we continue to use B.C. and A.D., for in effect we have abandoned the Incarnation as the real turning point for humanity.

Thus, for a committed Catholic, it is necessary in the first place to grasp the significance of what is meant by *Christendom*. Christendom was not merely a social order in which there were many Catholics: it was a social order in which there was an attempt to bring everything, public and private, into subjection to Christ the King. Religion existed not simply as one department of life permitting, for example, the economy to go its own way in pursuit of its own aims. Everything—political, economic, artistic—was to be subject to the Kingship of Our Lord. Only if that fact is grasped is there hope of correctly perceiving what happened when that principle of social unity was rejected, and thus of understanding the modern world, which is the offspring of that rejection of Christendom.

Any student of history can point to a number of notable changes that occurred over the centuries from about 1500 to about 1970. But which changes were most noteworthy and, more to the point, which were the more fundamental ones that led to the others? As I suggested above, most moderns will regard the political, economic, and especially the technological changes as most worthy of note. But these changes were in fact derivative. The fundamental changes were in the first place religious and secondly ideological. The rise of liberalism is the salient fact here. Liberalism brought about the privatization of religion in the Western world and led to the dissolution of a cultural order that was organized as a hierarchy, that is, the Church and her teachings (or some substitute in Protestant countries) as the apex, with everything subordinated and arranged under that cultural sovereignty. Liberalism in this context does not of course mean quite the same thing it generally denotes in the

United States. Thus, one of the essays here is devoted to explaining what is meant by that word. A crucial figure in giving an intellectual justification for this liberalism was John Locke, whose teachings have been of immense importance in the United States. The working out of Locke's theories in other areas, such as the arts, led to even more cultural disunity, although the connection of Locke's political and social ideas with the arts is not usually well understood.

Catholics, as might be expected, were not unaware of these changes while they were occurring. Although the French Revolution hindered and delayed an effective response on the part of the Church, in the nineteenth century Catholics set forth in answer to what was happening a restatement of the Church's position, based in large part on a revival of the philosophy and theology of St. Thomas Aquinas. This produced a brilliant era in the history of the Church, but unfortunately one that was cut short in the 1960s by missteps on the part of many within the Church herself.

As an American, I have long been fascinated by the peculiar ideological and cultural trajectory of my country. Thus, the special situation of the United States is given considerable attention here, particularly its understanding of itself and how that has affected Catholics. Some more recent chapters in American history are also considered, including the best example hitherto of a reasonably effective vehicle for Catholic involvement in American politics.

Finally, I offer an attempt to look at history in light of what we know from Divine Revelation about the course of man's life on this earth. Here one must be cautious, for it is easy to go beyond what is really known; and everything said must be seen as tentative. But because the intellectual atmosphere we live in has no conception of history as a sacred process from Creation to the Last Judgment, it does not seem without value to specifically remind ourselves of what we do know about this process.

Most of the essays in this book were previously published, but all have been revised to a greater or lesser extent. For the most part, I have kept their original historical context, even when subsequent events have introduced new ideas or controversies. I should note that several of the essays overlap to the degree that they consider the same sets of historical facts, although from different angles. This overlapping should in fact be helpful to a greater understanding of these complex historical events and trends.

Finally, my thanks go to Mr. Joseph Pearce for his generosity in writing the Foreword and to Mr. John Riess of Angelico Press for his helpfulness and the ease of working with him.

THOMAS STORCK

Sources

Chap. 1: Thomas Storck, "Christendom: God's Beachhead in a Rebellious World." *Homiletic & Pastoral Review* 102, no. 9 (2002): 31–47.

Chap. 2: "Religion in Christendom." Published here for the first time.

Chap. 3: Thomas Storck, "Liberalism's Three Assaults." *Homiletic & Pastoral Review* 100, no. 4 (2000): 8–16.

Chap. 4: Thomas Storck, "Europe, Christendom and the Faith." *Ethika Politika* (2014).

Chap. 5: Thomas Storck, "Reason, Traditionalism and the Enlightenment." *Ethika Politika* (2012).

Chap. 6: Thomas Storck, "The Social Order as Community." *Caelum et Terra* 6, no. 3 (1996): 15–22.

Chap. 7: Thomas Storck, "The Dissolutions of Modernity and the Response of Thomism." *Doctor Angelicus, Annuarium Thomisticum Internationale* 4 (2004): 191–206.

Chap. 8: Thomas Storck, "Seeking Beauty in Art: Some Implications of a Thomistic Statement About Glass Saws." *New Blackfriars* 92, no. 1040 (2011):431–442.

Chap. 9: Thomas Storck, Review of *The Making and Unmaking of the English Catholic Intellectual Community, 1910–1950*, by James R. Lothian. *The Chesterton Review* 36, no. 1/2 (2010): 149–159.

Chap. 10: Thomas Storck, "The World, Modernity and the Church." *Ethika Politika* (2014).

Chap. 11: Thomas Storck, "A Proposal for Europe." *TCR News and Reports* (2006).

Chap. 12: Thomas Storck, "Christendom or the West." *TCR News and Reports* (2006).

Chap. 13: Thomas Storck, "Postmodernism: Catastrophe or Opportunity—or Both?" *Homiletic & Pastoral Review* 101, no. 4 (2001): 9–19.

Chap. 14: "The Catholic Vocations of the Americas." Published here for the first time.

Chap. 15: Thomas Storck, "Government, Society and the Common Good." Anamnesisjournal.com (2012). Used with the permission of the Anamnesis Foundation.

Chap. 16: Thomas Storck, "John Locke, Liberal Totalitarianism, and the Trivialization of Religion." *Faith & Reason* 26, no. 3 (2001): 227–248.

Chap. 17: Thomas Storck, "The Catholic Failure to Change America." *Ethika Politika* (2014).

Chap. 18: Thomas Storck, "The End of the New Deal Coalition and the Transformation of American Politics." *Ethika Politika* (2012).

Chap. 19: Thomas Storck, "Change and Return." *Caelum et Terra* 1, no. 1 (1991): 7–8.

Chap. 20: Thomas Storck, "A Biblical Theology of History." *Homiletic & Pastoral Review* 107, no. 1 (2006): 16–22.

Chap. 21: Thomas Storck, "The Apostasy of the Gentiles." *Homiletic & Pastoral Review* 105, no. 10 (2005): 53–61.

1

What Was Christendom?

IT IS VERY EASY for a Catholic to come near to despair as he regards the shape of twenty-first-century life. Everywhere the laws of God are ignored, disdained, and ridiculed while sin and wrongdoing are not only practiced but also justified, encouraged, recommended, and praised. The institutions that form and define our culture—in religion, government, education, the fine arts—are for the most part in definite opposition to much of the moral law and to the Catholic view of life. Meanwhile, the voice of the Catholic Church, the true oracle of God, is confused and muted because of the raging dissent, indifference, and turmoil within her ranks. Of course, sin has always been pervasive on earth; if it had not been for sin we should have had no need of a Redeemer. But what is especially troubling about this pervasiveness now is not that men sin, but that sin is publicly accepted and justified and virtue derided. It is the *public* and *official* acceptance, and even promotion, of sin by institutions, by our culture as a whole, and at the same time the rejection of a Catholic way of life, that is especially disturbing. In this essay, however, I will argue that even this should not surprise us over much if we reflect on certain facts about our world.

In C.S. Lewis's novel, *Out of the Silent Planet*, Professor Ransom is carried to Mars and there converses with that planet's angelic ruler. The angel tells Ransom that Earth is the "silent planet," long subjected to the rule of its evil chief angel, and that there is no communion between Earth and the rest of the cosmos, which is inhabited by unfallen beings and good angels. All this is simply an imaginative retelling of the truth that Our Lord told us, that Satan is the prince or ruler of this world.[1] In other words, since this world has been given over to the powers of darkness, we should not expect peace and goodness, for "here we have no lasting city, but we seek the city which is to come" (Hebrews 13:14). And

---

1. Satan is called the ruler of this world several times in St. John's Gospel, 12:31, 14:30, and 16:11. St. Paul refers to Satan as the "god of this world" (2 Corinthians 4:4) and as the

especially and in particular, here on this earth *Christendom* will never be stable and lasting.

Christendom is sometimes used to mean those countries in which most of the population is Christian or at least has Christian traditions or is used roughly to describe the totality of Christians existing throughout the world. But it really means something much more important than this. Christendom is nothing else but the attempt to make real, even in this fallen world, the social reign of Jesus Christ the King; to subject every part and aspect of human life to His authority; to shape public life and, as far as may be done, private life so as to reflect His reign. Pope Leo XIII briefly described such a situation in the following words:

> There was once a time when States were governed by the philosophy of the Gospel. Then it was that the power and divine virtue of Christian wisdom had diffused itself throughout the laws, institutions, and morals of the people; permeating all ranks and relations of civil society. Then, too, the religion instituted by Jesus Christ, established firmly in befitting dignity, flourished everywhere, by the favor of princes and the legitimate protection of magistrates; and Church and State were happily united in concord and friendly interchange of good offices. The State, constituted in this wise, bore fruits important beyond all expectation, whose remembrance is still, and always will be, in renown, witnessed to as they are by countless proofs which can never be blotted out or even obscured by any craft of any enemies. (Encyclical *Immortale Dei*, no. 21)

In other words, a truly Christian state of affairs would involve a political and cultural order subordinate to the reign of Jesus Christ. It would not simply be such obvious offenses against the law of God as abortion or divorce that would be prohibited, but aspects of social life that are often overlooked by many modern Catholics, such as the economic order, would be regulated for the glory of God and the welfare of mankind. As Pope Pius XI put it:

> It is therefore very necessary that economic affairs be once more subjected to and governed by a true and effective guiding principle.... To that end all the institutions of public and social life must be imbued with the spirit of justice, and this justice must above all be truly operative. It must build up a juridical and social order able to pervade all economic activity. (Encyclical *Quadragesimo Anno*, no. 88)

"prince of the power of the air" (Ephesians 2:2). Cf. also Satan's words, who, after showing Our Lord "all the kingdoms of the world ... said to him, 'To you I will give all this authority and their glory; for it has been delivered to me, and I give it to whom I will.'" Luke 4:5–6 and Matthew 3:8–9.

In other words, when Christendom flourished, the political order, the economic order, artistic activity, the legal system, all of these in their own particular and proper ways, were conceived of as subordinate to Almighty God. Indeed, the entire life of man was to be lived within an order that extended from the inanimate world through plants and irrational animals to man, the highest and rational animal, through the various orders of angels to the Holy Trinity. But it was not merely man as an individual who was part of this order, but the human community. The state *as such* owed allegiance to Jesus Christ and to His representative on earth, the Sovereign Pontiff. This beautiful order was expressed theologically by St. Thomas, especially in his *Summa Theologiae*, and by Dante in his *Divine Comedy*, as well as in a host of other writers, theologians, philosophers, and poets. Even in a document written after the Middle Ages had begun to decline, the Prologue to Chaucer's *Canterbury Tales*, one can see the entire array of society, the activity of each man and woman, meant to serve God and the common good in its unique way.

This Christian civilization had been gradually built up over many centuries, from the beginning of the Christianization of the Roman Empire under Constantine until the High Middle Ages. But at the moment when it seemed the Church had finally succeeded in establishing a social order somewhat in keeping with the teachings of Jesus Christ, it began to unravel. As Christopher Dawson wrote:

> The fourteenth century was an age of division and strife, the age of the Great Schism, which saw instead of the Crusades the invasion of Europe by the Turks and the devastation of France by England. And at the same time the intellectual resources of Western society which had been so much strengthened by the extension of the university movement no longer assisted the integration of Christian thought but were used negatively and critically to undo the work of the previous century and undermine the intellectual foundations on which the synthesis of the great thinkers of the previous age had been built. It is as though the spiritual tide which had been steadily making for unity for three centuries had suddenly turned, so that everywhere in every aspect of life the forces that made for division and dissolution were predominant.[2]

Another historian spoke of it in this way:

> The influence of the Church had never seemed greater than in the third quarter of the thirteenth century, and some modern historians have claimed that the pontificate of Gregory X (1271–1276) marked the peak of papal power.

2. Christopher Dawson, *Religion and the Rise of Western Culture* (New York: Sheed & Ward, 1950), 238–39.

Yet the young men who witnessed the execution of Conradin, who studied under Thomas Aquinas, who accompanied St. Louis on his last crusade, were hardly more than middle-aged when the medieval papacy received a blow from which it never fully recovered. In an open conflict between the head of the Church and the kings of France and England, the secular rulers carried off the victory. As a result of this victory the popes deserted Rome and established themselves on the borders of the kingdom of France. The prestige of the papacy was tarnished and the leadership of the Church was shaken. The popes of the fourteenth century could no longer make all important social activities serve the cause of Christianity. They were placed on the defensive and had to devote most of their energy to the task of preserving the machinery of ecclesiastical government.[3]

How brief was the pinnacle of the Catholic Middle Ages! how often in the course of history has the attempt to establish or preserve a Christian civilization proven elusive! how often has the "prince of this world" defeated the best attempts to organize or maintain a Catholic social order on this earth! As the Middle Ages continued to decline, suffering not only from the effects of the Great Schism, but from a series of worldly popes and the corruption of philosophical and theological instruction by Nominalism, heretical movements increased their activity in all corners of Europe until suddenly in 1517 Martin Luther issued his challenge to some aspects of the doctrine of indulgences, a challenge occasioned by an indulgence that was being preached in various parts of Germany and that masked a rather shady financial deal between the new Archbishop of Mainz[4] and Pope Leo X.

With the success of Luther's revolt in north Germany and Scandinavia and of other Protestant movements in parts of Switzerland and France, the geographical basis for reestablishing the fullness of Christendom throughout Europe was destroyed. Shortly thereafter, the intensely Catholic country of England was separated from the Faith owing to the pride and lust of her king, Henry VIII. Then after the short reign of Henry's son, Edward VI, Queen Mary Tudor began the restoration of the Faith in England, to the great joy of most of the people. But her premature death in 1558 left unfinished her efforts at restoration, efforts that were then entirely undone by her treacherous half-sister, Elizabeth.

---

3. Joseph R. Strayer and Dana C. Munro, *The Middle Ages, 395–1500* (Pacific Palisades, CA: Goodyear Publishing, 5th ed., 1970), 418–19.

4. Albert of Brandenburg, also Archbishop of Magdeburg and administrator of the diocese of Halberstadt. He was only twenty-six years old and had been a bishop since the age of twenty-two!

Later, the failure of the Spanish Armada in 1588, caused in part by "Protestant winds" that blew King Philip's ships off course, and later still the failure of Louis XIV of France to heed the request of Our Lord, transmitted through Saint Margaret Mary Alacoque, that he publicly honor the Sacred Heart of Jesus and thereby obtain victory over his enemies, contributed to the final demise throughout Europe of a Catholic social and cultural order.[5] And although the Faith remained the official basis of the polity in Catholic Europe until the French Revolution of 1789, and remained so even longer in much of Latin America, by then rationalism had sapped the foundations of this social order, which became a mere shell of Christendom. Though the peasants in many places continued to live Catholic lives and observe Catholic customs, no one could say that eighteenth-century Europe was a Catholic culture. The aristocracy, most intellectuals, even many of the higher clergy, espoused ideals that were not Christian, ideals that matched the disordered lives many of them led.

Of course, the Church did not cease to exist with the Revolution of 1789. In fact, in many ways there was a revival of Catholic life in the nineteenth and early twentieth centuries; however, one important difference was that Catholic life from the Revolution on rarely encompassed entire social orders.[6] Catholicism was now, for the most part, a matter of individual or family commitment. Although Catholic intellectual life in the nineteenth and early twentieth centuries entered on a period of brilliance, this renewed Catholicism failed to become the framework in which whole nations lived, in which their political, intellectual, and social life was conducted, as it had been during the Middle Ages. The revival of personal commitment to the Faith and of Catholic thought was, of course, both excellent and necessary, but it should have been the springboard to a new political, intellectual, and social conversion of the entire Western world. Instead, after beginning to run out of steam in the 1950s, it vanished abruptly after the Second Vatican Council.

But should we be surprised by all of this? Should we be surprised that it is only in brief periods that the fullness of Catholic life triumphs? Should not the state of our world, as a *fallen* world, make us expect exactly this? Not that we should fall into the Protestant error of condemning God's creation. As many passages of Holy Scripture make

---

5. Among other things, Louis XIV was told to put an image of the Sacred Heart on his flag and to build a chapel dedicated to the Heart of Jesus, and in turn he was promised success to his arms. It is not certain, however, whether this communication ever reached the King.

6. Of course, there were valiant attempts to revive Catholic political and social structures in places as varied as Ecuador, Austria, Spain, and Quebec, to mention only a few.

clear, especially the beautiful hymn in Daniel 3:52–90, the physical cre-ation is engaged in a ceaseless praising of God and still retains the approbation that God pronounced upon it in Genesis 1. It is mankind that has sinned, and it is the order that we have established that always tends away from God.[7]

Christendom, then, whenever and wherever it has been established, has been a heroic attempt to reclaim a part of the world from the Devil's power, to make effective even now the Kingship of Jesus Christ, a King-ship that in its fullness will not be known till after the Second Coming. Since men have a constant tendency to sin, the clerics and statesmen who in the past ruled over Christian social orders faced an uphill battle to maintain that happy state of affairs; and one wonders whether God gives extraordinary graces at one period of the world's history that for His own reasons He withholds at other times. As in the passage from Christopher Dawson that I quoted above, it seems as if everything that had been working for good suddenly changed and began working for discord and evil:

> It is as though the spiritual tide which had been steadily making for unity for three centuries had suddenly turned, so that everywhere in every aspect of life the forces that made for division and dissolution were predominant.

It is not possible to understand entirely God's purposes in history. The best we can do is sometimes to get a glimpse of them. But our duty always remains. Whether in favorable or unfavorable times, we always have the duty of trying to make Jesus Christ King of both our own lives and of the life of our social order and even of the entire world. Even though the social reign of Jesus Christ the King will never rest upon secure foundations in this world, still we must do all we can to achieve a Christian social order. As St. Paul wrote (1 Corinthians 15:25), "*Oportet illum regnare*"—He must reign!

---

7. Of course, man's sin has affected all of creation. Cf. Romans 8:19–23. Cf. also these words of Josef Pieper, "In his Commentary on St. John's Epistle, St. Thomas remarks that we can find in Sacred Scripture three different meanings for the term 'the world': first, 'the world' as the creation of God, and second, as the creation perfected in Christ; last, as the material perversion of the order of creation. To 'the world' in this last-named sense, and to this world only, may one apply the saying of St. John: 'The world is seated in wickedness' (1 John 5:19). It is precisely the claim of St. Thomas that the first meaning of 'world' (as creation) may not be identified nor interchanged with the third ('world' as material perversion of the order of creation); the world as creation is not seated in wick-edness." *The Silence of St. Thomas* (Chicago: Henry Regnery, 1965), 31.

2

Religion and Life in Christendom

There's one did laugh in's sleep, and one cried 'Murder!'
That they did wake each other; I stood and heard them:
But they did say their prayers, and address'd them
Again to sleep.
            Macbeth, Act II, Scene 2

THE ABOVE LINES are part of the account that Shakespeare's Macbeth gave to his wife of his murder of King Duncan. He is speaking about the two sleeping attendants of the King as he crept into the room to kill him. Though of course the speech is fiction, nevertheless it had to be believable to the audience. What I think is noteworthy about it is that two common attendants or soldiers awakened in the middle of the night should say their *prayers* before going back to sleep. Could this scene be imagined in modern literature, or indeed in modern life? But during the centuries of Christendom the Faith had sunk so deeply into men's minds and actions, both individual and corporate, that it is difficult for us to grasp how thoroughly Christian that society was, "when religion and civilization were so closely united that religious institutions were the main organs of culture and almost every form of social activity possessed a religious sanction."[1] Moreover, this traditional attitude persisted so that several decades after the Faith had begun to collapse in England the old ways of behavior could still be portrayed by Shakespeare and be understood by his audience.

This is not to say that there was not plenty of sinning, by both princes and private persons, in that culture so profoundly shaped by the Church's Faith. Sin will be committed until the end of the world, but in a sense that is beside the point. What is not beside the point is to try to

---

1. Christopher Dawson, *Medieval Essays* (Garden City, NY: Image, 1959), 53.

understand what was the depth of the Christianization of everyday life in Christendom—how thoroughly the Faith ruled everything and permeated both private and public life. In fact, this attempt is necessary if we are to grasp how profoundly the coming of modernity altered the social life of mankind.

The first bar to our understanding of what the civilization of Christendom was and what it meant is the fatal modern divorce between private and public life, especially as regards the Faith. Catholics with any pretensions to orthodoxy realize of course the grave difficulties—the ongoing crisis of faith—that exist in the Church today. I fear, however, that among too many the desire is merely to restore the *status quo ante* 1963 or so. The notion that personal orthodoxy and rectitude of behavior is all that is needed for a healthy Catholic world is in need of correction. Although personal orthodoxy and piety are obviously necessary, they are not enough: for unless the Faith is incarnated in public life and public discourse; in institutions; in a civilization's art, literature, and education, we do not have a Christian civilization, nor even the precondition for a healthy Catholic life.

Although the so-called religious revival of the 1950s is far behind us and largely forgotten, we can nevertheless learn something about how religion is regarded in America by looking at the 1950s. Will Herberg's book, *Protestant, Catholic, Jew: An Essay in American Religious Sociology*,[2] first published in 1955, reveals much about the American approach to religion, an approach that remains pretty much the same. Based on answers obtained from public-opinion polls addressing church attendance and the importance of religion, as well as on other data, a religious revival seemed to be occurring.[3] But an odd fact about this revival is that it seems to have had very little to do with the doctrine of any form of Christianity or even with God. What I mean by this can be illustrated with a few quotations from Herberg. In the first, he presents the following from an article that appeared in *Parade* magazine in 1954:

> "It was back in those days," a prominent American churchman writes, recalling his early years, "that I formed a habit that I have never broken. I began saying in the morning two words, 'I believe.' Those two words *with nothing added* ... give me a running start for my day, and for every day."[4]

---

2. *Protestant, Catholic, Jew: An Essay in American Religious Sociology* (Garden City: Anchor Books, 1960). First edition 1955, revised edition 1960. My references are from the revised edition.

3. Ibid., passim, but especially 1–4 and 46–64.

4. Ibid., 89. Emphasis added by Herberg.

Herberg quotes the President as follows:

> "Our government makes no sense," President Eisenhower recently declared, "unless it is founded in a deeply felt religious faith—*and I don't care what it is.*"[5]

Herberg writes:

> This contentlessness of American religion is curiously illustrated by the confessions of faith of a hundred "thoughtful men and women in all walks of life," published in 1952 . . . in the volume *This I Believe*, edited by Edward P. Morgan. As one reads these statements, perplexity grows. The great majority of the hundred men and women who present their "philosophies of life" are unquestionably professed Christians or Jews, yet barely half of them found it necessary so much as to mention God, and only ten made reference to their formal religious beliefs. These eminent citizens proclaimed their faith in many and diverse things—in "brotherhood," "service," "idealism," and "spiritual values," in "life," "reason," and "tolerance," in "freedom," "self-reliance," "democracy," and, of course, in "faith"—but only incidentally, if at all, in God.[6]

There are many more such references; and, indeed, Herberg's entire book, even at a remove of more than fifty years, is well worth reading. But what is relevant to our inquiry here is what results from such a contentless religion. For naturally such a religion *must* be a private affair, since there are no doctrines to be shared. Such a faith is intensely private by necessity. Thus comes about the frequently heard notion that religion is simply too personal a matter to be discussed.

With such ideas about what religion is, Americans of course cannot understand how a faith could ever inform an entire culture. We make religion personal, so personal in fact that it sometimes has no effect even on our individual conduct ("I am *personally* opposed to abortion, but I would never think of acting on my belief, even voting in accordance with it."), whereas the culture of Christendom made religion so public and corporate that it affected the actions even of lax Christians.

In the culture formed by the Faith, from the foundation of the Middle Ages until, in some parts of the Catholic world, into the nineteenth century, all of our life, action, and thought was meant to be subsumed under Catholic faith and morals. This did not mean a proliferation of "pietistic" acts and writings, however. Such caricatures of genuine Catholic living occur when the relation between the Faith and our life is not organic but forced and artificial. If our literature, for example, is really

---

5. Ibid., 84. Emphasis added by Herberg.
6. Ibid., 274.

informed by a Catholic sense of the real drama and the choices and their eternal consequences that make up so much of life, and yet is able to see even the most tragic of circumstances in the light of the Gospel, then, without pretending to have easy answers for every situation, it can effectively present Jesus Christ as the hope of the world and the end of every human person. But if an essentially secular outlook is ornamented by a few references to faith or morals, then the result is truly worthy of rejection—precisely in the name of the true Faith.

How did the medievals achieve their authentic Christian culture?

> For the people of that time [i.e., the Middle Ages] religion or the Faith ran through the whole of life, in the sense of being inextricably entangled with it. The teaching of Christian tradition was not always lived up to nor ever lived up to perfectly, but the Church as the institution which in their eyes had been given them to be the living embodiment of that teaching could never wholly be put out of their lives. In the village, the church as a building was the centre of the village life, round it and in it moved the important events of life, individual and communal. It had no rival. Even in the towns, where at the beginning of the thirteenth century there were less visible signs of the domination of the Church, it was impossible to get away from the influence of the Faith. However much the medieval preacher might inveigh against the evils of men's lives, and however distressingly he might lament the ignorance and superstition of so many even of his audience, he could not but be conscious that life nevertheless was lived in surroundings that for ever bore witness to the Faith.[7]

Anyone acquainted with medieval literature or art or architecture knows that this is true.

The foundations of this corporate sense of the Faith were those publicly recognized facts that were pretty much accepted without question by the whole society. Around those the intellectual and emotional life of nearly everyone revolved. Blessed John Henry Newman, in his book, *Certain Difficulties Felt by Anglicans in Catholic Teaching*, strikingly described this as actually observed by him in contemporary Italy.

> Now, it being considered, that a vast number of sacred truths are taken for granted as *facts* by a Catholic nation, in the same sense as the sun in the heavens is a fact.... A bad Catholic does not deny hell, for it is to him an incontestable fact, brought home to him by that supernatural faith, with which he assents to the Divine Word speaking through Holy Church....

---

7. Bede Jarrett, *Social Theories of the Middle Ages, 1200–1500* (Westminster, MD: Newman, 1942), 213.

Hence, the strange stories of highwaymen and brigands devout to the Madonna.... We know the dissolute character of the medieval knights and of the troubadours; yet, that dissoluteness, which would lead Protestant poets and travellers to scoff at religion, led them, not to deny revealed truth, but to combine it with their own wild and extravagant profession. . . .

Once more, listen to the stories, songs, and ballads of the populace; their rude and boisterous merriment still runs upon the great invisible subjects which possess their imagination. Their ideas, of whatever sort, good, bad, and indifferent, rise out of the next world. Hence, if they would have plays, the subjects are sacred; if they would have games and sports, these fall, as it were, into procession and are formed upon the model of sacred rites and sacred persons. If they sing and jest, the Madonna and the Bambino, or St. Joseph, or St. Peter, or some other saint, is introduced, not for irreverence, but because these are the ideas that absorb them.... And hence, I say, in their fairs and places of amusement, in the booths, upon the stalls, upon the doors of wine-shops, will be paintings of the Blessed Virgin, or St. Michael, or the souls in purgatory, or of some Scripture subject. (vol. I, lecture 9)

One curious example of how the Faith permeated all of life concerns what were called firework books, late medieval instruction books for master gunners.

The temporal instruction was paramount, but the firework books give more than lip service to the spiritual. Anyone working with such devilish instruments as guns and gunpowder should never forget his Christian responsibilities. The vision of God should be always before the gunner's eyes—even when he squinted along the wrought iron or the cast bronze of one of his own dire creations.[8]

Can anyone imagine an instruction book for firearms written today that contained any reminder at all of one's "Christian responsibilities," that adverted to the fact that all of life and all of our actions must be performed in the light of our last end? The reason that books of the Middle Ages could do so was that to a fully Catholic mind no aspect or department of life had an end independent of man's last end. The principle that unifies such a society is a hierarchy of ends. As Pius XI wrote in his encyclical *Quadragesimo Anno*,

For it is the moral law alone which commands us to seek in all our conduct our supreme and final end, and to strive directly in our spe-

8. William Reid, *The Lore of Arms: a Concise History of Weaponry* (New York: Facts on File, 1984), 52.

cific actions for those ends which nature, or rather, the Author of Nature, has established for them, duly subordinating the particular to the general. If this law be faithfully obeyed, the result will be that particular economic aims, whether of society as a body or of individuals, will be intimately linked with the universal teleological order, and as a consequence we shall be led by progressive stages to the final end of all, God Himself, our highest and lasting good. (no. 43)

In other words, it is wrong to say that various departments of life have their own autonomous ends. Political activity or the economy or artistic creation or education or marriage has each its own proper end, certainly; but these ends are arranged in a hierarchy at the apex of which is "the final end of all, God Himself, our highest and lasting good." As a result, the various activities of mankind must be subordinate to God and to our everlasting union with God. We cannot exempt any part of our lives from God's law, and this includes our social or communal actions, and especially our political and economic activity.

If we Catholics are really interested in converting the world to the true Faith, then we must understand what exactly we should be aiming at. Unless we realize that the conversion of individuals requires the conversion of culture—in fact, the remaking of society so that our institutions and customs reflect the teaching of the Gospel—we shall achieve nothing lasting. Christopher Dawson pointed out the great difference between medieval missionary methods and those of more recent times:

> The great missionary expansion of the nineteenth century was everywhere based on the principle of individual conversion.... There is a fundamental contrast between this approach and the collective or communal form of expression which had dominated the Christian world for upwards of a thousand years. Western Christendom was not built up by the method of individual conversions. It was a way of life which the people accepted as a whole, often by the decision of their rulers, and which when accepted affected the whole life of society by the change of their institutions and laws....
>
> Moreover it may well be claimed that the missionary Churches of the Dark Ages produced a richer harvest even in the sphere of culture than anything that the modern missionary movement can show. There is little in the new non-occidental Christianity that can be compared with Bede and Boniface, with the religious art of Northumbria or with the new vernacular Christian literature. For in the case of Anglo-Saxon England, the mass conversion of the people meant the rebirth of culture....[9]

9. *Christianity in East & West* (La Salle, IL: Sherwood Sugden, 1981), 99–100.

There is no question here of forced conversions, certainly, which are always wrong. Rather, in cases where entire peoples converted following the example of their rulers, they accepted with more or less sincerity of heart what seemed to them the best pattern of worship and life they could find, and subsequently they began to see reality through a new lens, a lens that made better sense of things than their former pagan way of life. Their mental outlook changed so that now "a vast number of sacred truths [were] taken for granted as *facts* ... in the same sense as the sun in the heavens is a fact...." Gradually the lives of individuals began to conform, in a greater or lesser degree, to these new truths, which had become simply the norm for thinking and acting, even if no one lived up to that norm perfectly. What changed with the coming of modernity was that "religion ceased to provide a focus of social unity; but it became instead a major basis for the distinctive identity of specific communities, classes, factions in a divided society." Although "[m]any people found their loyalty to their churches intensified in the process,"[10] this opened the door for religion, and specifically for the Catholic faith, to become an ideology, an adjunct of a political program or a badge of a social class. Even if in some circumstances this seemed like a gain for the Church, in the long run it was not; for it created an image in the minds of many that the clergy was merely the servant of a political cause or, what is worse, of a social class. Thus, the bitter attacks on the Church by anti-clericals in the nineteenth century frequently had their origins in some political question, a question about which Catholic doctrine in many cases had nothing to say one way or the other.

The reason for studying the Middle Ages is that this period did attempt, imperfectly to be sure, to remake society after the pattern of the Gospel. Not everything the medievals did was right or wise, and we can learn both from their achievements and from their mistakes, but we shall never learn how to remake society by imitating times or places when the Faith was privatized and public life was organized according to alien principles. For as Pope Leo XIII noted,

> There was once a time when States were governed by the philosophy of the Gospel. Then it was that the power and divine virtue of Christian wisdom had diffused itself throughout the laws, institutions, and morals of the people; permeating all ranks and relations of civil society. (Encyclical *Immortale Dei*, no. 21)

---

10. Hugh McLeod, *Religion and the People of Western Europe, 1789–1989* (Oxford: Oxford University Press, 2nd ed., 1997), v.

3

Liberalism's Three Assaults

Liberalism, constructed upon an erroneous faith in the individual's ability to achieve the good without the assistance of authority, represented the secularization of an atomistic tendency already present in embryo in the sixteenth-century heresiarchs. It treated the human person as though he were a self-sufficient entity, a citadel threatened only by the evil from without. At first, roused by a rapacious bourgeoisie anxious to reduce Church and State restrictions on the growth and use of personal wealth, liberalism sought merely to prohibit authority over economic matters. Soon, however, more advanced brethren objected not simply to the *object* of authority's exercise, but to authority in itself, at least when wielded by men other than those freely admitted by the autonomous individual. Still more progressive liberals began to include among authorities to be tamed the leaders of subsidiary corporate entities, and even fathers of families. Finally, certain spirits, the most radical of all, could not bring themselves, out of misconstrued love for the individual, to endure the impudence of what were but intellectual and internal authorities: Away with the tyrannies of standards of beauty, of conceptual truths, of the structure of logic and linguistic forms![1]

OFTEN it can be confusing to try to understand the troubles of the present day. We see a great variety of conflicts, conflicts about politics and economics, about all kinds of social policy, about what are sometimes called the "culture wars." Is there a unifying thread, some framework, that ties all of this together? Our media like to portray every controversy as a conflict of liberal versus conservative, but the discerning observer sees that most often this dichotomy makes no sense and that in

---

1. John Rao, "Catholicism, Liberalism, the Right: A Sketch from the 1920s," in *Faith & Reason* 9, no. 1 (spring 1983): 12.

fact the pre-occupation with this alleged fundamental division of ideas often seems designed to confuse Catholics for the sake of someone else's political agenda rather than to cast light on reality. But nevertheless there is a thread that ties together the cultural history of our time, and even of the generations that preceded us. In this chapter, then, I wish to advance an explanation not only of the conflicts of our own era, but also of the last several hundred years, an explanation grounded in the success of one movement: liberalism. Liberalism here, however, means something much broader than our present-day American use of that word, and we should do well simply to put aside its ordinary meaning as we begin to consider the topic. We shall be using the word in the sense in which it is used in most of the world, the same sense incidentally in which it is used in papal documents. Liberalism, understood after this manner, is the chief enemy of the Church, having successfully assaulted Christian civilization on three levels and at three periods. Unfortunately, its triumph in each case has been nearly complete. Moreover, in the course of the three hundred and fifty or so years over which this has taken place, the struggle of liberalism with its opponents has produced so many eddies and backwaters and contrary currents that, without this essential framework from which to examine things, these conflicts are likely to seem like a mix of unrelated events and movements.

At the outset, let me roughly define *liberalism*, providing a definition that we shall clarify as we go along. A good working definition might be as follows: liberalism is that general movement in Western civilization that has sought freedom from the restraints imposed by Christian teaching and that has therefore attacked Catholic culture, first on the level of Christian economic morality, secondly on the level of the political rights of God, and lastly on the level of the human person itself. Corresponding to these three intellectual assaults have been (first) the overthrow of the guilds and the establishment of capitalism; (secondly) the overthrow of traditional Catholic regimes; and (thirdly) the assault on humanity through such things as divorce, contraception, abortion, euthanasia, and even the natural and complementary division of mankind into two sexes. Liberalism is responsible for the modern world and its pervasive secularism and is perhaps Satan's greatest success since the tempting of Adam and Eve in the Garden of Eden. To begin, let us look at each of these three assaults in turn.

The economic assault was liberalism's first attack.[2] Yet, it is in the eco-

2. Some may wonder why I do not include the Protestant revolt as the first manifestation of liberalism. Although Protestantism, along with the philosophical error of nominalism, is certainly one of the ultimate factors that gave birth to liberalism, it did not

nomic sphere that we are most liable to become confused by the different meanings of *liberal*. Milton Friedman in his book extolling the virtues of free-market capitalism wrote:

> It is extremely convenient to have a label for the political and economic viewpoint elaborated in this book. The rightful and proper label is liberalism. Unfortunately, 'As a supreme, if unintended compliment, the enemies of the system of private enterprise have thought it wise to appropriate its label', so that liberalism has, in the United States, come to have a very different meaning than it did in the nineteenth century or does today over much of the Continent of Europe.
>
> As it developed in the late eighteenth and early nineteenth centuries, the intellectual movement that went under the name of liberalism emphasized freedom as the ultimate goal and the individual as the ultimate entity in the society. It supported laissez faire at home as a means of reducing the role of the state in economic affairs and thereby enlarging the role of the individual; it supported free trade abroad as a means of linking the nations of the world together peacefully and democratically.[3]

In other words, liberalism, as I am using it here, and as indeed it is used in most parts of the world, includes many of the doctrines of what Americans call conservatism. But, as Friedman knew, it is not a conserving force, but rather the opposite.

During the Middle Ages, Catholic teaching had strongly impressed on society the necessity of keeping in check the powerful human desire for economic gain, just as much as the powerful human desire for sexual pleasure. R. H. Tawney writes thus of the medieval attitude:

> Material riches are necessary; they have a secondary importance, since without them men cannot support themselves and help one another; the wise ruler, as St. Thomas said, will consider in founding his State the natural resources of the country. But economic motives are suspect. Because they are powerful appetites, men fear them, but they are not mean enough to applaud them. Like other strong passions, what they need, it is thought, is not a clear field, but repression. There is no place in medieval theory for economic activity which is not related to a moral end, and to found a science of society upon the assumption that the appetite for economic gain is a constant and measurable force, to

---

usually at first have as its aim the overthrowing of traditional morality. In some ways, as in the seventeenth-century Protestant doctrine of the divine right of kings, it even seemed to oppose the new trends. Protestantism certainly contained the seeds of liberalism, but in the beginning it kept those seeds well hidden.

3. *Capitalism and Freedom* (Chicago: University of Chicago Press, 1962), 5.

be accepted, like other natural forces, as an inevitable and self-evident *datum* would have appeared to the medieval thinker as hardly less irrational or less immoral than to make the premise of social philosophy the unrestrained operation of such necessary human attributes as pugnacity or the sexual instinct.

And a little later:

At every turn, therefore, there are limits, restrictions, warnings, against allowing economic interests to interfere with serious affairs. It is right for a man to seek such wealth as is necessary for a livelihood in his station. To seek more is not enterprise, but avarice, and avarice is a deadly sin. Trade is legitimate; the different resources of different countries show that it was intended by Providence. But it is a dangerous business. A man must be sure that he carries it on for the public benefit, and that the profits which he takes are no more than the wages of his labor.[4]

And as another writer put it:

We can, therefore, lay down as the first principle of mediaeval economics that there was a limit to money-making imposed by the purpose for which the money was made. Each worker had to keep in front of himself the aim of his life and consider the acquiring of money as a means only to an end, which at one and the same justified and limited him. When, therefore, sufficiency had been obtained there could be no reason for continuing further efforts at getting rich, whether as merchant or beggar, except in order to help others. . . .[5]

Accordingly, medieval man created institutions and structures to implement these ideas of economic restraint. The most important of these, the craft guild, embodied the quintessential Catholic idea of regulating the economy without direct governmental intervention. Belloc, for instance, summarizes the work of one of the guilds—the fishmongers'—thus: "The . . . Fishmongers' Guild of London regulated the trade in fish, fixed prices, checked undue competition, prevented the wealthier fishmonger from eating up his smaller brother and so on."[6] The Middle Ages looked to justice and stability as their economic ideals and sternly rebuked and even punished those whose excessive desire for gain led them to take advantage of their fellow men.

4. R.H. Tawney, *Religion and the Rise of Capitalism* (New York: Harcourt, Brace, 1926), 31–32.

5. Bede Jarrett, *Social Theories of the Middle Ages, 1200–1500* (Westminster, MD: Newman, 1942), 157–58.

6. Hilaire Belloc, *The Crisis of Civilization* (Rockford, IL: TAN Books and Publishers, 1992 [1937]), 109.

But, as could be expected, many chafed under these kinds of restraints. And by a variety of means they succeeded in overturning the entire medieval system. By both direct and indirect means in both Catholic and Protestant countries, this structure of customs and institutions, whose linchpin was the craft guild, was destroyed between approximately 1600 and 1800. What happened is described thus by Belloc:

> What had been for centuries a Christian and therefore satisfactory equilibrium in human relations, gradually developing a free peasantry in the place of the old slave-state, ordering by rule and custom the economic structure of Society, regarding men as connected by status, rather than by contract, guarding against excessive competition, insistent upon stability, disappeared as a result of the mighty shock delivered in the early 16th century. There came in the place of the old stable medieval civilization..., and in place of the old social philosophy which for centuries had satisfied mankind, a new state of affairs the various parts of which developed at various rates, but all of which, combined, came in the long run to form the modern world [which is] a social state based upon unbridled competition, one eliminating the old idea of status and regarding only contract, and presenting [the] phenomenon of industrial capitalism....[7]

The result of these changes was summarized by Pope Leo XIII thus:

> The ancient workmen's Guilds were destroyed in the last century, and no other organization took their place. Public institutions and the laws have repudiated the ancient religion. Hence by degrees it has come to pass that Working Men have been given over, isolated and defenseless, to the callousness of employers and the greed of unrestrained competition. The evil has been increased by rapacious Usury, which, although more than once condemned by the Church, is nevertheless, under a different form but with the same guilt, still practiced by avaricious and grasping men. And to this must be added the custom of working by contract, and the concentration of so many branches of trade in the hands of a few individuals, so that a small number of very rich men have been able to lay upon the masses of the poor a yoke little better than slavery itself. (Encyclical *Rerum Novarum*, no. 3)

This overthrow of the Church's economic teaching was the first triumph of liberalism. Though it happened in different localities and sectors of the economy at different times, it was all but complete by the first third of the nineteenth century. Moreover, this overturning of traditional Catholic economic morality did more than change the economic

---

7. Ibid., 100–101.

scene. As the apologist for free-market capitalism and Austrian economics, Ludwig von Mises, wrote: "With the spread and progress of capitalism, birth control becomes a universal practice."[8] As we shall see below, hatred of the Church's economic morality is connected by intimate bonds with hatred of all of Christian teaching.[9]

Even before liberalism's first assault was completed, the second assault had begun. It prevailed in England in 1688, and a hundred years later in France in 1789.[10] The political assault is particularly hard for Americans to understand because this expression of liberalism is part of the air we breathe. As Friedrich von Hayek, another avowed liberal and noted free-market economist, writes as follows:

> ... what in Europe was called 'liberalism' was here the common tradition on which the American polity had been built: thus the defender of the American tradition was a liberal in the European sense.[11]

What was the traditional Catholic teaching that liberalism sought to overturn in its political assault? It is clearly stated as follows by Pope Leo XIII in his encyclical, *Immortale Dei*, of November 1, 1885:

---

8. *Human Action: A Treatise on Economics* (New Haven: Yale University, 1949), 665. Mises also says, "Those fighting birth control want to eliminate a device indispensable for the preservation of peaceful human cooperation and the social division of labor. . . . The philosophers and theologians who assert that birth control is contrary to the laws of God and Nature refuse to see things as they really are" (ibid., 668).

9. In the Apostolic Exhortation, *Ecclesia in America* (1999), John Paul II described neoliberalism as a "system . . . based on a purely economic conception of man, this system considers profit and the law of the market as its only parameters, to the detriment of the dignity of and the respect due to individuals and peoples" (no. 56).

10. The French Revolution not only abolished the monarchy and murdered the King and Queen, but also abolished the guilds and prohibited workers from forming unions or going on strike. The revolutionaries also intensified the enclosure movement, that is, the taking of land from the rural poor for grazing purposes, and established internal free trade. This is another clear indication of the interconnection of the varying forms of liberalism. Alfred Cobban, *A History of Modern France*, vol. I (Baltimore: Penguin Books, 2d ed. 1961), 171–72.

11. "Why I Am Not a Conservative," in *The Essence of Hayek*, edited by Chiaki Nishiyama and Kurt R. Leube (Stanford: Hoover Institution Press, 1984), 282.

Condé B. Pallen, in his translation and adaptation of Felix Sarda y Salvany's work, *Liberalism Is a Sin* (Rockford, IL: TAN Books and Publishers, 1993 [1899]), using a somewhat different, though related, definition of liberalism, nonetheless says: "In America [liberalism] would scarcely seem to exist at all, so ingrained is it in our social conditions, so natural is it to the prevailing modes of thought, so congenial is it with the dominant religious notions about us. . . . Indeed it is the very constituent of the pseudo-religious and pseudo-moral atmosphere we daily breathe" (156).

Man's natural instinct moves him to live in civil society, for he cannot, if dwelling apart, provide himself with the necessary requirements of life, nor procure the means of developing his mental and moral faculties. Hence it is divinely ordained that he should lead his life—be it family, social or civil—with his fellow-men, amongst whom alone his several wants can be adequately supplied. But as no society can hold together unless some one be over all, directing all to strive earnestly for the common good; every civilized community must have a ruling authority, and this authority, no less than society itself, has its source in nature, and has, consequently, God for its author. Hence it follows that all public power must proceed from God. For God alone is the true and supreme Lord of the world. Everything, without exception, must be subject to Him, and must serve Him, so that whosoever holds the right to govern, holds it from one sole and single source, namely, God, the Sovereign Ruler of all. *There is no power but from God* (Romans 13:1). (No. 3)

What is Leo saying here? In the first place, in clear opposition to John Locke and other social contract theorists, the Pontiff teaches that society is the natural condition of man; it is not something brought about by some kind of political pact or bargain. Moreover, it is not just for man's material comfort that society is necessary, but for "developing his mental and moral faculties." And because society is necessary, because man is social, man is also political, not in the modern sense of having a natural turn for the wheeling and dealing of politicians, but in the classical sense of needing a government, something "directing all to strive earnestly for the common good." And thus this governing power is both natural and from God, the Author of nature. Governments are not so much "instituted among men" as simply *there*, a necessary aspect of human community, and they certainly do not *ultimately* derive "their just powers from the consent of the governed" but from God.

Many people reading the above passage from Leo XIII would conclude that he was upholding monarchies, or even arguing for the notion of the divine right of kings (a largely Protestant idea). Leo was not especially promoting one form of government over another. He goes on to say, "The right to rule is not necessarily ... bound up with any special mode of government. It may take this or that form, provided only that it be of a nature to insure the general welfare." In Catholic Europe there had long been republics, such as Iceland, Switzerland, and San Marino; and there is no reason why the ruler or rulers may not be chosen by popular vote. Leo, rather, is promoting something much more radical, namely, the idea that governments are from God, that they therefore have duties toward God, that they rule in His name. They are not some human contrivance, some expedient devised when men first came together in society; moreover, their fundamental nature and powers have been fixed by God and are not subject to human will.

Although governments must take care that they not swallow up the whole of society or assume that they are the normal and natural party to directly alleviate every human ill, the notion that governments are only a necessary evil is pure liberalism. It ignores the truths that Pope Leo taught and that indeed have been taught consistently by Catholic tradition since the New Testament.[12] Governments are necessary goods, and their rule reflects some of the glory of God himself.[13]

But the various revolutions that shook Europe and the Americas between the seventeenth and nineteenth centuries taught that governments were pure creations of the governed and, indeed, ruled in their name and were, in a sense, their servants. Although the doctrine that governments ought to rule for the benefit of their subjects is at least as old as Plato and is solidly sanctioned by the Catholic faith, still it was liberalism that destroyed any notion of the ruler or rulers as holding power from God, and therefore (in a sense) to be feared as from God. There is a big difference between a benevolent parent and a hired manager who simply fulfills the will of his employers.

The latest assault by liberalism is the assault on the human person; it is the assault we are living with today, the contemporary and latest project of liberalism. Its roots, however, are in the nineteenth-century propaganda for divorce and were presaged by the disordered lives of many of the eighteenth-century liberals. As an organized movement it first championed divorce; divorce was followed by contraception, contraception by abortion, abortion by euthanasia, euthanasia by homosexual conduct, homosexual conduct by the entire abolition of the two created human sexes. All these assaults are really attacks on the primal truth of the Book of Genesis: "Male and female he created them" (Genesis 1:27). The creation of man as male and female is a truth about marriage and thus excludes divorce; is about fertility and thus excludes contraception and abortion; is about human life and thus excludes euthanasia; is about the holiness of natural marital sex and thus excludes homosexual acts; and especially excludes the notion that the two created sexes are arbitrary impositions on mankind.

---

12. See, for example, Romans 13:1–7 and 1 Peter 2:13–17.

13. "Hallowed therefore in the minds of Christians is the very idea of public authority, in which they recognize some likeness and symbol as it were of the divine Majesty, even when it is exercised by one unworthy." Leo XIII, Encyclical *Sapientiae Christianae* (1890), no. 9.

Many people are unaware of the attempt to label the two created human sexes as arbitrary and unjust impositions on humanity, but this is exactly what cutting-edge liberals are trying to do today. Their first tack was the attempt to separate sex from gender, that is, the biological fact of the two human sexes from their social and cultural expressions, which they term *genders*, and which they claim to be purely social constructions in no way grounded in nature. Then, using a thing like "sex-change operations," they begin to deny the very stability and reality of the two created sexes. After that, they claim that whether or not one undergoes such an operation, one's subjective feeling about what sex/gender one is trumps the physical facts of one's body. And from that it is only a short step to the notion that male and female are only two out of a nearly infinite number of possible expressions of human sexuality.

> Kate Bornstein is neither a man nor a woman but "hir" own special transgressive creation—and, inevitably, something of a travelling circus. "Ze" was born male, raised as a boy, opted for a sex-change in adulthood, and became a woman. A few years later, she got tired of being a woman, so she stopped—but didn't want to become a man again. And I think many of us can identify with that. Perhaps this is why "Ze" has become an evangelist for the joys of being transgendered.[14]

Just as the early liberals resented the fact that God decreed justice and restraint in economic relations and later liberals resented the fact that the state had God for its author and was accountable to Him, so now the latest wave of liberals resents the fact that God has created the human race as male and female. Even if people mutilate their bodies to try to change what God has created, this does not and cannot change the facts. "Male and female he created them." There are two sexes; and the social expression of our sexuality, while to some extent dependent on cultural mores, must be rooted in the biological facts if it is to be healthy. Whether liberalism will identify any more frontiers it will hope to cross God and Satan only know. We do know, however, that wherever God has established order liberalism will seek to destroy it and fulfill its own

---

14. *The Independent* (London), March 8, 1998. Consider also the following from the article, "Patriarchy Is Such a Drag: the Strategic Possibilities of a Postmodern Account of Gender," in *Harvard Law Review* 108, no. 8 (1995): 1993: "Whereas family and marriage are merely legally conferred statuses, conception, pregnancy, and childbirth, as biological processes, seem to be archetypes of naturalness. But procreation is much more like marriage and family than this focus on biology suggests: each is an experience as well as an institution" (1982); and "Biological sex is revealed to have no inevitable meaning, but only the social meaning attached to it on the basis of gender identity."

desires however much they fly in the face of God's law, human happiness, or even common sense and sanity.

The spirit of liberalism is at bottom opposed to the spirit of Catholicism. Ultimately, it is the spirit of Lucifer, of one who opposes all of the order created by God, in heaven or on earth, and even (in principle) himself. It is fundamentally the principle of the supremacy of the will, the principle of I want, of *sic volo, sic jubeo, sic pro ratione stet*. Instead of accepting the order established by God and by his representatives on earth, liberalism tears down whatever is opposed to its restless striving to fulfill its desires.

Though the different assaults that liberalism has perpetrated at different times may seem unrelated, and in fact may be manifested in different people, they all result from this same spirit. The fact that certain people hold only parts of the liberal creed (and may even explicitly reject other parts) tends to obscure the links between these different manifestations of liberalism. But in some of its representatives one can find the full liberal spirit. Above I quoted the statement of the free-market economist, Ludwig von Mises, on capitalism and birth control. Mises is refreshingly explicit in making clear his fundamental ideas about human acts and morality.

> The ultimate end of action is always the satisfaction of some desires of the acting man. Since nobody is in a position to substitute his own value judgments for those of the acting individual, it is vain to pass judgment on other people's aims and volitions. No man is qualified to declare what would make another man happier or less discontented. The critic either tells us what he believes he would aim at if he were in the place of his fellow; or, in dictatorial arrogance blithely disposing of his fellow's will and aspirations, declares what condition of this other man would better suit himself, the critic.[15]

Here is liberalism unabashed: the refusal to make "value judgments" on human behavior, the exalting of the human will into the final principle of action.[16] The connection between such a fundamental attitude toward human moral acts and free-market individualism is not widely recognized in this country, but it is nonetheless true, for both indicate the same attitude toward the Divine order. That is, both have the same inner form, though both differ outwardly considerably. Both are expressions of the essentially unruly human will.

---

15. *Human Action: A Treatise on Economics*, 18–19.

16. Mises' disdainful statements about religion further illustrate the liberal mind in action. After explaining that (in his view) advertising can entice a consumer to try a

If there is to be a return to God's order for created beings, then this return will have to be accomplished on all levels. It is not enough to simply defeat the latest assault of liberalism, unless we likewise attempt to overcome the two earlier assaults, because they are all rooted in the same thing. One can see this in advertising, for example, which was illegal in Catholic nations during the Middle Ages and even into the eighteenth century.[17] Advertising has been one of the chief means by which sexual images and enticements have made their way very publicly into our culture: on the sides of busses, into our homes through the electronic media, and so on. It is natural that the free market should exploit the sexual urge to sell its products, for both the misuse of the economic process and the misuse of sex are aspects of the same liberalism. So in accomplishing its goal of luring consumers to buy goods they may well not need, advertising also very often works against chastity, thus nicely combining the first and third assault of liberalism into one.

At the present moment it does not appear likely that the culture of the West will experience a conversion, at least any time soon. But we can always seek to convert our own hearts and minds. As Catholics we have to understand what liberalism is and fortify ourselves internally against its varying manifestations. Otherwise, we shall be dupes of one or more kinds of liberalism. The Devil is very clever, and one of his cleverest ploys has been to make liberalism seem as if it were really two or three separate and unrelated movements, thus dividing the opposition. So, some who are very much opposed to liberalism's assault on the human person are nevertheless defenders of liberalism's assault on economic morality, and vice versa. Satan wants to keep mankind distracted with as many side issues as he can to prevent us from seeing the main question. But the magisterium of the Church has never been distracted, and

---

product only once and that if the product is not good, the consumer will not buy it again, he goes on to say. "Entirely different are conditions in those fields in which experience cannot teach us anything. The statements of religious, metaphysical and political propaganda can be neither verified not falsified by experience. With regard to the life beyond and the absolute, any experience is denied to men living in this world." *Human Action: A Treatise on Economics*, 318. Though it is true that experience conceived after an empiricist manner can rarely tell us about religious truths (except for miracles), still I think his contemptuous tone is obvious here.

Earlier, Mises, after a reference to "the Roman Catholic Church and the various Protestant denominations" says the following: "The pompous statements which people make about things unknowable and beyond the power of the human mind, their cosmologies, world views, religions, mysticisms, metaphysics, and conceptual phantasies differ widely from one another" (ibid., 180–81).

17. Amintore Fanfani, in *Catholicism, Protestantism and Capitalism* (New York: Sheed & Ward, 1939), 79–81, instances the case of France.

in the writings of several Supreme Pontiffs one can find consistent denunciations of all the assaults of liberalism. Thus, it behooves us, as usual, to study and learn from the authentic teaching of Christ's vicars. Only then shall we hope to understand the signs of the times and fighting the good fight against our real enemies

4

Europe, Christendom, and the Faith

HILAIRE BELLOC is famous, and in some quarters infamous, for the statement in his book *Europe and the Faith* that "The Faith is Europe, and Europe is the Faith."[1] Of course Belloc, like any intelligent man, knew well that this statement was not literally true, at least not in any statistical sense. That is, there were millions of Catholics outside Europe and millions of non-Catholics within Europe. This is even more the case today than when Belloc wrote. There is a sense, however, in which this statement is true, for Europe is that place in which under God's providence the Faith was given both time and space to develop itself intellectually and culturally to form Christendom, the outward and visible sign of God's internal and invisible work in human souls. Although originally the Church's cultural orbit had included parts of both Africa and Asia, and many important early Fathers and other theologians were north African or Middle Eastern, after the Mohammedan invasions these areas were to some degree cut off from contact with the rest of the Catholic world. In the case of Latin north Africa, the Church dwindled away to nothingness. Thus, Europe was left as the only place where, although amid difficulties certainly, Catholic life could develop in a more or less natural or proper manner. In this way it is true to say that the Faith is Europe and Europe is the Faith, since it was only there that Catholic social and cultural life had the chance to attain any degree of maturity, in turn giving the European continent a cultural unity it otherwise would probably have lacked.

Such an outward social and cultural manifestation of Catholic faith has always been characteristic of the Church. Except in cases of persecution it is normal for a Catholic social order to arise, and we take for granted the immense number of intellectual, literary, artistic, musical,

---

1. (Rockford, IL: TAN Books and Publishers, 1992 [1920]), 2.

architectural, and other expressions of Catholic faith that were produced within Christendom. But there is one additional and almost always necessary element in this outward expression of the Faith: the political aspect. Ever since the Emperor Constantine's initial recognition of the Church with the Edict of Milan, the Catholic Church has enjoyed a complex relationship with the various political powers of this world. Before Constantine, of course, the Church was generally an object of persecution by the Roman government, but after Constantine all this changed. Now the government became, in a sense, the patron and protector of the Church. That this patronage had a negative side no one can deny, but that in general it was the providentially appointed means for protecting the Church and allowing a Christian civilization to develop also seems to me beyond denial. Because of this complex relationship with the powers of the world, a relationship often both positive and negative at the same time, it can be perplexing to evaluate any particular instance of this relationship; thus, it seems to me that we should be careful about either condemning it wholesale or on the other hand failing to acknowledge or downplaying its negative aspects.

In evaluating the pros and cons of the political patronage that various rulers have bestowed on the Church over the centuries, we should remember that without such patronage only rarely would Catholic cultures have been able to develop. I shall address the present-day situation below; however, regarding the past, up to a few hundred years ago, the military or political triumph of an anti-Catholic power usually brought with it persecution of the Church, the destruction of any outward manifestations of Catholic life, and often even the slow death of the Faith in the private life of individuals. Tertullian's dictum that the blood of the martyrs is the seed of the Church has certainly proven true at times, but it can hardly be regarded as an axiom to be applied uncritically to all times and places. In the lands conquered by Moslems or in those parts of Europe that embraced Protestantism, the Church was subjected to varying degrees and kinds of persecution and in some cases the Catholic population was reduced to nil. All this is adduced simply to point out that, whatever harm state protection and patronage of the Church has brought with it, it also provided needed space for the Church and Catholic life to exist and develop. The sad state of the Church in Catholic Europe today is often taken as proof that ultimately such official protection does more harm than good; but when we compare Latin Europe today with such once-Catholic lands as Scandinavia or Asia Minor, we might conclude that more than one opinion is possible.

In Christian Europe there existed a succession of political powers that provided this patronage even into the nineteenth century, albeit less consistently as the centuries progressed: the Roman Empire both east and west; Charlemagne's Frankish empire; most European kingdoms during the Middle Ages; thereafter, Habsburg Spain, together with the Holy Roman Empire; and, lastly, France. During this time, of course, large sections of Europe were lost to the Church in the Protestant revolt at about the same time as there began a Catholic expansion into the New World and into parts of Asia and Africa. Necessarily, Catholic life in these regions was derivative of European Catholic life. In one region, though, there were enough time and resources to permit the creation of a genuinely new province of Christendom. This was Latin America, where a Baroque Catholic culture was created—in its main lines certainly a European transplant, but in a new environment and among new peoples. As Christopher Dawson wrote:

> Nowhere are the vitality and fecundity of the Baroque culture better displayed than in Mexico and South America, where there was a rich flowering of regional types of art and architecture, some of which show considerable indigenous Indian influence. This power of Baroque culture to assimilate alien influences is one of its characteristic features, and distinguishes it sharply from the culture and artistic style of the Anglo-American area.[2]

This assimilating power of the Spanish Baroque was so great that, as one scholar put it with reference to music:

> It is very difficult in Bolivia, Peru, and Ecuador to separate the musical elements of Indian origin from those of the European tradition.... The elements of the two cultures combined to form inseparable units.[3]

Although Latin America did offer fresh space for Catholic cultural development, it, like all the newly discovered or colonized lands, continued to depend upon Europe both politically and intellectually.

In Europe, as I noted, important and increasingly powerful states had already loosed themselves from Catholic unity. Protestant England, together with Holland and for a time Sweden, became the chief loci within Europe aiming at the destruction of Catholic civilization. These countries not only became political and military rivals to Catholic powers, but also erected an alternative model of Western cultural life, a model that has exerted a powerful intellectual appeal to many. Subsequently, the United States became the foundation of this Protestant culture worldwide. Speaking of this, Belloc wrote, "The strength of the

---

2. *The Dividing of Christendom* (Garden City, NY: Image, 1967), 162.
3. Bruno Nettl, *Folk and Traditional Music of the Western Continents* (Englewood Cliffs, NJ: Prentice-Hall, 2d ed., 1973), 191.

Protestant culture now lies out of Europe, in the United States."[4] These various Protestant powers worked by seizing bits of Catholic territory all around the world; by sending out Protestant missionaries into Latin America and other Catholic lands, where they have contributed to the destruction of Catholic faith and culture; and, perhaps most importantly, by offering an alternative model of Western culture that appeals strongly to modern materialist man. The increasing industrial might and wealth of this model offered a kind of spurious argument in its favor, an argument summarized by Belloc as follows:

> The Catholic Church is false because nations of Catholic culture have declined steadily in temporal wealth and power as compared with the nations of an anti-Catholic culture, which, in this particular instance, means the Protestant culture.[5]

Although today neither Great Britain nor the United States as nations has any interest in Protestant theology, both of them continue to reflexively oppose Catholic interests, indeed any remnants of Catholic culture existing in the world today. In fact, part of the anti-Hispanic feeling that animates so many Anglo-Americans, even Catholics, has its roots in this feeling of the cultural superiority of Protestant civilization.

Although Protestant civilization in general still exists as a power supporting, I do not say Protestantism as a religion, but Protestant culture, today there is no Catholic power. In fact, with the partial and weak exception of a few Latin American nations,[6] the Church and Catholic culture have no true political props today. In the late nineteenth century, Pope Leo XIII and other far-sighted Catholic thinkers saw that the Church could no longer depend for her external support upon Catholic princes. In both the political and the cultural realms it was now the mass of the Catholic people, more and more living in democratic regimes and possessing some voice in their governments, who would be the external support for the Church, if anyone would be. At first this new arrangement seemed to work tolerably well. The last third of the

---

4. "The Two Cultures of the West," in *Essays of a Catholic* (Rockford, IL: TAN Books and Publishers, 1992 [1931]), 244.

5. *Survivals and New Arrivals* (London: Sheed & Ward, 1939), 80.

6. When Argentina first observed March 25 as the Day of the Unborn Child to symbolize its rejection of abortion, her President, Carlos Menem, wrote to the heads of state of all the Latin American countries, and of Spain, Portugal, and the Philippines, inviting them to join in this observance. He noted that "the common historical roots of our nations bind us together not only on matters of language but also in an understanding of man and society based on the fundamental dignity of the human person" (*Catholic World News*, March 25, 1999). This is an echo of the Hispanic world's former status as the geopolitical bulwark of Catholicism.

nineteenth century and the first half of the twentieth were one of the most brilliant periods in Catholic letters and philosophy, a period made further illustrious by the efforts of popes from Saint Pius X to Pius XII to realize the liturgy's potential as a school for Christian living. Despite the interruptions of two world wars, Catholic thought exerted an influence on politics in more than one country; a number of official or unofficial Catholic political parties existed; and some few regimes were more or less consciously devoted to carrying out a Catholic program in their public policy, while even in Protestant countries popular Catholic life flourished in a great variety of associations and institutions. Catholics exercised sometimes considerable influence on the political process.

Unfortunately, in the second half of the twentieth century, the Church deliberately, if uncomprehendingly, inflicted a grave wound on herself. Although, apart from a few ambiguities, the conciliar documents themselves are unproblematic, it does not seem to admit of reasonable disagreement that the conduct of the Second Vatican Council, and much more its aftermath and application, have generally been a disaster for the Church, a disaster at once pastoral, intellectual, and institutional. As a result of this disaster the popular Catholic life that had existed was largely destroyed. Although Catholic culture is much broader than simply catechesis and the reception of the sacraments, it depends upon such formal elements of Catholic life and without them it cannot last. It is thus hard to envisage any ready way out of our present situation, since both the formal and the popular sides of Catholic life have been affected. So, how can we respond to that situation, in which the Church neither enjoys the patronage of any powerful government nor commands widespread enthusiasm and loyalty on the part of the Catholic people at large? In such circumstances how can the Church and Catholic life be maintained, nourished, and extended?

Unfortunately, the measures that can be suggested to achieve this end seem woefully inadequate. Attention to a beautiful and historically rooted liturgy and the cultivation of a consciousness of the Catholic intellectual tradition, including an emphasis on the Church's social teaching, new or restored Catholic schools at all levels, and constant popular education through the media—these seem to me to be the chief means that are possible and have some hope of success. None of them is easy to establish; and of those that have been initiated, many are already more than tainted by alien influences: e.g., in the United States, by fatal compromises with the worldview of classical liberalism on the part of uncomprehending Catholics unable to distinguish between a Catholic view of the social order and that of classical liberalism, simply because the latter seems to be at odds with the trajectory of more recent and obviously harmful liberalism. That both forms of liberalism are rooted in the same errors is seemingly impossible for many to grasp.

I am not hopeful for the immediate future. As to the long term, there is no doubt and there should be no fear, for it is Jesus Christ who is head of the Church, his Mystical Body. How long this long term may be is hardly our concern—short or long it is not in our hands. Meanwhile, success should not be the norm of our activity, but simply faithfulness, faithfulness to the mandate given to the Church by her Founder to go out into the world and proclaim the Gospel to every creature.

5

Reason, Traditionalism, and the Enlightenment

THE HISTORY OF IDEAS is often illuminating not only of the past but of the present as well. That is, if we come to understand what people thought and why in some former era, we might learn something helpful to us today. Especially is this the case if we still live in the wake of those past intellectual or cultural movements and they continue to exercise a determining influence on our thinking. Let us look at some aspects of the history of thought since the eighteenth century in order to see some of its relevance to discussions in the present.

In many ways the Western world is still living intellectually in the so-called Enlightenment of the eighteenth century, the era in which intellectual life largely dissociated itself from any form of the Christian religion. That is the reason why it is usually assumed at the highest levels of academic or cultural discourse that the claims of the Christian revelation are hardly worth mentioning, let alone seriously considering. Before the Enlightenment most of the leaders of European thought were Christians, but since that time this has only rarely been the case. I shall not be discussing here the causes or history of the Enlightenment, but simply tracing some of its effects on subsequent thinking, addressing especially how the Enlightenment concept of reason continues to affect us.

The thinkers of the eighteenth century had an understanding of reason that was but a partial and desiccated conception, a kind of either/or approach to reality, whereas reality demands something fuller and richer. Its shallow metaphysics, such as that found in Locke or Hume, were the outcome of the sterile conflict between rationalists and empiricists, a conflict that Kant attempted to solve but only papered over. By accepting the nominalists' denial of the mind's ability to go beyond the particular to the universal, they were forced either to limit knowledge to perception (empiricists) or to choose an altogether different starting point for philosophy (rationalists). Kant's subsequent limitation of what is knowable to essentially a projection of our own minds is perhaps the worst possible attempt at a solution of this impasse. The Aristotelian and Thomistic realization that our knowledge does indeed begin with sense perception but does not end there had been written out of the debate centuries before, and many people seem to have been unaware that it was even an option.

Given the sort of philosophizing that took place in the eighteenth century, it was not surprising that thinkers such as Edmund Burke or Joseph de Maistre, who were horrified by the Enlightenment's offspring, the French Revolution, sought to take refuge in something that seemed safe—tradition. The only conception of reason they were familiar with could be better termed ratiocination, for it was simply a consideration, often superficial, of phenomena, and stopped short of an attempt to reach being itself. The reaction against such a degraded notion of reason manifested itself in adherence to tradition and went so far that some writers asserted that the only way of knowing the existence of God was by a tradition handed down generation to generation from Adam, since the human mind was incapable of discovering this by its own unaided reasoning powers.

There are a number of objections that can be raised against this traditionalism. One of these is put in the following way by G. K. Chesterton:

A cultivated Conservative friend of mine once exhibited great distress because in a gay moment I once called Edmund Burke an atheist. I need scarcely say that the remark lacked something of biographical precision; it was meant to. Burke was certainly not an atheist in his conscious cosmic theory, though he had not a special and flaming faith in God, like Robespierre. Nevertheless, the remark had reference to a truth which it is here relevant to repeat. I mean that in the quarrel over the French Revolution, Burke did stand for the atheistic attitude and mode of argument, as Robespierre stood for the theistic. The Revolution appealed to the idea of an abstract and eternal justice, beyond all local custom or convenience. If there are commands of God, then there must be rights of man. Here Burke made his brilliant diversion; he did not attack the Robespierre doctrine with the old medieval doctrine of *jus divinum* (which, like the Robespierre doctrine, was theistic), he attacked it with the modern argument of scientific relativity; in short the argument of evolution. . . . "I know nothing of the rights of men," he said, "but I know something of the rights of Englishmen." There you have the essential atheist. His argument is that we have got some

protection by natural accident and growth; and why should we profess
to think beyond it, for all the world as if we were the images of God![1]

This quotation shows in a striking manner, albeit with some inexacti-
tude, that the attempt to oppose the Enlightenment by using an argument resting fundamentally on tradition will ultimately fail. The
universal claims of the Enlightenment must be met by equally universal
claims, grounded in truths of human nature, and finally in truths about
metaphysics and about the nature of God.

Although a number of Catholic thinkers had joined in this disparage-
ment of reason, the Church never accepted this approach. Even before
Pope Leo XIII's endorsement of a revival of the thought of St. Thomas
Aquinas in his 1879 encyclical *Aeterni Patris*, the Church had asserted a
proper understanding of man's reasoning powers in the First Vatican
Council of 1870, in which it was solemnly defined that the existence of
God could be demonstrated "by the natural light of human reason."[2]
But with the pontificate of Leo XIII (1878–1903), the project of a revived
Thomism began to oppose Enlightenment modernity at its intellectual
foundation, for Richard Weaver was surely right when he traced the
beginnings of modern intellectual error back to the medieval nominalists.[3] This Pope Leo saw likewise, and his political and economic teachings were based on the philosophy of St. Thomas. Political discussion is
always grounded in metaphysics and theology, whether perceived or
not; and we cannot oppose the characteristic doctrines of modernity
without consciously having a philosophy, a philosophy moreover
adopted not because it is convenient or useful but because it is true.

Pope Leo was explicit about the connection between the seemingly
abstruse doctrines of philosophers and the everyday political, economic, and social life of humanity. He wrote,

> Whoever turns his attention to the bitter strifes of these days and seeks
> a reason for the troubles that vex public and private life, must come to
> the conclusion that a fruitful cause of the evils which now afflict, as
> well as of those which threaten us, lies in this: that false conclusions
> concerning divine and human things, which originated in the schools
> of philosophy, have crept into all the orders of the State, and have been
> accepted by the common consent of the masses. For since it is in the
> very nature of man to follow the guide of reason in his actions, if his
> intellect sins at all his will soon follows; and thus it happens that loose-

---

1. *What's Wrong With the World* (San Francisco: Ignatius Press, 1994), 179.
2. Vatican Council I, Constitution *Dei Filius*, chap. 2, and canon 2 (Of Revelation).
3. In his *Ideas Have Consequences*.

ness of intellectual opinion influences human actions and perverts them. (Encyclical *Aeterni Patris*, no. 2)

All of Leo's later encyclicals dealing with the foundations of the political order or of socio-economic affairs, such as the famous *Rerum Novarum* (1891), flowed from the fundamental principle enunciated here, that right thinking results in right action, and if our ideas are not correct our actions will surely not be correct either.

Philosophy is important, indeed crucial, because in the end no political order or social theory is defensible that is not grounded first in a philosophy of man and finally in a metaphysics, including a doctrine of God. This does not mean that an appeal to tradition in certain circumstances is not fitting. It does mean, however, that tradition is never the final court of appeal, and any role for tradition is the role allotted to it by reason. Whenever someone claims by nature a right or a duty, whether this claim is correct or is absurd, it is not enough to answer by an appeal to custom, to history, or to established institutions of any kind. At their back there must always be reason, "since it is in the very nature of man to follow the guide of reason in his actions."

For example, in the debate over same-sex marriage in the United States, the chief locus of controversy has seemed to lie in the interpretation of passages from Holy Scripture. Although as a Catholic I certainly accept the authority of Scripture, I do not think it is appropriate to make this question revolve around biblical exegesis. For one thing, not everyone accepts the authority of the Bible nor is there general agreement about how to understand the sacred text or who has the ultimate authority to expound its meaning. More fundamentally, most of the moral code in Scripture that continues to apply to mankind today does so because it is simply a statement of the natural law, the ethical principles rooted in our very human nature or whatness. Opponents of same-sex unions must be able to advance better reasons than simply the scriptural texts if they want ultimately to have a reasonable basis for the opinions they hold, as well as a chance, however slim it may be, of influencing public opinion.

The debate over same-sex marriage and homosexuality is simply one instance of the necessity for having a reasoned intellectual foundation for our thinking. Too many people assume that Christians have no such reasoned foundation nor even aspire to have one. However this may be the case with some, this is clearly not true for all Christians, since the Catholic Church insists that the act of faith is a reasonable act, not dependent upon some sort of leap of faith. But my purpose in writing here is not to engage in controversy with other Christians on such matters, rather merely to point out the absolute necessity that we be able to base our thinking on a reasonable philosophical foundation.

Enlightenment ratiocination is not reason as understood in the scholastic tradition. The usurping of the title to reason by the disciples of the Enlightenment ought not to mean that their opponents acquiesce in that claim. Rather, we should be able to show how our use of reason is both more true to the demands of the intellect and does not depend upon tradition or a misuse of what people call "faith." Even if no one pays any attention to our explanations, fidelity to God himself and to our own intellectual integrity demand this. Otherwise, our thinking will merely rest upon sand and will deserve whatever scorn our contemporaries care to cast upon it.

6

The Social Order as Community

Introduction

THERE HAS LONG BEEN a persistent desire on the part of mankind to imagine or to construct a paradise on earth, a utopia in which all of our problems and conflicts would vanish or at least diminish. Most people have heard of some of the nineteenth-century American examples, such as Brook Farm in Massachusetts or New Harmony, Indiana; but there have been many before and since. Those who know Ronald Knox's book, *Enthusiasm*, will remember that numerous heretical sects made attempts to construct such a Kingdom of God on earth throughout the centuries. While it is certainly true that such utopians and visionaries have always existed, it seems to me that there is a special reason why today, and indeed for the last century of so, longings for an ideal community are more apt to arise in people's hearts than previously.

Let me quote from an article in the July 29, 1995, issue of *America*. This is a description of a 60s-style gathering of a group called the Rainbow Family that has taken place every year since 1972 and last year was held near Taos, New Mexico.

> On the first day of the gathering, I watched dozens of young people pound drums and hundreds more dance in half-naked or fully naked abandon.

The writer interviewed one regular attender of these gatherings as to their aim.

> Robbie told me that the Rainbow Family is about the conscious and positive evolution of humankind. It's about world peace and healing our poor, damaged Mother Earth. It's about making us into better people. It happens like a miracle—it's just love, all these wounded, strange, crazy people learning how to love one another. Jesus, he said, would feel at home at the gathering.
>
> When I asked Robbie what he wanted the human race to evolve into,

he responded: "The ideal is what the Lakota Nation, the Cherokee Nation, the Taos Nation and other Indian nations have. That kind of unity with diversity. The ability to know who you are in a society and on the earth. Knowing that you are related to every human being you may come across." Loving and sharing, he said, are at the heart of so-called "primitive" societies.

It is easy to see through the pretensions of the Rainbow Family. To imagine that a real human community can be created by a week of dancing in a field, and that people's deep defects and faults can be eliminated so easily is to ignore the fact of original sin and has always been the hallmark of such utopians. I think that if the members of the Rainbow Family ever had to sit down and make some hard decisions of the sort that every community eventually has to make, they would soon be disabused of their notion that feelings of peace and harmony are a substitute for clear thinking and hard-won moral virtues.

But nevertheless I would not mock such a gathering, for I think that it is a witness to the very deep and laudable desire on the part of human beings for community, an echo in fact of our lost happiness in the garden of paradise. I would suggest also that there is something specially wrong with the modern world that makes it probable that our desire for community will be more intense, and at the same time more unsatisfied, than has been the case in other ages or in parts of the world less affected by modernity.

The Founders of Modernity

What specifically is it about the modern world that would intensify such desires for community? It is this: the modern Western world is built on principles that deny or reject the possibility or desirability of community as the foundation for social life. The men of the eighteenth century who more or less created the modern social order did so in conscious rejection of the social community that had been built, imperfectly it is true, by Catholic civilization over many centuries. They consciously rejected so much of our Catholic heritage that as a result the public order of the modern West has become based on principles much more anti-Catholic than most of us recognize. Specifically, they willed to create a social order not based on mankind viewed as a brotherhood, but on other and less communitarian principles. They aimed at creating what some of them candidly termed a "commercial republic." Before examining in more detail what they actually said or did, let us look at this term, *commercial republic.*

In itself there is nothing wrong with commerce. Though it obviously should be subordinate to the more primary economic acts of producing and consuming, there is certainly a need for buying, selling, trading, even importing and exporting. But should we want to define our commonwealth, our nation, by its commercial activity? Economic activity itself is a subordinate activity of man; and within economic activity, commerce properly so-called is still more subordinate. Why then would anyone want to raise it to the pinnacle and put it on the masthead of his civilization?

The answer to this lies in the abandonment by the men of the eighteenth century of the idea of founding a civilization upon a religious or metaphysical principle. In part because of a century or more of unfortunate religious strife, but still more, I think, because of new philosophies that either mocked or ignored Europe's traditional religious sense, many thinkers turned to something as ancillary as commerce to find the basis for their new order of things. I hope to show that during the eighteenth century a new concept of civilization and the social order became widespread in Europe and her colonies and that we are still living with that concept today.

The men of the eighteenth century whom I shall be quoting and to whom I shall be referring intended to create a new basis for society, and in their thinking we can see with what force they turned against all that the Church had hitherto created in European culture. I shall be quoting from their writings, as well as from some modern commentators who happen to be in agreement with them. In the first place I shall be making use of material gathered from an essay by Prof. Ralph Lerner.[4] The interesting thing here is that Prof. Lerner, although seeing the same doctrines that I do in these eighteenth-century writers, views them as the prophets of a great new age for mankind whereas I consider them as having helped to destroy whatever was left of Christian civilization and community. So, insofar as part of my evidence has been selected for me, it has been selected by an opponent of my position. Perhaps this will make it more objective. At any rate, it is representative of its age and will, I think, serve to show what the real foundations of the present social order are.

First of all, then, what eighteenth-century thinkers are we talking about? I shall be speaking of a group of writers, primarily John Locke, Montesquieu, Adam Smith, David Hume, and our own Benjamin Franklin, Thomas Jefferson, and Benjamin Rush. All these men are representatives of the so-called Enlightenment, whether of England,

---

4. "Commerce and Character: the Anglo-American as New-Model Man," in *Liberation South, Liberation North*, ed. Michael Novak (Washington: American Enterprise Institute, 1981), 24–49.

France, Scotland, or the English colonies in North America. Despite all the differences in their thought, Prof. Lerner calls them "a band of brethren in arms,"[5] for they all worked to overthrow the West's remaining heritage of Christian civilization and substitute something new. To begin, Prof. Lerner says that these innovators

> saw in commercial republicanism a more sensible and realizable alternative to earlier notions of civic virtue and a more just alternative to the theological-political regime that had so long ruled Europe and its colonial periphery.[6]

These men had a profound desire to overturn traditional European social life. They were impatient with "constraints and preoccupations based on visions of perfection beyond the reach of all or most" and "saw fit, rather, to promote a new ordering of political, economic, and social life."[7] What was the old order they wished to replace? "The old order was preoccupied with intangible goods to an extent we now hardly ever see. The king had his glory, the nobles their honor, the Christians their salvation...."[8] But "Eighteenth-century men had to be brought to see how fanciful those noncommercial notions were."[9]

David Hume, for example, found it quite understandable that men would fight over their economic self-interest, but he found it utterly inexplicable that they should ever have any

> controversy about an article of faith, which is utterly absurd and unintelligible, is not a difference in sentiment, but in a few phrases and expressions, which one party accepts of without understanding them, and the other refuses in the same manner.[10]

Hume believed that Christianity had nourished a spirit of persecution "more furious and enraged than the most cruel factions that ever arose from interest and ambition."[11] So that, as Prof. Lerner says, "fanaticism prompted by principle was incompatible with civility, reason, and government."[12] And also,

> ...where the ancient polity, Christianity, and the feudal aristocracy, each in its own fashion, sought to conceal, deny, or thwart most of the

---

5. Ibid., 25.
6. Ibid., 24.
7. Ibid., 25.
8. Ibid., 26.
9. Ibid.
10. Ibid., quoted on 28.
11. Ibid.
12. Ibid.

common passions for private gratification and physical comfort, the commercial republic built on those passions. . . .

In seeking satisfaction under the new dispensation a man needed to be at once warm and cool, impassioned and calculating, driven yet sober. Eschewing brilliance and grandeur, the new-model man of prudence followed a way of life designed to secure for himself a small but continual profit.[13]

Prof. Lerner continues, "The contrast with and opposition to the Christian and Greek world could hardly have been greater."[14]

One can also see this in John Locke. In his (first) *Letter Concerning Toleration* (1689), Locke bases his argument for civic toleration of all religions on the following supposition:

> The commonwealth seems to me to be a society of men constituted only for the procuring, preserving, and advancing their own civil interests.
>
> Civil interests I call life, liberty, health, and indolency of body; and the possession of outward things, such as money, lands, houses, furniture, and the like.[15]

He reiterates this point in his *Second Essay Concerning Civil Government* as follows:

> The great and chief end, therefore, of men uniting into commonwealths, and putting themselves under government, is the preservation of their property; to which in the state of Nature there are many things wanting.[16]

Rulers are not to be involved in matters beyond these "civil interests," and the general tenor of Locke's argument is that religion is a purely private matter that does not even affect men's moral conduct. As Locke says,

> If a heathen doubt of both Testaments, he is not therefore to be punished as a pernicious citizen. The power of the magistrate and the estates of the people may be equally secure whether any man believe these things or no. I readily grant that these opinions are false and absurd. But the business of laws is not to provide for the truth of opin-

---

13. Ibid., 30.
14. Ibid., 33.
15. Page 3. All references to the Letter are to the edition published in the *Encyclopaedia Britannica Great Books* series (Chicago: Encyclopaedia Britannica, 1952), vol. 35.
16. *Concerning Civil Government*, 53; edition published in the *Encyclopaedia Britannica Great Books* series (Chicago: Encyclopaedia Britannica, 1952), vol. 35.

ions, but for the safety and security of the commonwealth and of every particular man's goods and person.[17]

The point here is not that we should pine for the restoration of the Inquisition—simply that when men unite to form political communities, it is a fatal mistake to assume that things such as God or human morality are of no concern to the community, as such. St. Thomas, for example, wrote that law was concerned "to lead men to virtue," though not in a tyrannical manner. But for Locke and the other thinkers of this movement, law is concerned only with the protection of property—and liberty. This one only intangible good, liberty, that the men promoting the new social order valued as a public good will turn up again as we view the results of their work.

What is the result of narrowing the basis of the social order to material things? Montesquieu wrote,

> We see that in countries where the people move only by the spirit of commerce, they make a traffic of all the humane, all the moral virtues; the most trifling things, those which humanity would demand, are there done, or there given, only for money.[18]

Prof. Lerner sums up Montesquieu's thought as follows:

> For Montesquieu, a regime dedicated to commerce partook less of a union of fellow citizens, bound together by ties of friendship, than of an alliance of contracting parties, intent on maximizing their freedom of choice through a confederation of convenience. It was in this character of an alliance that men found themselves cut off from one another or, rather, linked to one another principally through a market mechanism. It was a world in which everything had its price—and, accordingly, its sellers and buyers. Not surprisingly, the habits of close calculation and "exact justice" appropriate to one kind of activity were extended to all kinds, and political community was replaced by a marketplace of arm's-length transactions.[19]

We can see in these statements, admittedly with differing emphases depending on which eighteenth-century writer is being quoted or referred to, an utterly this-worldly notion of life with two chief aspects: first, a rejection of what Prof. Lerner calls "intangible" goods—in Hume, for example, an utter disdain for the notion that it could ever be reasonable to disagree over a mere article of faith, a metaphysical abstraction,

---

17. *A Letter Concerning Toleration*, 15.

18. *The Spirit of Laws*, 146; edition published in the *Encyclopaedia Britannica Great Books* series (Chicago: Encyclopaedia Britannica, 1952), vol. 38.

19. "Commerce and Character," 44.

"which one party accepts of without understanding them, and the other refuses in the same manner"—and second, in Locke, an explicit restricting of religion to the private sphere. Religion has no importance in the public life of a nation or culture.

This is in fact the crucial point: no culture exists or can exist without a set of ruling ideas. When everything that smacks of the transcendent is eliminated from the public life of a culture, something has to take its place. In our case it is largely commerce and the ideals and ideas that commerce fosters. Moreover, the liberty that accompanies such a commercial society is a liberty whose chief effect is the dissolving of traditional ties and the destruction of traditional communities, whether that takes place because of direct attacks on the family and chastity or indirectly because of an economic system that works as a solvent in hundreds of ways: driving mothers out of the home, exploiting sex to sell products, moving families about to seek employment, or emptying rural areas of farm families.

It is important for us to see how this rejection of any but a materialistic basis for society plays out in everyday life. One example, taken from a writer of the eighteenth century, is the following: Benjamin Rush, a signer of our Declaration of Independence, wrote an essay entitled, "Observations Upon the Study of the Greek and Latin Languages," in which he wrote,

> We occupy a new country. Our principal business should be to explore and apply its resources, all of which press us to enterprise and haste. Under these circumstances, to spend four or five years in learning two dead languages, is to turn our backs upon a gold mine, in order to amuse ourselves in catching butterflies.[20]

Once one rejects "intangible" goods, it is only the cash calculus that counts. Latin and Greek will not open trade routes or help in land speculation, therefore they must go.

The more recent heirs to the same tradition of a commercial society exhibit the same attitude toward tangible and intangible goods. Consider this example from John Kenneth Galbraith's 1958 book, *The Affluent Society.*

> In the autumn of 1954, during the Congressional elections of that year, the Republicans replied to Democratic attacks on their stewardship by arguing that this was the second best year in history. It was not, in all respects, a happy defense. Many promptly said that second best was not good enough—certainly not for Americans. But no person in

---

20. Quoted in Lerner, "Commerce and Character," 45.

either party showed the slightest disposition to challenge the standard by which it is decided that one year is better than another. Nor was it felt that any explanation was required. No one would be so eccentric as to suppose that second best meant second best in the progress of the arts and the sciences. No one would assume that it referred to health, education, or the battle against juvenile delinquency. There was no suggestion that a better or poorer year was one in which the chances for survival amidst the radioactive furniture of the world had increased or diminished. Despite a marked and somewhat ostensible preoccupation with religious observances at the time, no one was moved to suppose that 1954 was the second best year as measured by the number of people who had found enduring spiritual solace.

Second best could mean only one thing—that the production of goods was the second highest in history. There had been a year in which production was higher and hence was better. In fact in 1954 the Gross National Product was $360.5 billion; the year before it had been $364.5. This measure of achievement was acceptable to all. It is a relief on occasion to find a conclusion that is above faction, indeed above debate. On the importance of production there is no difference between Republicans and Democrats, right and left, white or colored, Catholic or Protestant.[21]

Doubtless there were a few Americans in 1954 who rejected the notion that we ought to measure our welfare by purely materialistic measures—but whatever *they* may have thought, public discourse in this country is conducted solely in terms of material goods.

More recently the very respectable free-market-oriented weekly magazine, *The Economist*, published in London, continued this same tradition of putting tangible goods above everything else. In an editorial in the September 9, 1995, issue, on "The Disappearing Family," the editors opined as follows:

> Anxiety about the state of the family is nothing new. A constant of modern history is the perception of social decay: the "breakdown of the family" has seen long and distinguished service. Another constant is the fact of material progress. The association between the two is unsurprising. Economic progress gives people opportunities they were hitherto denied, which provokes social change. And social change almost always seems to be regarded initially as for the worse.
>
> In thinking about the family today, it is well to keep that history in mind. Over the past 30 years almost all rich countries have seen big increases in the rate of divorce. Expanding opportunity is doubtless

21. (New York: Mentor, 1958), 101.

one of many causes. More women have a career and the financial independence that goes with it: far fewer are forced to choose between misery in a failed marriage and destitution. And divorce laws have been greatly eased, reflecting demands for greater freedom from the control once exercised over private behaviour by church and state. If divorce has gone up for reasons such as these, the change must be counted, at least in the first instance, as a gain.

A bit later it goes on to say,

Simply, it is too soon to say of society at large that the rise in divorce, and the increase in single-parent households associated with it, has gone so far that the loss outweighs the gain. Without compelling evidence that the net harm is great, and perhaps not even then, governments have no business imposing their moral choices on citizens. This remains true even if it is mainly adults who benefit from more divorce and mainly children who lose....

I submit that there is a direct and clear road from the statements of the eighteenth-century writers I have quoted or referred to above and these contemporary attitudes toward tangible and intangible goods. In the Galbraith quotation and in the editorial from *The Economist* we see the consequences of rejecting any intangible goods—except unrestrained freedom, the only intangible eagerly embraced by the modern world, which is also the only intangible good mentioned by Locke. "A constant of modern history is the perception of social decay," *The Economist*'s editorial writer says. Perhaps that is because a constant of modern history is the reality of social decay, a hypothesis that he does not consider. Note that "material progress" is what makes possible this increased freedom and social change. "Economic progress gives people opportunities they were hitherto denied...." Fewer women "are forced to choose between misery in a failed marriage and destitution." I pass over the well-known fact that divorced women and their children do experience, if not always destitution, at least a much lower material standard of living, and simply point out that if "material progress" gives people the opportunity to simply walk away from difficult relationships instead of doing the hard work of trying to make them work out, then that is hardly a gain. Of course there are some relationships in which people cannot reasonably or even safely remain—and in those cases a Christian civilization should offer all the support, of every sort, that is necessary. But it is not increased divorce, or indeed any divorce at all, that is needed here to promote human welfare.

As my last examples, I take first a statement by the president of the American Enterprise Institute, Christopher DeMuth, as quoted in the *Washington Post* on February 23, 1996. Mr. DeMuth said,

It's certainly true that capitalism sometimes conflicts with the preservation of established cultural values. The gale of creative destruction not only destroys old firms, but old methods of doing things. Another word for that gale is progress.

The old things that are destroyed by capitalism are not just inefficient firms or industrial methods invented in a prior era. They include things such as families and communities and even Christian civilization itself. Nor, as some like to pretend, is all this the result of some recent bad turn in our history, a falling off from an earlier and so-called Christian America, a land that never was. No, it is inherent in the commercial republic constructed at the end of the eighteenth century by the Founders of our present regime, who consciously and carefully rejected traditional European civilization in order to attempt to build the *Novus Ordo Seclorum*, the New Order of the Ages.

And finally, I quote from a very recent statement by Associate Justice of the U.S. Supreme Court, Antonin Scalia. In the same speech in which he opined that the state should permit abortion if that is what the electorate wants, Justice Scalia gave his view of the task of government, which was summed up as "protecting person and property and ensuring the conditions for prosperity."[22] This, of course, is nothing but a restatement of John Locke and demonstrates the fact that conservatives in America are simply one variety of Lockean liberals.

Perhaps the best summation of the commercial republic can be found in the Argentine writer, Julio Meinvielle, in his book, *From Lamennais to Maritain*.[23]

> We might also point out that a society under the banner of Money, such as the Anglo-American commercial society, or under the banner of Work, such as Soviet Russia, will be structurally *atheistic*; for even though the merchant and the worker may believe in God, they do not believe in Him in their capacity as merchant or worker but just as private persons; that is, because they are more than just merchants or workers. For that very reason, a society which exalts Money or Work as the supreme value of life is necessarily atheistic as a society.

Critics of Capitalism

The capitalist system has triumphed in the modern world, but not everyone has rejoiced at that triumph. In fact, the critics of capitalism have been many and have represented many differing and opposed

22. Quoted in the *Arlington Catholic Herald* (May 16, 1996), 12.
23. (Buenos Aires: Ediciones Theoria, 2nd ed., 1967) (Translation privately prepared for the Theology Dept., Christendom College.)

points of view. Of course, socialists and communists have been against capitalism, but its opponents have also included many very traditional Catholics, such as Hilaire Belloc and G.K. Chesterton, men no one can accuse of being influenced by what we call the Left. Nor is it surprising that so many have been able to see that the mere production of material goods cannot possibly be the purpose of the social order or the state and that the social atomism resulting from making competition and contract the basis for society is profoundly contrary to the nature of man.

This widespread opposition to capitalism has been of concern to some of its defenders. For example, Michael Novak, a writer to whom I shall be referring more than once, writes, "Although the evidence of the immense benefits for . . . moral progress ushered into history by capitalist economies lies before their eyes, they [i.e., anticapitalist intellectuals] go on as if it does not exist."[24] The defenders of capitalism commonly talk as if only the left and a few naive fellow travelers, mostly ecclesiastics, were enemies of the capitalist economic order; and so they have attempted to explain this opposition, or explain it away, in various ways. For example, one free marketer, Ernest van den Haag, explains this opposition as an example of irrational commitment to ideology:

> Union leaders, socialists, academic egalitarians, Marxists, totalitarians, and millenarians of every kind have a strong emotional investment in their policies and theories which ultimately leads to ideological and finally to material investment. They cannot be persuaded by any argument, however well it shows that the policy they favor is contrary to the public interest, ineffective or both. The attempt of economists to tutor the emotionally committed is as doomed to failure as the attempts of philosophers to tutor the insane.[25]

Van den Haag goes on to say that "rational knowledge is of little help in dispelling the resentment against the market—or the longing for an ideal system in which a just government justly rewards moral merits."

> On closer analysis this longing rests on nonrational fantasies: Each of us secretly hopes that his essential superiority will be recognized in an ideal system. Albeit unconsciously, revolutionaries as well as reformers place this hope on an ideal government, which functions as a true *parens patriae*, a just and omniscient parent—just as a gambler places

24. Michael Novak, *This Hemisphere of Liberty: a Philosophy of the Americas* (Washington: AEI Press, 1990), 63.

25. Ernest van den Haag, ed., *Capitalism: Sources of Hostility* (New Rochelle, NY: Epoch Books for the Heritage Foundation, 1979), 12. Another similar work is Ernest W. Lefever, ed., *Will Capitalism Survive?* (Washington: Ethics and Public Policy Center, 1979).

his hope on Dame Fortuna, who inexplicably but certainly and justly will love him best, and prefer him—as mother should have done.[26]

Another writer in the same volume says,

> I suggest that the root of much—perhaps not all, but much—of the hostility to free markets comes from man's difficulty in dealing with the most human of activities, the making of conscious choices.[27]

I could continue in this vein, quoting other writers' accounts as to the true sources of opposition to capitalism, but what I believe to be those true sources is perhaps apparent in what I have said above: human beings have a powerful, though faulty, longing for justice and brotherhood. Modernity and the economic system it fosters, capitalism, can never produce either. Therefore the resentment against capitalism arises.

The Romanticizing of Capitalism

Now, some defenders of capitalism seem to have seen this inadequacy. They understand that capitalism must win at other levels besides the merely materialistic, and so several efforts have arisen to romanticize capitalism. One such effort can be found in Mr. Novak's book, *Toward a Theology of the Corporation*.[28]

> In thinking about the corporation in history and its theological significance, I begin with a general theological principle. George Bernanos once said that grace is everywhere. Wherever we look in the world, there are signs of God's presence: in the mountains, in a grain of sand, in a human person, in the poor and the hungry. The earth is charged with the grandeur of God. So is human history.
>
> If we look for signs of grace in the corporation, we may discern seven of them—a suitably sacramental number.[29]

What are these seven "signs of grace"? They are creativity, liberty, birth and mortality, social motive, social character, insight, and the rise of liberty and election. Novak continues, "In these seven ways, corporations offer metaphors for grace, a kind of insight into God's ways in history."[30]

Now, in fact most of what Novak says about the theology of the corporation seems to me simply inflated nonsense. The interesting thing

---

26. *Capitalism: Sources of Hostility*, 27.
27. Ibid., 47.
28. Michael Novak, *Toward a Theology of the Corporation* (Washington: American Enterprise Institute, 1981).
29. Ibid., 37.
30. Ibid., 43.

about it is not his pseudo-theology, but the fact that he feels the need to offer one at all. It suggests that he might feel that many of the objections made against capitalism and its lack of community have merit. For example, here is his explanation of "social character," one of the corporation's "signs of grace":

> The corporation is inherently and in its essence corporate. The very word suggests communal, nonindividual, many acting together. Those who describe capitalism by stressing the individual entrepreneur miss the central point. Buying and selling by individual entrepreneurs occurred in biblical times. What is interesting and novel ... is the communal focus of the new ethos: the rise of communal risk taking, the pooling of resources, the sense of communal religious vocation in economic activism.[31]

The attempt to harness the desire for community for the sake of capitalistic business enterprises has had more success than it deserves. It forces us, however, to address the question of what capitalism really is and what kind of social order it creates. Is it one of atomism and strife or, as Novak asserts, is it a communal and corporate one? Pirate crews were also communal, and slave gangs worked corporately. Much more than verbal similarity is needed to show that capitalism is the communitarian force that Novak makes of it here.

Is There a "Catholic Whig Tradition"?

Mr. Novak makes another and more serious attempt to put capitalism in a communitarian and less harsh light. He writes as follows:

> ... beginning in the seventeenth and eighteenth centuries ... a group of Western European moralists became skeptical of the moral biases of the aristocratic class and developed the thesis that a regime based upon commerce, and pursuing plenty as well as and even more than power, offered the most reasonable route to the moral betterment of the human race.

He says further, "Where earlier generations found the pursuit of plenty, of wealth, and of commerce morally inferior, they found it morally superior to the foundations of any previous regime."[32] Novak posits and attempts to discover what he calls a "Catholic Whig tradition," that is, a line of Catholic thinkers who were more or less in agreement with the eighteenth-century project of refounding the social order on a new

---

31. Ibid., 40–41.
32. *This Hemisphere of Liberty: a Philosophy of the Americas* (Washington: American Enterprise Institute, 1990), 63.

basis. Let us see what this supposed Catholic Whig tradition is and whether in fact there is any such thing.

I shall begin by following Novak as he conducts his search. One cannot understand Latin American thought, he begins, "unless one understands the Catholic intellectual traditions of southern Europe and Latin America...."[33] So far so good. He points out that this is true even of Latin American thinkers who reject the Catholic faith. Let me quote the following fine passage of Novak's:

> Moreover, I have encountered in my travels many writers and scholars in Latin America who, while not Catholic, find the language of northern Anglo-Saxon political economy too emotionally and culturally thin, too materialistic in its timbre, too individualistic in its intonation, too drily pragmatic. For many in Latin America, the smell of incense at the High Mass, the flickering candles and their smoke, the bells, the sonorous hymns, and the taste of the Lord's Body on the tongue convey a sensibility that is far thicker than that received in the bare white Puritan churches of New England.... A highly cultured people, furthermore, necessarily carries with it a profoundly conservative sensibility. Painfully aware of the richness and complexity of the past, they revel in holding onto that past and recreating it. Partly, they live in memory as birds in air. Their imaginations need the past as certain fauna live only in the tangled jungle; one sees this vividly in Latin American novelists. Thus, nearly all Latin Americans, even the most radical, nourish a conservative consciousness, sometimes under the banner of "national identity." They identify themselves with past events, heroes, movements, struggles. Progressives in Latin America are seldom purely progressive; most want to carry their past proudly with them as they advance.[34]

I can easily agree with what Mr. Novak has written here. He reveals the existence of an intellectual tradition that is utterly unknown to most North Americans. With reference to socio-political thought, this tradition begins in Plato and Aristotle, then continues with Catholic thinkers, including Augustine, Aquinas, Bellarmine, and later on Joseph de Maistre and Juan Donoso Cortes. It is a tradition that is worthy of being better known among Anglo-Saxons, especially Anglo-Saxon Catholics; and in many important respects, it is totally opposed, in both its starting points and in its conclusions, to our own traditions of political thought. Novak says as much (in a different book), with reference to Latin America:

33. Ibid., 1.
34. Ibid., 1–2.

a socialist order is closer to their own past. It is less pluralistic and more centralized, and it allows for a more intense union of church and state than does the democratic pluralism of the North American type.[35]

(One can accept this without thereby becoming an advocate of socialism, for socialism was simply one more and flawed attempt to construct a community without God. Just because capitalism is wrong does not make socialism right.) Having admitted that many Latin Americans would "find the language of northern Anglo-Saxon political economy too emotionally and culturally thin, too materialistic in its timbre, too individualistic in its intonation, too drily pragmatic," Novak posits the existence of the "Catholic Whig tradition" in order to offer something to Latin Americans that is not entirely alien to their heritage and yet promotes capitalism. Curiously, he takes his cue in this matter from Friedrich von Hayek, a quintessential libertarian and secularist, who defines Whig as one who favors "a free economy (and democracy and pluralism)."[36] What Novak endeavors to do is to take the writers whom I quoted in the first part of this essay, tone down what they said a bit, and enroll Thomas Aquinas and other Catholic thinkers among them. A few examples of his manner of proceeding follow.

> "The God who gave us life gave us liberty." The words are Thomas Jefferson's, but the thesis is that of Thomas Aquinas. For Aquinas, man is the glory of the universe, an image of God on earth, made to be like God in his liberty.[37]

What is the problem with this? When St. Thomas wrote about man and his freedom, he was simply stating the truth of man's freedom of choice; he was not making a political statement. It is otherwise with Jefferson. *Liberty* as used here by Jefferson and by Aquinas mean different things. Novak describes the eighteenth-century innovators thus:

> One of the great achievements of the Whig tradition was its new world experiment, the *Novus Ordo Seclorum* (the new order of the ages). Its American progenitors called that experiment the commercial republic. The Whigs were the first philosophers in history to grasp the importance of basing government of the people upon the foundation of commerce. They underpinned democracy with a capitalist, growing economy.[38]

---

35. *Liberation South, Liberation North*, 4.
36. *This Hemisphere of Liberty*, 2.
37. Ibid., 115.
38. Ibid., 11.

In his attempt to justify Aquinas's standing as a Whig, Novak has to fudge a good deal. For example, he makes the point that Thomas accepted the created world and rejected the supernaturalistic Augustinianism common to many earlier Catholic thinkers. Thus Aquinas "legitimated . . . all that is good about human nature and its strivings."[39] But does this make him a Whig? In what sense is it just to say that St. Thomas legitimated the "strivings" of human nature?

Mr. Novak continues,

> By no means would it be legitimate to ask if Thomas Aquinas were a Whig in the same sense as Thomas Jefferson, James Madison, Edmund Burke, Adam Smith, Lord Acton, or Friedrich von Hayek. The more exact question is, What did Thomas Aquinas hold that might embolden those who today cherish the Whig tradition to count him in their number? There are six propositions of Aquinas that seem particularly compelling to the Whig temper.[40]

What are those "six propositions"? They are (1) "Civilization is constituted by reasoned conversation"; (2) "The human being is free because he can reflect and choose"; (3) "Civilized political institutions respect reflection and choice"; (4) "True liberty is ordered liberty"; (5) "Humans are self-determined persons, not mere individuals (group members)"; and (6) "The regime worthiest of the human person mixes elements of monarchy, aristocracy, and democracy."[41] Most of these six theses are not peculiar to the Whig tradition; number six, for example, has been a staple of political philosophers since pagan antiquity, and numbers two, four, and five are likewise hardly peculiar to the Whigs. In fact, Novak does not really attempt to make a serious argument here. He does not attempt to show that these theses are uniquely Whig nor that, to the extent St. Thomas held any of them, this fact should make us "count him" in the same tradition as that of John Locke. By Novak's method of reasoning, almost every classical political philosopher could be counted as a Whig.

It would be extremely tedious to examine in detail each of Novak's six points; so, let us look briefly at his discussion of just one of them to see his method of proceeding.

"Fourth Thesis: True liberty is ordered liberty." After some platitudes on the need for restraint and the moral virtues, he says the following:

---

39. Ibid., 111.
40. Ibid., 113–14.
41. These six theses are on pages 114–19 of *This Hemisphere of Liberty*.

The proudest boast of the young Whig republic, the United States, was the legendary manly strength (virtue) of its leaders, notably George Washington, James Madison, and Thomas Jefferson—and also the virtue of its people, who were asked in an unprecedented way to reflect and to deliberate upon the ratification of the Constitution under which they would live and to maintain sufficient virtue to keep the republic from the self-destruction into which all earlier republics had speedily fallen.[42]

In the first place, this paragraph has really nothing to do with the rather vague discussion of virtue which precedes it, nor does it have anything to do with St. Thomas. In typical Novak fashion, no argument is made. Nothing is even asserted. All depends upon a vague power of association and suggestion.

Moreover, Novak shifts back and forth, as it suits his purposes, between a narrow and an expansive definition of *Whig*. No one of the six points is especially characteristic of the Whig tradition as defined by Hayek, for example. Throughout, Novak implies much more about Aquinas than he dare assert and asserts much more than he proves.

There are undoubtedly thinkers whom one can call Catholic Whigs—Lord Acton, for example, would seem to be one, and Novak himself fits the definition well. The important question, of course, is whether it includes exponents of authentic Catholic tradition, such as St. Thomas Aquinas. And if Novak's case is the best one that can be made for including Aquinas among the Whigs, then definitely St. Thomas cannot be labeled as such. Certainly Aquinas says things that Whigs said, and that nearly everybody would say, such as that tyranny or totalitarian government is an evil or that order is better than chaos. But this does not make him a Whig.

Catholic Alternative

We have looked at various attempts to refashion human society. Some of these attempts at least gave a nod in the direction of the solidarity of mankind as the necessary foundation of any social order whereas others denied it. Before finishing, let us turn to what the Catholic Church proposes on these matters.

Catholic social thought has always seen society as a unity, a unity based on true mutual interests, on justice and on charity. Here is a vision of community, yet a vision that does not fail to take into account our fallen human nature. Just as labor and capital are not inherently in

42. Ibid., 117.

conflict, so all the other natural groupings of human society can and ought to work together so as to form a community not just of individuals but of nations. As Pope Pius XII said in his first encyclical, *Summi Pontificatus* (October 20, 1939), the evils of his own day were caused in the first place by "forgetfulness of that law of human solidarity and charity which is dictated and imposed by our common origin and by the equality of rational nature in all men, to whatever people they belong." Pope Pius goes on to speak of the "truth which associates men as brothers in one great family." He continues,

> And the nations, despite a difference of development due to diverse conditions of life and of culture, are not destined to break the unity of the human race, but rather to enrich and embellish it by the sharing of their own peculiar gifts and by that reciprocal interchange of goods which can be possible and efficacious only when a mutual love and a lively sense of charity unite all the sons of the same Father and all those redeemed by the same Divine Blood. (No. 43)

Here is a vision of human community and solidarity as powerful as anything that the Rainbow Family can come up with. It is opposed both to the Whig version of civilization founded on mere exchange of goods and to those who forget the fact of original sin. The entire social teaching of the Church is based on this vision of human solidarity. Nor does the most recent social encyclical, *Centesimus Annus*, change anything in this regard, despite some of its tendentious commentators, who have created a widespread belief that somehow the Church now takes a more benign view of a society based on the free market than she previously did.[43]

The most sober Catholic, if he has truly formed his mind with Catholic truth, will not deny this vision of human community; while the most optimistic Catholic, if he is orthodox, will realize that our vision of community must be tempered by the realities of our sinful state. The social teachings of the Church present this chastened vision of community, tempered by the reality of personal sin and the creation of structures of sin, structures that both institutionalize evil and tend to make all of us cooperators in evil. Because of this, I suggest that when a Catholic considers the foundations of society, he ought to be at once hard-

---

43. In fact, this encyclical contains several eloquent denunciations of the very commercial civilization that Mr. Novak and his friends celebrate. For example, "The atheism of which we are speaking is also closely connected with the rationalism of the Enlightenment, which views human and social reality in a mechanistic way. Thus there is a denial of the supreme insight concerning man's true greatness, his transcendence in respect to earthly realities . . . and, above all, the need for salvation. . . ." (no. 13).

headed and a dreamer, both realistic and utopian. If a Catholic is confronted by those who desire a total reshaping of civilization, a civilization refounded on some new principle, be it the *Novus Ordo Seclorum* of the commercial republicans or the trans-historical paradise of the Marxists, he should reply in these words of St. Pius X, from his encyclical letter, *Notre Charge Apostolique*, of August 25, 1910:

> No, Venerable Brethren, We must repeat with the utmost energy in these times of social and intellectual anarchy when everyone takes it upon himself to teach as a teacher and lawmaker—the City cannot be built otherwise than as God has built it; society cannot be set up unless the Church lays the foundations and supervises the work; no, civilization is not something yet to be found, nor is the New City to be built on hazy notions; it has been in existence and still is: it is Christian civilization, it is the Catholic City. It has only to be set up and restored continually against the unremitting attacks of insane dreamers, rebels and miscreants. (No. 11)

Christian civilization is not something existing in the air, something that is a blueprint only, something that forever eludes us. No, it has existed. Its effects and remnants still exist in parts of the world. It is of course true that this historic Christian civilization had many faults. Although it is the case that these faults could, in principle at least, have been dealt with within the framework of Catholicism, it is also the case that a Catholic will realize that the search for a perfect civilization is vain. If the Catholic city had faults, then let these be corrected as well as possible; but if they are never entirely corrected, that does not mean that the social order should be scrapped and begun over again. It is rather a matter of setting right, restoring, protecting. The more keenly Catholics of the past saw the defects of Christian civilization the more keenly they should have tried to correct them, but at the same time understanding that there was no magic formula that would usher in the new order. It was simply a matter of the hard work of shoring up and improving what they already had.

On the other hand, however, a Catholic is a kind of utopian, a dreamer of dreams of perfection, without contradicting anything that I have just said. For he longs for the perfect "civilization of love" (to use a phrase of Paul VI and John Paul II), the social order that is true community. He longs to cooperate with the Holy Spirit in renewing this earth. In doing so, though, he really is longing for the heavenly Jerusalem coming down from above, for only there can the true Catholic city be found. As the epistle to the Hebrews tells us, here on earth we have no lasting city, but we seek the city that is to come; and in desiring that city that is to come, we at the same time work to establish and maintain the earthly Catholic city, hoping perhaps that in some way the earthly city can be transformed by the spirit of that city coming down from Heaven. Thus, we acknowledge with St. Pius X our mundane task of continually restoring what we have, while at the same time longing for what we do not yet have.

At the heart of the Church is the sacrifice of the Mass, an act of reconciliation between God and man, between individual men, between man and the rest of creation. Thus, at the heart of any civilization formed and informed by the Faith are reconciliation, unity, community. This is the vision of the social order that the Church has always held out to mankind. If the participants in the Rainbow Family gatherings do not understand this—do not understand that the Church is their ally, even their guide, in whatever of good that they are seeking—then perhaps the fault lies with us Catholics. How can we convince others that the Church is not simply another institution of bourgeois society, but the only real alternative to that society? Well, perhaps we had best start by convincing first ourselves, next our fellow Catholics, and then the rest of mankind.

7

The Dissolutions of Modernity
and the Catholic Response

IT IS A COMMONPLACE to speak of the medieval synthesis, an intellectual integration of all reality, of the entire cosmos, of all things in heaven and in earth and under the earth, into a unity, something understandable, in which all the parts were related to one another and in which man, as a microcosm of the whole, embodied the world of matter and spirit, of intellect, will, and affection. Externally, this unity was realized, imperfectly it is true, in the unity of Christendom under Pope and Emperor, in the sacralizing of life within the liturgy and the sacraments of the Church, in the subordination of economic activity for the common good by feudal land tenure and by the urban craft guilds. Of course, it is also a commonplace that this unity no longer exists. My intent in this essay is to describe, with rather broad strokes, some of the elements and results of the disruption of this unity and of the response to this disruption and dissolution that was made by Catholics. I shall be talking about intellectual causality and sometimes making things more schematic than they were or not paying strict attention to historical chronology. I shall not be concerned much with external aspects of the disruption, such as the Black Death, the schism of the Church under two rival claimants to the Papacy (1378–1417), or even the Protestant revolt. I shall speak chiefly of intellectual disruptions to the medieval intellectual synthesis.

Before beginning, I should say a word about this synthesis: its highest exemplar was without doubt St. Thomas. As Josef Pieper wrote,

> In this synthesis of a theologically founded worldliness and a theology open to the world, a synthesis Thomas forged with the full energies of his inner being, a culmination was reached. Here was the structure toward which the whole intellectual effort of Christian thinking about the world ... had been aiming and toward which this whole era of

Christendom was directed: the *coniunctio rationis et fidei*, the conjunction of reason with faith.[1]

Without downplaying the many efforts of other thinkers, one may say that in St. Thomas all their contributions find in a sense their true home, the universality of vision that assigns each to its proper place and allows it to peacefully coexist with its neighbors. But let us now turn to our consideration of the beginnings of the modern world.

In his book, *Society and Sanity*, Frank Sheed makes a seemingly off-hand remark about the modern world which goes to the heart of most of what I shall be talking about. Sheed wrote, "I know that to the modern reader there seems something quaint and old-world in asking what a thing is for; the modern question is always what can I do with it."[2] The loss of any conception of inherent purpose is a common thread running through most of the things I shall be addressing.

In the first place, I have to say a word about the connection between a thing's having a nature and a thing's having a purpose. As Frank Sheed said, moderns are not accustomed to asking what the purpose of a thing is. And this is because moderns are not accustomed to thinking that things have a nature, a whatness, of their own. Moderns instead will think that a thing is what I make it to be. It has no inherent nature of its own that I have to respect. For unless one thinks that a thing has a nature, it is hard to maintain that it has a purpose, for purpose comes from nature. As the scholastic axiom says, *agere sequitur esse*, action follows being. If we look at any of the organs of the human body, for example the eyes, the nose, and so on, we can see what their purpose is because we first examine what they are, what they are like, what they are fitted for, how they ordinarily function. From this we can intuit something about their nature and thus their purpose.

The first step in destroying the idea of nature was to destroy the universality of the nature. One of the recurring questions in early Greek philosophy was that of the relationship between the one and the many. What do I mean when I say that X is a horse and Y is a horse and Z is a horse? What do they have in common that makes them all horses? The mature answer, as given for example by Aristotle and St. Thomas, was that they all shared the same universal nature; hence, in answer to the question, What is that?, it was proper to say, X *is* a horse, Y *is* a horse, Z *is* a horse. Being a horse is what they essentially were, whatever accidental differences, such as color or size, they might have had; and this

---

1. *Guide to Thomas Aquinas* (Notre Dame, IN: University of Notre Dame Press, 1987), 132.

2. *Society and Sanity* (New York: Sheed & Ward, 1953), 110–11.

"horseness" existed equally in each individual horse. Now the nominalist philosophers of the late Middle Ages began to destroy this notion of the reality of universal natures by arguing that only individual things exist and that universals have no extra-mental existence in the individual things themselves, the logical result of this being that universals are reduced to simply being "names [*nomina*] or ideas with which nothing in reality corresponds."[3] From this it follows that we have all these animals that curiously resemble each other and we call them all horses, but this is not to say that they are all really the same kind of thing, philosophically speaking. It is simply a convenience. But if this is so, then the essential reality of these horse-like beings cannot be determined by their natures, their whatness, for they really have none, at least none that is knowable to us.

What is the connection between seeing universals in this way and a loss of the sense of purpose? Well, this can best be illustrated with regard to human beings. If anything about myself as a human being is simply something shared with all other human beings, I am a humble receiver of something that is bigger than I am and to whose purposes I should try to be obedient. But if in fact I do not identify my deepest self with a shared humanity, but am unique, not just as a person, who I am, but as *what* I am, then everything about me is subject to my will. As we shall see, in our day this notion has worked itself out with particular virulence with reference to mankind's sexual powers.

Moreover, if we ignore or deny the reality of universals, we have only individual things to deal with, things that can be weighed and measured and whose conduct can be observed, but concerning which we can never say anything about how they *ought* to be acting because we do not know what their nature, and thus their purpose, is. It is often said that it is impossible to go from an *is* to an *ought*, meaning that from simply examining something, we cannot make a moral judgment about what that thing should be or do. But this is not true. From examining the eye, for example, I can safely say that it was meant for seeing and that an eye that cannot see is a defective eye, a bad eye; not morally bad, of course, as it has no will, but ontologically bad. In the case of something subject to the human will, such as our human acts and institutions, I can say that something is not only ontologically bad but also morally bad also, as any human act is an act of the human will. If things do not have common natures, I cannot make these kinds of judgments. The ramifications of this will become clearer later.

3. Jacques Maritain, *An Introduction to Philosophy* (London: Sheed & Ward, 1947), 119. Of course this simplifies the complexities of the nominalists' positions.

Now, the notion of purpose was deeply embedded in human thought in the pre-modern period. Whether it was knowledge, political authority, economic activity, or sexuality, generally among the first questions that was asked was, What is it for? And this question, as we saw, presupposed that it had a certain determinate whatness of its own. Otherwise, it could not have an inherent purpose, and its purpose would be whatever we made it to be.

Thus, the heart of the modern assault on mankind lay in the denial of universals and thus of determinate natures and of inherent purposes. This denial creates a flux in which only individual things exist and in which morality, insofar as it might exist, is something imported into reality, as may be seen in the term *value judgment*. Even many supporters of Christian morality use the term *values*, but to do so is to turn the argument over to our adversaries; for a "value" is something that subjectively appeals to me. Thus, I have my values; you have yours. They are essentially things added to reality, and therefore we have the well-known contrast of facts and values. According to this conception of things, only individual facts exist; there are those facts some of us like (value) and those some of us dislike. It is really a matter of taste, much like one's favorite kind of ice cream. The earlier notion, however—the notion that was destroyed by the coming of modernity—saw purpose as inherent in reality, because things really had natures. It was not unscientific to speak of a thing's whatness; in fact, this was what a science chiefly studied.[4]

Now let us look at a few of the ways in which this loss of the recognition of purpose worked itself out in human affairs.

Politics

Since at least Plato the notion that the ruler governed not for his own gain, but for the common good of those whom he ruled, was a commonplace. Human beings obviously need to live in some kind of community, and this community obviously needs some kind of government. It was supposed that there was thus a natural relationship between ruler and ruled. Both needed each other; neither was held to be naturally out to exploit the other. This, however, is not the modern view. With Machiavelli the notion emerged that political thought, instead of dwelling on what was assumed to be the nature of the state, the ruler, and the people,

---

4. Of course, activities such as ruling or buying and selling do not have natures the way men or birds or flowers do. Perhaps one could say they have quasi-natures. At any rate, to look at them from the standpoint of nature and purpose is the only way to really understand them.

political thought, now loosed from the purposes inherent in the nature of any political thing, became interested simply in individual facts, such as how rulers got and kept power, it being presumed that the purpose of the ruler was to benefit himself. Whatever general principles were now studied in political thought were not deduced from the nature of authority or of the political community, but were taken by induction from the example of successful rulers or successful empires. Similarly in our own day, the academic discipline of political science is largely concerned with examining voting behavior, the behavior of various interest groups within a society, and so on. This approach is simply an updating of Machiavelli to the realities of modern democratic regimes.

We can see from this how the loss of the idea of universals has affected our approach to political questions. If the political community, rulership, and political authority each has a whatness, that is, something inherent in it that is true always and everywhere regardless of the many accidental differences in types of regime, then there is some standard against which we can compare and understand governments and states. This same standard can be appealed to in seeking to make political reforms or correct abuses; but if there are only individual things, we cannot go from *is* to *ought*. We can only compare individual things or facts with other things or facts as we count, measure, and narrate the eternal flux of human activity.

This is likewise true with regard to economic activity. If we ask ourselves why human beings have the need and capacity for external goods, the answer is obvious: human beings need such external goods not merely to exist physically, but in order to live lives that are fully human. Thus, these external goods exist for the sake of something else—the sake of what is more important in our lives: our family life, our community, intellectual, and spiritual life. We eat to live; we do not live to eat. So, economic activity, the activity by which we obtain external goods, is of its own nature strictly subordinate to the good life of each man and of the entire community. Logically then, if an economic system subverts the common good, if it makes the more important aspects of human life more difficult to attain, it would be violating its purpose and going beyond its merely subordinate role and thus should be changed.

This is not, however, how economic activity is seen today. Neither the so-called practical man, the entrepreneur, nor the economist in the tradition of Adam Smith, ever asks, What is the purpose of economic activity as a whole? He only asks what each individual's purpose is, and he assumes that the answer is buy cheap and sell dear—in other words, to enrich himself. This question he asks regardless of what it means to the moral or cultural health of the community or to the moral character of the entrepreneur himself. Wealth, however obtained, for whatever end and in whatever amount, is the purpose of economic activity, not simply the provision of those external goods the individual and society need.[5] If I can make money producing a good or service, so long as it is legal, I need never ask if the community really needs it; or if it is not in fact harmful to it, or if I am otherwise destroying any of the higher goods that pertain to the community.

All this is possible only because men were first convinced that the purpose of economic activity was whatever an individual wanted to make it. It had no inherent purpose to which he must in humility submit, because it had no inherent nature. And again, this was so because all that economists saw was this man selling and that man buying, this man producing and that man consuming. They were simply facts, facts from which we could make inductions to discover how to buy most cheaply or sell most dearly or produce and consume the most. There is no standard by which to judge any of these actions because there is no purpose inherent in them; there is no purpose because they have no nature.

Another area in which this modern approach has triumphed is with respect to sex, marriage, and the family. It is hard to see how anyone could deny that the inherent purpose of sex is the procreation of offspring. Clearly, if the human race were not meant to reproduce by means of sexual union, we should not have the physical capacity for sexual activity. The connection of the sex act with reproduction is obvious. But this is not what modern man thinks. Because our technology allows us to dissociate sex and the possibility or probability of procreation, we have largely forgotten that they are connected, and connected not because I or anyone else says they are but by their natures, by what they are. Sex is inherently connected with procreation. Of course, sex has other purposes too, but they are all related to and based on its primary or fundamental purpose: the production of children. For example, the tendency of sexual activity to produce profound bonds of affection between the man and the woman is clearly related to the need for husbands and wives, as fathers and mothers, to maintain an affectionate relationship through the difficulties and trials of rearing children. If sex

5. One can eat only so much food or wear so many clothes. These are all real economic goods that serve human life, but wealth as money can be multiplied without measure and without reference to any reasonable need or purpose. As St. Thomas Aquinas says (*Summa Theologiae*, I-II, q. 2, a. 1, ad 3), ". . . the appetite of natural riches is not infinite, because according to a set measure they satisfy nature; but the appetite of artificial riches is infinite, because it serves inordinate concupiscence. . . ."

were meant to be purely recreational, there is no reason why it should be connected with feelings of benevolence and love. It could be simply an economic transaction in which the two partners separated as soon as the transaction was completed.

Thus, having broken the tie between heterosexual activity and pro-creation, what stands in the way of admitting any sort of sexual activity? This is the reason, I think, for the lack of principled opposition to the legitimizing of homosexual activity.[6] Consider the absurdity of what is affirmed when people say that homosexual acts or a homosexual incli-nation is natural. It is as if one were to assert that my legs were not made for walking or my eyes for seeing if I choose to regard them otherwise; and if someone did have this disconnection between the obvious pur-pose of his body and his subjective inclinations, then clearly such a per-son would have some kind of psychological affliction. Even if it is true that some people are born with a homosexual inclination, this would mean nothing toward saying that such behavior was natural for them, any more than the fact that some people are born blind proves that it is not natural for every human being to see with his eyes. But when the modern world insists that it is somehow just as natural for two men or two women to pretend to a sexual union as for a man and a woman, this confusion of thought is explainable only when we remember the deep forgetfulness and even hostility of modernity toward natures and pur-poses.

The loss of recognition of universals is connected with a changed atti-tude toward what we usually call the natural world or simply nature. Indeed, the fact that we use that word *nature*, which properly refers to the whatness of anything, to mean the vast interconnected system of natures within which man dwells, suggests that our attitude toward uni-versals may be connected with our attitude toward the things of the nat-ural world. For one of the most important things that happened in the change from a medieval to a modern outlook was in our view of nature. With Galileo, and later with Newton, the view that things are best explained as determined by forces outside them rather than by their own natures, becomes the accepted explanation. As Dr. Vincent Smith wrote, "Newton was validating again Galileo's method of control, which regards a body as inert and as equivalent to the forces and factors maneuvering it from the outside."[7] And what does this lead to? It leads to

---

6. In the United States at least, most opposition to legitimizing such behavior comes from Protestants who do not seem to go beyond the biblical prohibition as simply an expression of divine positive law.

7. *Philosophical Physics* (New York: Harper & Brothers, 1950), 142.

the idea that, since things have no whatness of their own, at least no whatness that is knowable, we can understand a thing by understanding the forces that control it. And from that it is but a short step to asserting that we understand it only when we control it. Again, to quote Dr. Smith, "Empiriological physics must interfere with a phenomenon in order to understand it, and, in its purity, it can grasp only what it can control."[8] We can see the practical application of this in the notion that a psychologist, because he has performed experiments on man, can understand him better than the moralists and saints who have only observed him in action. And this Newtonian approach has had profound effects on things as diverse as our medicine and our farming practices.[9]

The meaning and the result of this changed attitude toward the world around us, an attitude brought about by abandoning the idea that things have determined natures of their own, is described in the following very interesting passage from C. S. Lewis:

> What was fruitful in the thought of the new scientists was the bold use of mathematics in the construction of hypotheses, tested not by observation simply but by controlled observation of phenomena that could be precisely measured. On the practical side it was this that delivered Nature into our hands. And on our thoughts and emotions . . . it was destined to have profound effects. By reducing Nature to her mathematical elements it substituted a mechanical for a genial or animistic conception of the universe. The world was emptied, first of her indwelling spirits, then of her occult sympathies and antipathies, finally of her colours, smells, and tastes. . . . The result was dualism rather than materialism. The mind, on whose ideal constructions the whole method depended, stood over against its object in ever sharper dissimilarity. Man, with his new powers became rich like Midas but all that he touched had gone dead and cold. This process, slowly working, ensured during the next century the loss of the old mythical imagination: the conceit, and later the personified abstraction, takes its place.

8. Ibid., 141.

9. Modern medicine and modern farming practices tend to treat their subjects, e.g. the human body or the soil, as so much inert material for the interaction of external forces, as (in the case of medicine) germs and antibiotics or (in the case of farming) pests or diseases and chemical fertilizers or pesticides. They always tend to treat the body or the soil as if neither had much of a role in promoting health. Thus, the body's ability, when properly stimulated, to repel disease or the role of the various microorganisms that inhabit the soil to promote healthy crops are downplayed. But as Aquinas wrote, "health is brought about through the power of nature with the assistance of art." *Expositio super Librum Boethii De Trinite*, q. 5, art. 1, ad 5 (as published in Thomas Aquinas, *The Division and Methods of the Sciences*, trans. by Armand Maurer. [Toronto: Pontifical Institute of Mediaeval Studies, 4th ed., 1986], 22).

Later still, as a desperate attempt to bridge a gulf which begins to be found intolerable, we have the Nature poetry of the Romantics.[10]

What Lewis says certainly reminds one of Descartes and his making merely dead machinery of living matter. It is only the mind that lives. Though I suppose few would claim to be pure Cartesians today, this view still has profound effects on us. What Lewis said about the Romantic poets, moreover, is true for others besides them. The entire modern "back to nature" movement has been an attempt to break out of the mechanistic world in which we feel we are doomed to live because of the immense prestige and power of modern experimental science. This "back to nature" movement, as Lewis said, was behind the Romantic movement in literature, not only in England but throughout Europe. In Germany it inspired the German youth movement of the early and mid-twentieth century and, for all their technology, heavily influenced the Nazis. And of course it was strong in the counterculture of the 1960s. It is wrong to call it simply an evil, rather it was a confused response to a prior evil. For Lewis's adjective "desperate" is correct, I think. Experimental science and the empiricist philosophy that goes so well with it have, at least in the United States, captured the subconscious mind of nearly everyone, so that we think of reason, science, conceptual knowledge, as mechanistic, technology oriented, and mathematically grounded. Consider that current saying: "It doesn't take a rocket scientist to understand such and such." Notice, we do not say, "It doesn't take a metaphysician," or "It doesn't take a theologian." We are witnessing to our deep belief that experimental science is the highest form of knowledge.

Those who are dissatisfied with that, who realize its inhibiting effects on the human spirit and despair of finding any rational alternative to empiricism, break out into Rousseau's idealization of the primitive or into Nazi worship of blood or the 1960s cult of sex, drugs and rock music, or into the postmodern disparagement of reason. But they are not fully to blame, for they had been taught to identify rationality with the desiccated philosophy of a Descartes or a Newton. They never knew Aristotle or Aquinas, so they turned from Galileo or Hume to Rousseau or Derrida.

Thus, someone like Wendell Berry, a writer whose insights and intuitions about man and society I greatly respect, but who apparently knows no scientific tradition other than empiricism, confounds rationality with empiricism and tends to denigrate reason and exact knowl-

10. *English Literature in the Sixteenth Century* (Oxford: Clarendon Press, 1954), 3–4.

edge in favor of a vague and cloudy subjectivism that in his case generally leads to healthy conclusions but is ultimately grounded in personal experience and poetry.[11]

So, here we find all the modern separation between reason and imagination, between philosophy and poetry. In the Middle Ages there was poetry that was philosophical, as in Dante or Chaucer; if you are convinced that rationality is dry and confining, you will champion a kind of poetry that eschews any grounding in philosophy. The same will be true of the visual arts and music. Anti-rationality, as in dada or surrealism, will seem plausible because the enemy you are fighting against is itself partial and distorted. The enemy, however, is not really reason and philosophy; it is only reason and philosophy as conceived by the heirs of Newton and Locke.

In fact, one of the chief triumphs of modernity has been the separation of the arts themselves from life. The traditional definition of art was *recta ratio factibilium*, that is, the right conception of things that are to be made. The making of pots and the making of sacred images were both within the same genus. Both were concerned with making something useful to the community and beautiful according to their use. No art was divorced from use. Music, for example, was useful—useful for worship of God, for dancing, for military marching, and so on. Of course, beauty was sought, but within the context of an external social purpose. All this changed with modernity. Today, for example, much of the visual arts and music are seen or heard only in special places—museums or concert halls—and have no relation to life. Having no relation to life, no social purpose, there are no canons by which to judge art or music except the ever-changing standards of the arts community and its hangers-on. In the past, a painting or a piece of music could be judged on how well it fulfilled a function, a function that was conceived as the purpose of that particular art form: did it truly help raise the mind of the worshipper to God, did it have a good beat so that we could dance to it? This is still the kind of standard we use for judging a pot: is it useful for cooking? But makers of pots, note well, are not unconcerned with beauty; they simply subordinate their concern with beauty to the function of the pot. A pot that was beautiful but that melted or leaked would not be a good pot. And our forefathers looked at all the arts this way. All art was expected to be functional. This is not to ignore beauty, but to realize the truth embodied in the title of Eric Gill's 1933 book, *Beauty Looks After Herself*.

11. See, for example, his work, *Life is a Miracle: an Essay against Modern Superstition* (Washington: Counterpoint, 2000), especially 95–103.

There is one more dissolution I want to talk about before I proceed to the Thomistic response. Although this dissolution can be traced to more than one source, I shall talk chiefly about its association with Immanuel Kant, who, of course, dissolved something very important, namely, man's nexus with reality. Here, however, I want to concentrate on another point in Kant's thought and another of his separations.

In his *Foundations of the Metaphysics of Morals*, Kant wrote, "Nothing in the world—indeed nothing even beyond the world—can possibly be conceived which could be called good without qualification except a good will."[12] In the first place such a doctrine destroys the entire structure of the human virtues; for instead of seeking to acquire virtues, that is, human perfections by which the entire man becomes good and is able more easily to do good acts, it is only the will that is good or evil.[13] The will is separated from the rest of the human being. The logical consequences of this doctrine are brought out in the passage from C. S. Lewis that I quoted above.

> The mind, on whose ideal constructions the whole method depended, stood over against its object in ever sharper dissimilarity. Man, with his new powers became rich like Midas but all that he touched had gone dead and cold.

Here in Kant is the application of these words within man himself. Now man will "stand over against" himself. No longer will the whole man—intellect, will, passions, the body itself—be a unity that can become better or worse; now the will stands over against all the rest of man, which becomes mere object, something to be studied and eventually to be manipulated.

This idea works itself out in many ways in many different thinkers during the next two hundred years. In Freud there is again a radical separation of man into parts: the superego, the ego, and the id. We are no longer integrated and cannot be. With B. F. Skinner's behaviorism, the subject, the I, is simply jettisoned, and only man as object is left.

One could talk at length about the natural connections that the modern world has severed and about the consequences of doing this—about how the severing of the intimate body/soul nexus has created the

---

12. Translated, with an introduction, by Lewis White Beck (Indianapolis: Bobbs-Merrill, 1959), 9. Emphasis in original.

13. On a fundamental level, Kant approaches this subject with an entirely different starting point from that of Aquinas. If we recognize that every being is good—"omne ens, inquantum est ens, est bonum"—we can see that Kant's "good will" is simply a special case of goodness, and one that he himself cannot place in any broader context of goodness or of being. It is simply posited and hangs in the air, as it were. See St. Thomas, *Summa Theologiae* I, q. 5.

pseudo-mind/body problem and how that has led to such perversions as so-called sex-change operations and to the current attack on the notion that there are only two sexes, male and female.[14] It is time now to look at the response that was made to the unfolding of modernity.

Modernity took mankind by surprise, meaning that, although people could see that something was afoot, the vastness of the change that was coming over the Western world (and eventually the entire world) was not well understood until about the second half of the nineteenth century and even the first half of the twentieth. By that time the change was essentially complete. Again, in an unsystematic fashion, let me highlight some of the responses that were made to emerging modernity by Catholics.

In a sense, one may say that Catholics tolerated the modern world to the extent they fell away from the teaching of St. Thomas. Roughly speaking, during the first part of our period—from the end of the Middle Ages till around 1850—the response of Catholics to emerging modernity was generally inadequate. Too often Catholics attempted to cooperate with the new trends in philosophy, political theory, and economics. They tried to harmonize them with the Faith, as they were half ashamed of the Middle Ages as a full-blown example of Christian society. Instead of taking the principles that had animated the medieval Christian social order and applying them to their own times and seeking to reshape the age, constructing Christendom anew, they tinkered piecemeal with Christian principles to make them fit the new order. On the practical level, they often surrendered. This is perhaps best symbolized by the suppression of the Jesuits by Pope Clement XIV in 1773. In the middle of the nineteenth century all this began to change. Catholics began proudly to reclaim medieval principles, especially those of Thomas Aquinas, and sought to show how they contained solutions to the various modern problems. Blessed Pius IX, and especially Leo XIII, provided leadership to these efforts. Let us look now at some specifics of this response.

14. On this see the following in "Patriarchy Is Such a Drag: the Strategic Possibilities of a Postmodern Account of Gender," in *Harvard Law Review* 108, no. 8 (1995): "Whereas family and marriage are merely legally conferred statuses, conception, pregnancy, and childbirth, as biological processes, seem to be archetypes of naturalness. But procreation is much more like marriage and family than this focus on biology suggests: each is an experience as well as an institution" (1982). And "Biological sex is revealed to have no inevitable meaning, but only the social meaning attached to it on the basis of gender identity" (1993).

Obviously, the most important facet of an adequate Catholic response to modernity must be the philosophical. This is so because philosophy, and above all metaphysics, is alone able to order other subjects, such as political philosophy, economics, and the arts, toward their true ends. Divorced from their moorings in reality—in the ultimate reality of God and in the more proximate reality of mobile being and especially human nature—such subjects inevitably drift into self-seeking, as we saw above. In the area of philosophy things went slowly at first. Although many theologians and philosophers continued to comment on the text of St. Thomas throughout the seventeenth and even into the eighteenth century, Catholic philosophy gradually became corrupted by Cartesian and other alien and false elements. It was Leo XIII who gave impetus to a change that was already beginning. Although at the First Vatican Council in 1870 the Council Fathers had reaffirmed—against those who would undervalue reason and base everything on faith or tradition—that the Church was not afraid of rightly using reason and philosophy, it was really Leo's encyclical *Aeterni Patris* of 1879, which called for a new Thomism equal to the philosophic challenges of modern times and able to show by a true use of reason philosophy's true path, that provided the necessary stimulus to the Thomistic revival. As this revival got underway it not only devoted itself to a recovery of the true text and authentic meaning of St. Thomas but also faced up to the challenges of modern thought, producing a host of philosophers and historians of philosophy, such as Maritain and Gilson.

With St. Thomas, as was said above, we find not only "a synthesis [and] culmination [of] the whole intellectual effort of Christian thinking about the world," but more importantly an openness to reality that surely must be the hallmark of any true philosophy. Errors in philosophy generally oppose other errors; one extreme breeds another. Philosophizing that starts from reality itself can lead to a restoration of that right thinking that must precede any restoration of right living, either individual or social. Only by turning again toward that which is could Catholic philosophy ever hope to overcome the layers upon layers of error introduced by so many false philosophies. For this reason Leo XIII wrote that Thomas "single-handed ... victoriously combated the errors of former times, and supplied invincible arms to put those to rout which might in after-times spring up."[15] John Paul II acknowledges the "special place" that Aquinas holds in the long history of Christian wisdom.[16]

15. Encyclical *Aeterni Patris*, no. 18.
16. Encyclical *Fides et Ratio*, no. 43.

Let us now turn to some specific areas in which the principles of Thomism can be applied. We shall consider first the political. Since at least Thomas Hobbes in the seventeenth century, the notion had been gaining acceptance that man's nature is not really social and political; that therefore society and the state are formed by contract; and that, since men themselves create the state, it derives its authority from them. As the American Declaration of Independence puts it, "governments . . . [derive] their just powers from the consent of the governed." In John Locke and Rousseau we have complete statements of this social contract theory. Although Pius IX's *Syllabus of Errors* of 1864 condemns in one magnificent statement the notion that the Roman Pontiff "can and ought to, reconcile himself, and come to terms with, progress, liberalism and recent civilization,"[17] the document deals mostly with specific and narrow questions, not examining or censuring the foundations of that liberalism that was everywhere prevailing.

With Leo XIII all that changes. Leo not only saw the need to recover Thomistic metaphysics but he also restated in the face of modernity the traditional principles of the theory of the state, again derived chiefly from St. Thomas.[18] In a series of encyclicals beginning in 1885—chiefly *Immortale Dei*, *Libertas*, and *Sapientiae Christianae*—he taught again that it was natural for man to live in civil society and that it is natural for society to have some kind of ruler. Therefore, whatever sort of ruler a society has and however that ruler is chosen, he receives his authority from God, not ultimately from the people. Leo also reaffirmed that the state as such has duties to God and thus must acknowledge the true religion.

Leo's restatement of Thomistic and Catholic political principles as against those of modern liberalism found expression in a host of Catholic writers and movements of the first half of the twentieth century. The establishment of the Feast of Christ the King by Pius XI in 1925 set the seal of the Papacy on these efforts. One of the restatement's most impressive purely political monuments may be found in the Irish Constitution

---

17. ". . . cum progressu, cum liberalismo et cum recenti civilitate."

18. Already in *Aeterni Patris* Leo had noted that "the teachings of Thomas on the true meaning of liberty, which at this time is running into license, on the divine origin of all authority, on laws and their force, on the paternal and just rule of princes, on obedience to the higher powers, on mutual charity one toward another—on all of these and kindred subjects have very great and invincible force to overturn those principles of the new order which are well known to be dangerous to the peaceful order of things and to public safety." *The Great Encyclical Letters of Pope Leo XIII, 1878–1903: Or a Light in the Heavens* (Rockford, IL: TAN Books and Publishers, 1995 [1908]), 54–55.

of 1937, which, though not without faults,[19] is a notable Catholic document. Its preamble begins with these words:

> In the Name of the Most Holy Trinity, from Whom is all authority and to Whom, as our final end, all actions both of men and States must be referred, We the people of Eire, humbly acknowledging all our obligations to our Divine Lord Jesus Christ. . . .

Article 44 reads, "The State acknowledges that the homage of public worship is due to Almighty God," and Article 6 affirms that all governmental powers derive from the people *under God*. Other articles acknowledge the family "as the natural primary and fundamental unit group of Society," require the State "to ensure that mothers shall not be obliged by economic necessity to engage in labour to the neglect of their duties in the home," forbid the enactment of divorce legislation, acknowledge the Family as "the primary and natural educator of the child," and guarantee the right to home schooling. Other articles encourage social justice and attempt to orient the economic system toward the common good of the society, rather than viewing it merely as a means of private enrichment. In the Irish Constitution we find the mature fruits of the Catholic social and political movements of the previous hundred years.

Economics

During the Middle Ages, writers such as St. Thomas discussed with great insight the moral aspects of economic activity and made it clear that this activity must be subordinated to the common good of man, in fact, to the political in the classical sense of that word. The purpose of the human community was virtue, not riches.[20] But as time went on, economic activity became more and more complex. The largely static economy of the medieval urban centers and of the manor gave way to more trade and to new and more complex kinds of contracts and other business arrangements. Moralists of the sixteenth and seventeenth centuries made a real effort to keep up with what was going on in the world

---

19. Its chief fault was its failure to identify Catholicism as the "religion of the State" as such. It simply stated (Article 44, I, ii) "The State recognizes the special position of the Holy Catholic Apostolic and Roman Church as the guardian of the Faith professed by the great majority of the citizens." This sort of language, which recognizes simply a statistical fact, derives ultimately from the Organic Articles which Napoleon I added to his 1801 Concordat with the Church. In 1972 this clause of the Irish Constitution was repealed in a referendum.

20. One of number of handy summaries of St. Thomas's thought on these matters is his treatise, *De Regimine Principum*.

of the marketplace and to give moral guidance on the new forms of economic life. It was necessary to let men know what was sin and what was not. Yet, I would suggest that their approach, though well-meant, was insufficient, for they were essentially letting the marketplace take the lead and responding with the requisite guidance called for by their position as confessors and directors of souls. With the exception of the taking of usury, which again was authoritatively condemned by Pope Benedict XIV in 1745,[21] Catholic writers of the sixteenth through the eighteenth centuries failed to sound a clarion call for a Christian economy, seeming not to realize the degree to which the new economy of personal enrichment was removing the whole realm of economic activity from any inherent relationship to the pursuit of the common good. Of course I am not suggesting that Catholics should have closed their eyes to the new economic phenomena growing up around them and simply repeated texts of St. Thomas verbatim. Rather, they should have attempted to distill the essence of what Thomas had said and tried to rally Catholics to understand the purpose of economic activity and oppose the attempt to divorce it from any connection with the common good. The response was piecemeal, sometimes yielding, sometimes, especially with usury, holding firm, but apparently not grasping how fundamental were the changes taking place. Even on usury, the Holy Office and the Sacred Penitentiary beginning in 1822, and especially in the 1830s, allowed penitents who in doubtful or bad faith had taken moderate usury to keep their gains if they repented of having acted in doubtful or bad faith and were prepared to submit to any future decision of the Church.[22] This is not to say that the doctrine of the Church on usury had or has changed, simply that the economic facts had become so complicated that the authorities despaired of being able to apply the doctrine of Benedict XIV to the complexities of a capitalist economy.[23]

Around the middle of the nineteenth century this began to change as Catholics became bolder in proclaiming the virtues of the medieval economic order. Pius IX took steps to restore the guilds in the Papal States after they had previously been abolished by Pius VII in 1801.[24] At about

21. In the encyclical, *Vix Pervenit*.

22. Patrick Cleary, *The Church and Usury. An Essay on Some Historical and Theological Aspects of Money-Lending* (Dublin: M.H. Gill & Son, 1914), reprinted (Palmdale, CA: Christian Book Club of America, 2000), 168–75.

23. On these points see John P. Kelly, *Aquinas and Modern Practices of Interest Taking* (Brisbane: Aquinas Press, 1945), especially 33–37. See also my article, "Is Usury Still a Sin?" in *Communio: International Catholic Review* 36, (3) (Fall 2009).

24. See Joaquin Azpiazu, *The Corporative State* (St. Louis: B. Herder, 1951), 78–83.

the same time, writers such as Bishop von Ketteler of Mainz and later the Roman Pontiffs beginning in 1891 with Leo XIII's *Rerum Novarum*, turned the full force of their attention to an application of Catholic principles to modern conditions, so that something like a clarion call for a Christian reconstruction of the social and economic order was made. With Pius XI's encyclical *Quadragesimo Anno* of 1931, this call for a Christian reconstruction of society is made explicit.[25] Indeed, *Quadragesimo Anno* is as radical a Catholic document as one could want in its subjection of socio-economic questions to a truly Catholic scrutiny. And of course by then, the Distributists in England, including Chesterton, Belloc, and Fr. Vincent McNabb, were attacking capitalism with at least as much vigor as the Marxists were. Actual attempts to create economic systems based on a Catholic understanding of man and society were made in Portugal, Austria, Ireland, Spain, and elsewhere.[26] Thus, by the end of the nineteenth century and in the first half of the twentieth, there existed a body of Catholic thinkers and writers who well understood what had happened to the world. They saw how fundamental was the change from the pre-modern world to the modern, and they understood exactly what in the intellectual realm the Church must do to counter modernity. In philosophy, politics, economics, and art—in all the various endeavors of mankind—they were formulating an intelligent and attractive Catholic response to modernity, grounded in the thought of Thomas Aquinas. In fact, as men began in the twentieth century to exhibit dissatisfaction with earlier forms of modern thought, for example, the mechanistic conception of reason that I discussed earlier, Catholics could show how the principles of Catholic thought often contained exactly what people, in their confused way, were looking for and that all the objections against earlier and now passé forms of modernism had already been made by St. Thomas and were contained in Catholic tradition. Unfortunately, this critique was not carried on. As the world changed, Catholics faltered and it seemed as if the Church herself had forgotten the lessons of the previous hundred years. An examination of what has happened in the Church since the mid-1960s, however,

---

25. On the question of usury, Leo XIII reaffirmed the Church's condemnation of it in *Rerum Novarum*, and the 1917 Code of Canon Law renewed the teaching of Benedict XIV in its full rigor (canon 1543).

26. A comprehensive statement of economics in the tradition of Aristotle and Thomas was made by the Jesuit Heinrich Pesch (1854–1926), especially in his monumental *Lehrbuch der Nationalökonomie* (Freiburg: B. Herder, 1905–1923), English translation by Rupert Ederer (Lewiston, NY: Edwin Mellen Press, 2002). Of course, a host of other writers contributed many lesser or more specialized studies.

is outside the scope of this book. One can only say that the patrimony of the Catholic intellectual revival—a revival that was at bottom a response to modernity—is still ours and simply awaits our intelligent and vigorous use.

8

Seeking Beauty in Art:
Some Implications of a Thomistic
Statement About Glass Saws

Beauty has nothing to do with art! This sounds monstrous!
—Eric Gill[1]

IT IS CURIOUS that some of the most important statements in St. Thomas Aquinas are said only in passing, seemingly tossed off in the course of an argument but of immense importance and interest. For example, his often-cited statement that "grace does not abolish nature" is said in the course of a reply to an objection in an article that discusses whether sacred doctrine makes use of argument.[2] Another example of this is the passage I wish to consider here, a comment likewise contained within a discussion concerned with another point, but pregnant with its own meaning. This statement, also in the *pars prima* of the *Summa Theologiae*, contains in germ a conception of art very different from that which is common today, and one moreover that I believe has implications for our social and even economic practices and institutions. This remark occurs as part of his discussion of the *dispositio*, that is, the arrangement and qualities of the human body. In the course of this discussion Thomas notes that every artist (*artifex*) intends the best disposition of what he is making according to its purpose or end. He writes, "And if such a disposition has with it some defect, the artist is

1. *A Holy Tradition of Working: Passages from the Writings of Eric Gill* (West Stockbridge, MA: Lindisfarne Press, 1983), 79. Originally from *Work and Property*, 1937.
    2. "Cum enim gratia non tollat naturam...." (*Summa Theologiae*, I q. 1, a. 8, ad 2).

not concerned; just as the artist who makes a saw for cutting makes it from iron, so that it is suitable for cutting; he does not care to make it from glass, which is a more beautiful material, because such beauty would be a hindrance to its purpose."[3]

On the face of it, St. Thomas's explanation is simply common sense. Who would make a saw out of glass? But if we proceed further in our consideration of this passage, we see that making a saw out of glass, even though that would result in a more beautiful object, would in fact be an impediment to art itself, the art of the saw maker, that is. In fact, the pursuit of beauty here is in opposition to art. But why is this a difficulty? It may be thought that the kind of art represented by saw making has nothing to do with beauty and that beauty is only a concern of the fine arts. But if we look at Thomas's well-known definition of art as *recta ratio factibilium*, the right conception of a thing that is to be made, we can see the connection.[4] In this definition of art is included both the art of the maker of saws and that of the maker of pictures, symphonies, or statues. Though certainly these arts differ, they differ as species of a genus; and in our understanding of that genus, art, lies an understanding of the place in society of the fine arts, of beauty, as well as of the artist.

However, we must deal with a difficulty in that usually the fine arts are no longer conceived as art in the sense of *recta ratio factibilium*, and thus their connection with the more humble arts of making pots or bottles or saws is entirely forgotten or denied. The fine arts are now commonly regarded as concentrating on beauty directly and for its own sake, although as a matter of fact this pursuit of beauty has sometimes led to an entire loss of beauty or, rather, to its subordination to the taste or whim of the artist. At any rate, it seems to me that, unless the Thomistic conception of art is recovered, there will be no possibility of doing away with art objects that have neither beauty nor purpose and sometimes even offend our aesthetic sensibilities, and at the same time of regaining for the artist a healthy place in a social order.

Perhaps the best way to approach this matter is by quoting from the English artist and essayist, Eric Gill (1882–1940), who, although if not

3. *Summa Theologiae* I q. 91, a. 3.

4. *Summa Theologiae* I-II q. 57. In article three Thomas states that "ars nihil aliud est quam 'ratio recta aliquorum operum faciendorum,'" and in article four he writes, "ars est 'recta ratio factibilium.'" This latter wording is repeated elsewhere, including in the *Prologus* or *Prooemium* to the *Secunda Secundae* and in the *Summa Contra Gentiles*, lib. I, cap. 93.

usually classed as a philosopher, nevertheless was one of the most faithful and radical disciples of St. Thomas on art.[5] Gill wrote,

> Music, if it be separated from occasion (the wedding, the funeral, the feast, the march and the Mass) is, like modern abstract painting and sculpture, nothing but a titivation of the senses, and all that can be said of worshippers at the Queen's Hall is that they have possibly more refined tastes than those of children dancing to a barrel organ. But whereas the children, like new-born lambs, dance for exercise, the devotees of the concert are more like debauchees at a Roman feast—and if music entered the stomach instead of the ear, owners of concert halls would have to supply spumatoria. They have no use for music—they only want to enjoy it. Music as we know it today, in its latest developments, is nothing but a refined sensationism, a refined debauchery, psychological auto-erotism *à deux, à trois, en masse*. The history of music during the last 400 hundred years is the history of the progressive divorce of music from occasion, and the high talk musicians indulge in is no higher and no more precious than that which birth-controllers use to extol physical union.... From Palestrina to Bartok and Stravinsky the history of music is a progress from meaning made attractive by music, through Handel and Gounod who straddled the fence, to music made attractive by meaning nothing at all.[6]

In order to better understand what Gill means here, we must look further at St. Thomas's definition of art as *recta ratio factibilium*. Something is to be made, but of course made for a purpose. If this is so, that purpose must govern everything about the making: the material used, its external form, and so on. If it is a saw, it must be made of some strong material, not of glass, even if glass is more beautiful. But again, an objection will be raised: Why should we care if the saw is beautiful? Indeed, can we really say that a saw is or could be beautiful? Let us explicate this again from Eric Gill.

---

5. In this respect Gill seems to me to follow St. Thomas more closely than an acknowledged Thomist and philosopher, Jacques Maritain, in his *Art and Scholasticism*. Although Maritain begins by rightly remarking (21) that "the ancients did not give a separate place to what we call the fine arts" and notes the entire dependence of all the arts on their essential meaning as *recta ratio factibilium*; nevertheless, he seems to forget this and in the rest of his book to treat the fine arts as having a direct relationship with beauty, seemingly different in kind from that of the other arts. In any case, he does not stress the essential unity of all the arts and what follows from such a unified conception of art. *Art and Scholasticism and the Frontiers of Poetry* (Notre Dame, IN: University of Notre Dame Press, 1974).

6. *A Holy Tradition of Working*, 89–90. Originally from *Work and Property*, 1937.

The idea that the distinction between art and fine art is that art is skill applied to the making of useful things and fine art is skill applied to the making of things of beauty, is clearly unreasonable—because there is no reason why useful things should not be beautiful, and there is no reason to suppose that beautiful things have no use. Are tables and chairs and houses and pottery necessarily ugly? Are portraits and statues and church paintings and wall decorations necessarily useless?[7]

To some extent, we recognize this in daily life. Manufacturers of automobiles and even of bottles do take steps to produce objects that are pleasing to look at. But this recognition lacks an explicit realization that the relationship of both the more humble arts and of the fine arts to both use and beauty is essentially the same.

All human arts must be rooted ultimately in our capacity and need for external objects of various sorts and for various purposes: houses, pots and pans, saddles, candles, music, pictures, and so on. Yet, when we make any such thing, our natural instinct is to make it as beautiful as possible. No one, all things being equal, would make an ugly pot if he could make a more beautiful pot that was equally useful. But as Thomas pointed out in the passage I quoted at the beginning, beauty when seen as something abstract or as something pursued for its own sake should not be what the artist aims at. A glass saw might be beautiful, but not very useful for sawing. It is only *beauty in relation to some end*, that is, some *use*, that art properly aims at.[8] When beauty is pursued as an abstraction and as the only goal of an art, it means that the relation of that art to any use has been forgotten; and when it is thus divorced from use and instead beauty is pursued for its own sake, then, paradoxically, the art can even end up destroying beauty itself, a point which I shall discuss further below.

The fine arts were originally accompaniments of important human activities, especially worship of God or the gods. Naturally, beauty in the fine arts, as in any other kind of art, was desired, but it is beauty for a particular purpose. Music for the liturgy is not the same as music for a march or a dance. Each has its own particular kind of beauty, because

---

7. Ibid., 93–94. Originally from *Sacred and Secular*, 1940.
8. In the fine arts, the artist works toward the same generic end as in the other arts, a certain use enhanced with appropriate beauty. How then do the fine arts differ? It would appear that in the accomplishment of that end, however, the fine arts allow for greater freedom because their end is less determined. For example, although there is comparatively little variation in the way a saw can be made if it is to be useful, a composer of music for the liturgy or for a dance has greater freedom with regard to accomplishing his end, and thus more opportunity for greater and more direct engagement with beauty.

each has its own particular use. A musician would fail as an artist if he pursued beauty but made his work less useful for its purpose. "We must not forget that until the end of the eighteenth century the great musicians were only artisans, members of a craft; that they were also great musicians is only incidental."[9] The impressive and beautiful, but liturgically useless, compositions of the last several centuries, such as Verdi's *Requiem* or even Bach's *Mass in B minor*, are actually less perfect as works of art because beauty was pursued at the expense of purpose, as if they were saws made of glass.

Now, it might be objected that, although the fine arts *can* be useful at the same time as being beautiful, there is nothing wrong with pictures or music that aim at beauty alone—at being looked at or listened to without reference to any other end than imply for the sake of esthetic pleasure. It might seem so if we limited our consideration to the works of art themselves and neglected the question of the social and cultural effects of art. Certainly the nineteenth century abounded in such works: symphonies, paintings, statues that, because they had no social role, were exhibited or performed in special places segregated from ordinary life, such as museums or concert halls. Many of them are indeed beautiful in the highest degree. But what comes of this? What effects do such works of art have on a culture?

In the first place, the fine arts when divorced from any social role become the property only of those who have leisure and education to attend to them. The rest of mankind, who formerly might have heard the most magnificent music at public worship or viewed paintings or statues of the highest order in their churches, no longer comes across such works in everyday life. Very often even those works that were intended to adorn churches or other public buildings are now found only in museums, and the best liturgical music is heard not during the liturgy, but as recorded music or in concerts. This produces a schism in a culture, about which I shall speak further below.

Secondly, now cut off from a public role—a role that in the past made them accountable to princes, bishops, cathedral chapters, or guilds—artists increasingly became responsible only to themselves. It is true that someone else usually has to pay the bill; but even when the content of the arts began to become esoteric and sometimes even ugly, the prestige of the fine arts, the desire to belong to or patronize the arts coterie—the "arts community," as it is called in the United States—exercises such an attraction that many of the rich are only too happy to pay large sums for

9. Alfred Einstein, "Early Concert Life," in *Essays on Music* (New York: Norton, 1956), 28.

works that it is difficult to believe anyone really finds attractive. To quote Eric Gill again,

> These special people are quite cut off from the ordinary needs of life and so they become very eccentric and more and more peculiar and their works become more and more expensive and so they are bought only by very rich people and so artists have become like hot-house flowers, or lap-dogs and so their works are more and more as peculiar as themselves and so we have all the new kinds of 'art movements' and so what we call Art (with a large A) is now simply a sort of psychological self-exhibitionism.[10]

In a way, the maker of fine arts became cut off from the common culture to the detriment of his art, of the culture, and sometimes even of his personal character.

> In the Middle Ages the plastic artist paid lip service at least to the lowest common denominators of experience. This even remained true to some extent until the seventeenth century. There was available for imitation a universally valid conceptual reality, whose order the artist could not tamper with. The subject matter of art was prescribed by those who commissioned works of art, which were not created, as in bourgeois society, on speculation. Precisely because his content was determined in advance, the artist was free to concentrate on his medium. He needed not to be philosopher, or visionary, but simply artificer. As long as there was general agreement as to what were the worthiest subjects for art, the artist was relieved of the necessity to be original and inventive in his 'matter' and could devote all his energy to formal problems.... Only with the Renaissance do the inflections of the personal become legitimate, still to be kept, however, within the limits of the simply and universally recognizable. And only with Rembrandt do 'lonely' artists begin to appear, lonely in their art.[11]

Left to himself, without the external but healthy discipline by which he must express beauty while at the same time achieving a social and public purpose, where was the artist to turn? In the first place he turned to his art, to the very process of creating.

> This constraint, once the world of common, extraverted experience has been renounced, can only be found in the very processes or disciplines by which art and literature have already imitated the former.

10. "Art in England Now...As It Seems to Me," in *It All Goes Together: Selected Essays* (New York: Devin-Adair, 1944), 91.

11. Clement Greenberg, "Avant-Garde and Kitsch," in *Art and Culture* (Boston: Beacon Press, 1961), 16–17. Cf. Maritain, *Art and Scholasticism*, 158–60, note 43.

These themselves become the subject matter of art and literature. If, to continue with Aristotle, all art and literature are imitation, then what we have here is the imitation of imitating.... Picasso, Braque, Mondrian, Miró, Kandinsky, Brancusi, even Klee, Matisse, and Cézanne derive their chief inspiration from the medium they work in.[12]

But just as the pursuit of sexual pleasure apart from any reference to its natural procreative function can eventually lead to perversion or even sexual boredom, if not in any particular individual, certainly in society as a whole, so the pursuit of beauty alone too often led to a kind of artistic perversion and even a boredom that sought in the most unlikely ways to stimulate both the artist and his viewers or listeners. What is the electronic music of a John Cage, for example, except the pursuit of ever more and more esoteric means for a music that has no purpose and thus no standard by which it can be judged? For the purpose of a thing, its final cause, is always a standard against which it can be judged: How well does it fulfill its end? If the fine arts have no purpose whatsoever, neither to adorn the worship of God or to provide a good beat for marching or dancing, or even (in the end) to please their viewers or listeners, how are we to judge them? Even the criterion of beauty is now gone, since the artist is free to disregard it if he chooses. A work of art with no purpose cannot really be judged at all. For while purely formal criteria may remain, which are not necessarily of no importance, they provide no sufficient standard against which to judge any particular work of art. A pot may fulfill any formal or technical criterion one likes, but if its maker has not sought utility together with appropriate beauty, he has failed in his chief duty.

If we look at the passage from St. Thomas again, he points out that a saw ought not to be made from glass because in that case it is not fitted for sawing. That is, when the genuine end of an art is recognized, the object created by the art will be sound and healthy and fulfill its end; in addition, the relationship of the artist and the things he makes to beauty will likewise be well ordered. An iron or steel saw can be as beautiful as its maker can contrive, provided that it is still useful for sawing. But if saw making were governed merely by the fantasies and whims of saw artists, saws might be made of glass or paper or anything at all. There is no limit except the inventiveness of the artist. But of course makers of saws have no pretensions. They do not aspire to do anything but make a useful object, perhaps beautified in such ways as they can manage. But

12. Greenberg, "Avant-Garde and Kitsch," 6–7.

the same is not true of the fine arts. There, since the social use of their art has largely vanished, the artists can now usually work free of the end inherent in their art and thus simply create with no constraint.[13] But with what result we shall see.

The loss of a social purpose in the fine arts led not only to the segregation of art and artist from society but also to the cultural schism I mentioned above, an enmity between high and popular culture, and made easier the eventual displacement of popular culture by mass culture. Let us see how this occurred in the arts that make use of language.

While the arts of painting, sculpture, and music were being separated from their social functions, something similar was going on in the arts that make use of the spoken word. The theater, of course, had had intimate connections with religious festivals, both in ancient Greece and in medieval and baroque Europe. Now, however, dramatic performances are akin to concerts and art museums, that is, they are special events separate from the rest of life and reserved for those with sufficient leisure and interest.[14] They are no longer part of the community's public and corporate life. An analogous process has occurred even in poetry.

Originally, there had been a very close relationship between music and poetry.[15] In ancient Greece the typical setting for poetry was "a fusion of word, music, and dance," which Prof. H. T. Kirby-Smith calls *mousike*;[16] for the poet produced both for and within a community, not in the privacy of his study. The bard's recitation was "a mixture of memorized recitation and improvisation," that is, the poem was in part made up on the spot, in part recalled from an immemorial tradition of previ-

---

13. In fact, the modern conception of art turns on its head the classical meaning of the term, which had subordinated the form of the thing made to its use. For example, "... we have often observed that the composer of art music is at liberty to choose from a wider variety of solutions to a particular problem than the composer of practical music. Indeed, it might be said that art imposes freedom upon the composer—freedom to determine for himself the limitations of the system within which he shall construct a design.... He need not take into consideration any extrinsic determinants that might confine his imagination...." Joseph Agee Mussulman, *The Uses of Music: an Introduction to Music in Contemporary American Life* (Englewood Cliffs, NJ: Prentice-Hall, 1974), 159. (Emphasis in original.)

14. Filmmaking, however, although it likewise does not fulfill a social role as I am using that term, nevertheless has obtained a wide popularity. It does so, however, (with few exceptions) as part of mass culture.

15. Prof. H. T. Kirby-Smith's book, *The Celestial Twins: Poetry and Music Through the Ages* (Amherst: University of Massachusetts Press, 1999), which I follow here, provides a masterly account of the relations between poetry and music from antiquity to the present.

16. Ibid., 9.

ous performances.[17] This is true, moreover, in every pre-modern culture. Based on studies of living epic traditions in the Balkans and Finland, Prof. Kirby-Smith writes,

> Authentic, or oral, epics, as they have been handed down to us, are transcriptions of a highly sophisticated oral performance; they are not scripts or texts written down in advance of performance by the performer.[18]

The words *performance* and *performer* here are important; for even if the bard did not always dance, his singing of the poem had more in common with a dance performance than with someone sitting down in his study to read the *Iliad*. Contrast that with the writing of poetry as a private act.

> Horace's poems give every evidence of being carefully labored, and Virgil is said to have spent an entire day reducing ten or twelve lines into a perfected one or two hexameters. In place of an hour's oral recitation—a mixture of memory and improvisation—one finds a year's meticulous labor as the literary epic took the place of the authentic, or oral, epic. The connection with music disappeared almost entirely.[19]

In the change described here, at least three distinct but related things were happening. The most obvious is the severing of the connection between music and poetry. But this change is simply the necessary result of the other two changes that were occurring. Those changes concern the social context in which poetry was produced and performed. In the second place then, instead of poetry as part of a public performance with evident social implications, we now have quiet writing in the study that brought about (at least eventually) equally quiet reading in the study. Thus, both the poet and his audience are now alone, solitary, no longer part of a community that nourished poetry and in reference to which the poet did his work.

Equally important is the third thing that happened here, which likewise follows from the creation and reading of poetry as a solitary act. This is the separation of high cultural poetry from popular poetry. Previously, the poetry sung by the bard had to be acceptable to all social classes, for the community for which the poet sang, and of which the poet was also a part, comprised the whole of the population. The poet had to provide entertainment for the masses, as well as for others. In

17. Ibid., 62.
18. Ibid., 61.
19. Ibid., 17.

England the type of dramatic entertainment that could please all social classes persisted until the closure of the theaters by the Puritan government in 1642. A good example of such a poet and dramatist is Shakespeare, whose plays include both scenes of slapstick as well as the most sublime poetry and tragedy.

Such changes in time brought about the complete disappearance of poetry from life. Now that poetic/musical performances were no longer the concern of society as a whole, poetry began that slow withdrawal from life that has been nearly completed in our time. To be sure, there were many vicissitudes in this process, new surges of popular poetry and music; but in the end, they came to nothing. The following scene in *Beowulf* of the bard's performance gives a picture of this lost type of entertainment, a poetic/musical performance that we have replaced with television:

> Then song and revelry rose in the hall;
> Before Healfdene's leader the harp was struck
> And hall-joy wakened; the song was sung,
> Hrothgar's gleeman rehearsed the lay
> Of the sons of Finn when the terror befell them.[20]

This kind of poetry naturally included music, just as so many variety shows on television include song and dance.

For our present purposes, though, the point to be noted is that the divorce of poetry from music signaled its divorce from everyday life, first retreating into the privacy of the study, then vanishing altogether. The things that I mentioned above which caused and accompanied the separation of music from poetry—the different context in which poetry was made and heard or read and the separation of high cultural poetry from popular poetry—are of course akin to what happened in the other arts. When poets, like painters, were functional artists, people still remembered that the fine arts were arts in much the same way as pot making or dressmaking are arts. They had public and social ends and public and social uses.

In the cultures of Homer and *Beowulf* and the Middle Ages, the best music and the best visual artistic works were part of life. People saw and listened to them as parts of ordinary community life; they adorned their churches and guild halls. Today, such artistic works have been removed from ordinary life and put into special times or places, such as concerts or museums or poetry readings, events that are not seen by the average

---

20. *Beowulf*, trans. Charles W. Kennedy (New York: Oxford University Press, 1940), 35.

person as something of interest. Although there was sometimes a distinction between high cultural and popular cultural works in the past, it was a distinction, not an enmity; and the two traditions continued to nourish each other.[21] Rustic villagers may not have danced to the works of John Dunstable or Josquin des Préz, but they still moved in a world in which high culture was not cut off from ordinary life but appealed to and sustained the entire people, since it was an integral part of the corporate life of the entire people.

In addition to the disastrous separation of the artist from a real social role, the removal of the arts from society both created that unnatural separation of high culture from popular culture, and—with the rise of our commercial and industrial civilization—brought about the death of popular culture. What is often called popular culture today is in reality *mass* culture. Popular culture is produced and performed according to traditions handed down in a particular place, and such an artistic tradition can hardly survive in today's world of electronic communication and mass-produced music and pictures. Ironically, though, it is in the products of mass culture that one finds functional art flourishing: music intended for dancing, poetry sung to music, paintings or statues intended to stimulate religious devotion or patriotic feelings. Unfortunately, largely cut off from healthy cultural roots and often produced with an eye solely to money, most of these rightly excite disdain in the minds of high-culture artists, who fail to see that they themselves have contributed to the conditions that have led to the predominance of such mass culture.

In speaking of the deleterious effects that the segregation of the fine arts and of the artist himself from an ordinary social role have had on the course of Western culture, we should not adopt too narrow a view of this. As in many matters, it is a question of what predominates. If the arts are generally seen in their rightful place as part of society and as having a social role, then the poetry or music that is enjoyed by an individual alone will not adversely affect things. Certainly there have always been

---

21. The influence of popular culture on high culture is well known and has continued even into our own time. Less widely realized is the existence of an influence in the opposite direction. "We also know little about the age of the various styles of folk music in Europe. Still, we are sure that for centuries there has been a close relationship between the art music of the continent and its folk music...." "The ballad was developed in Europe in the Middle Ages—first, presumably, by song composers of city and court—and evidently passed into oral tradition and the repertories of folk cultures thereafter." Bruno Nettl, *Folk and Traditional Music of the Western Continents* (Englewood Cliffs, NJ: Prentice-Hall, 2d ed., 1973), 38 and 52.

such private reading and music making, and this is as it should be;[22] however, when such private use of the fine arts is preponderant and seen as the norm, we shall experience the bad results of which I have spoken.

Although it is possible to chronicle the history of the various types and forms of the arts in a purely formal manner, noting how particular technical problems were successively approached and solved, nevertheless the forms of the arts are always symptoms and effects of social and cultural realities. The various ways in which artists work and exercise their art and in turn interact with the other members of society presuppose certain forms of social order and can in turn themselves be causes of social change. For example, the massive orchestral works of the nineteenth century were possible only because the institution of the concert had emerged in the preceding century.[23] The art museum was possible only because painting and statues were no longer created for some social use, whereas in turn the very existence of museums has meant that high-cultural objects are created with the intent of being kept out of sight in special buildings. The products of mass culture, on the other hand, are able to invade our public spaces. If all this is true, then it behooves those who are concerned with the arts not to overlook the effects of the social role of both arts and artist.

St. Thomas's off-hand remark about saws, then, implies an entire theory about art, as well as of the place of the artist and the arts in society. When the fine arts are divorced from their ends, when they pursue beauty without regard to social use, they become subject to the private

22. Apparently, however, there was originally some uneasiness about this on the part of artists. "Beethoven was the first example, and a dangerous one, of the 'free artist' who obeys his so-called inner compulsion and follows only his genius. A hundred years before, this attitude of the composer toward his art and toward the world was quite unheard of; in the case of J.S. Bach it appears that he was afraid to come forward with his most intimate and lonely works, the Inventions and Sinfonias, and later the Well-tempered Clavier and the Art of Fugue, without having some special pretext. Therefore he disguised them as pedagogical examples 'for the use and profit of the musical youth desirous of learning as well as for the pastime of those already skilled in this study.' Music that did not have a religious or social function still needed some excuse. Even Haydn and Mozart hardly ever wrote music that did not have some such defined purpose." Alfred Einstein, "Beethoven's Military Style," in *Essays on Music*, 244.

23. "The concert audience came into existence with the oratorios and concerti grossi and organ concertos of Handel. . . . In earlier times there was no audience in the modern sense. The church was the only place where a musician was able to reach a fairly large audience—but it cannot be said that the congregation was a real audience with an interest in musical and esthetic values. A church musician serves the church. A churchgoer is there for edification and music is only a means to an end. . . . In the past it was very difficult to listen to music just for enjoyment, as a 'connoisseur.'" Alfred Einstein, "Early Concert Life," in *Essays on Music*, 26–27.

whims of the artist. They also begin to be separated from the ordinary life of society, allowing the rise of mass culture, which is inimical to both high culture and a true popular culture. A recovery of the meaning of art as *recta ratio factibilium*, with all that is implied by it, can, however, make possible an integration of art and the life of the artist with the social order, to the health and benefit of all three.

9

The Making and Unmaking
of the English Catholic Intellectual
Community, 1910–1950[1]

PROF. LOTHIAN'S BOOK on the English Catholic intellectual community in the first half of the twentieth century is a timely and suggestive book for several reasons. First, he deals with a group of writers who are still much read, discussed, and admired, a group moreover that included several very colorful personalities, including Chesterton, Belloc, Waugh, and Gill. Secondly, although it does not become clear until the very end of his book, Prof. Lothian raises the question of what stance Catholic intellectuals and, *a fortiori* the Church herself, should take regarding the life of the world around them, the various currents of modern thought, and contemporaries who disbelieve Christian revelation. No one would deny, I think, that questions such as these have been in the forefront of the numerous intellectual battles within the Church since the 1960s and that they often underlie disputes about the liturgy, catechetics, the behavior of Catholic politicians, and many other matters about which controversy rages today. By raising these questions and situating them in the careers and works of an important group of thinkers and writers, Prof. Lothian's book could substantially promote a fruitful discussion of these matters.

It is important at the outset to recognize that this book is not simply a history of the Catholic intellectual revival in England, still less of the Catholic *literary* revival. Prof. Lothian insists that he is writing about an intellectual *community*, and that he is interested in their ideas, not in

---

1. The following is a review of Prof. James R. Lothian's *The Making and Unmaking of the English Catholic Intellectual Community*, 1910–1950 (Notre Dame, IN: University of Notre Dame Press, 2009).

their literary talents. "To view Catholic intellectuals through a literary lens is most often to restrict one's studies to the 'great writers,' selected via aesthetic criteria" (xv). Secondly, the author writes from a definite organizing principle. He selects his subjects and much of what he says about them with that principle in mind, a principle stated in the title of the book: the *making* and the *unmaking* of the community. Thus, this work also constitutes an interesting contribution to a sociology of intellectuals, quite apart from its implications for the life of the Church.

At the outset Prof. Lothian states his thesis in these words:

> It argues that the Catholic intellectuals in interwar England were not a disparate collection of individuals but a genuine community united not only by close personal ties but especially by ideology. The foundation for this community . . . lay in the ideas of Hilaire Belloc. . . . Belloc presented a unified and self-consciously Catholic theory of government, political economy, and history. [Belloc's] ideology made its first influential converts . . . in the persons of the Dominican priest and social critic Vincent McNabb (1868–1943), the sculptor and writer Eric Gill (1882–1940), and the prolific man of letters G. K. Chesterton (1874–1936). . . . The next generation of Bellocians [chiefly Douglas Jerrold, Douglas Woodruff, Christopher Hollis, Evelyn Waugh, and Arnold Lunn] ensured that Bellocianism remained the unifying ideology for this community. (xii–xiii)

Even though a new group of writers and thinkers, including Frank Sheed, Maisie Ward, and Tom Burns, "promoted, under the influence in part of . . . Christopher Dawson . . . an aesthetic and philosophical vision at odds with Belloc's agenda . . . [this] did not mean the end of the community" (xiii). Only under the stress of the Second World War and its aftermath was the Catholic intellectual community dissolved. Although Prof. Lothian devotes much space to what he considers the differences in outlook and interest between Dawson and those he influenced, on the one hand, and the "Bellocians" on the other, he stresses that the intellectual community remained united until the war and postwar years. In fact, the fracturing of the community during and after the war had almost nothing to do with any differences between Dawson and Belloc, either intellectual or personal.

It is not clear whether Prof. Lothian means to suggest that all, or nearly all, Catholic intellectuals in England at this time were part of a community united around what he calls "Bellocianism." Several important figures, such as Ronald Knox, C. C. Martindale, Maurice Baring, and Graham Greene, receive only a passing mention here; others do not appear at all although many of them were doing important work during this period and arguably could be said to represent interwar English

Catholicism as well as most of those who are treated in this book. Prof. Lothian does explain why he does not include Greene, saying simply that he was not sufficiently in sympathy with "Bellocianism," nor "closely connected personally" to the members of the community (388). Prof. Lothian can hardly be faulted for not discussing every writer of note, but it seems to me that some attempt to place the group of writers that constitutes the community under review within the larger context of English Catholic intellectual life would have been useful.

In the Prologue, after reviewing the relevant historiography of the period, Prof. Lothian turns his attention to the background of his work, the pre-1910 state of English Catholicism. Here he recounts the familiar emergence of English Catholics from the penal regime, the effect of the Oxford movement, the restoration of the hierarchy, Irish immigration, and the work and influence of Cardinal Manning toward the end of the nineteenth century. He gives some interesting concrete statistics of the growth of the English Catholic church in this period: 70,000 Catholics in 1780, 1.35 million by 1891; 469 churches in 1840, 1,387 in 1891; and 788 priests in 1851, 2,812 in 1900 (xix–xx). Prof. Lothian, however, reveals what seems to me the kind of intellectual ax he has to grind when he states that Manning had "more in common with the defiant 'fortress' Catholicism of Pius IX regarding the relation of English Catholics to the broader society than with the Liberalism of Mr. Gladstone, who after all sided with his friend Acton in 1870" (xxii). It is not clear what relevance Gladstone has to the internal constitution of Catholicism, in England or elsewhere, but I think it is a mistake to focus primarily on one side of Manning's thought, such as his opposition to Catholic attendance at Oxford or Cambridge. His work with the labor movement, which Prof. Lothian acknowledges, certainly shows a great desire to engage "the broader society." And although it is surely true that Belloc inherited through Manning, and passed on to those he influenced, "the antipathy toward the modern world that had come to characterize Catholicism in the second half of the nineteenth century," this antipathy hardly constituted an "impulse to turn away from" the contemporary world (xxiii). It is hard to imagine two men with a greater desire to engage their contemporaries than Belloc and Chesterton. Instead of situating Belloc and most of the other writers discussed in this book simply as heirs of Pius IX, it makes more sense, it seems to me, to see their work in large part as a response to the project of Leo XIII to engage the modern world, but to engage it from the point of view of a confident Catholicism that could yield on nonessentials while holding fast to what was essential.

After the Prologue, Prof. Lothian devotes chapter one to Belloc; chapter two to those he calls the first generation of Bellocians, Fr. McNabb,

Eric Gill, and Chesterton; and chapter three to the second generation, concentrating on Douglas Jerrold, Douglas Woodruff, Christopher Hollis, Evelyn Waugh, and Arnold Lunn. For each of these individuals he sketches something of their education, careers, and writings. Although it is obviously necessary to include such background, I think that much of this matter fails to build up the book's thesis and is at times merely an over-long recital of biographical facts.

In addition, one can make some other general comments on the contents of these chapters. First, it is essential to Prof. Lothian's thesis to make Hilaire Belloc the foundation of the English Catholic intellectual community and the real source of its ideas. Yet, to what extent were these ideas the common property of most literate Catholics of the time, and not just in England, and even of many non-Catholics? Distributism, for example, was rooted in the response to Leo XIII's *Rerum Novarum* and shared important features with continental theories such as Corporatism or Heinrich Pesch's Solidarism, as well as with Guild Socialism. Similarly, Belloc's admiration for the Middle Ages was hardly unique or original with him. Well before Leo XIII, Catholic thinkers in Germany and elsewhere were looking to medieval institutions as the source of ideas on how to deal with capitalism and the resulting exploitation and alienation of workers. Even Marx and Engels in the *Communist Manifesto* put in a good word for the Middle Ages, speaking of how the "bourgeoisie . . . has put an end to all feudal, patriarchal, idyllic relations." Belloc did indeed set out to rescue English historiography from its Whig, anti-Catholic bias, but that project was part of a much wider revival of interest in the Middle Ages that dated from the end of the eighteenth century and the beginnings of Romanticism. And although Belloc certainly had very considerable influence on Chesterton's sociopolitical ideas, the latter's interests ranged much wider than politics and economics. It seems to this reviewer that Prof. Lothian tends to present Chesterton as simply or primarily an exponent of "Bellocianism." Maisie Ward in her biography of Chesterton holds that Belloc was the decisive influence on his friend in matters political, economic, and historical. But "[i]n pure literature, in philosophy and theology he remains untouched by the faintest change" based on his association with Belloc. Certainly, Chesterton was as much at home in these fields as in sociopolitical matters. For that matter, it is a mistake to limit Belloc to "Bellocianism." Although Belloc's interests obviously centered on history and social affairs, such books as *Survivals and New Arrivals* and *Essays of a Catholic* range widely over other territory and constitute, in my opinion, a distinguished portion of his work.

Prof. Lothian devotes considerable space in these chapters to Belloc's and Chesterton's cautiously favorable attitude toward Mussolini and Fascism. He does this in part because he later stresses the even more favorable attitude of many of the later "Bellocians," especially Douglas Jerrold, who was naive in the extreme concerning Mussolini and Pétain. In chapter five he presents Jerrold as a counterpoint to the efforts of Christopher Dawson and others to promote liberal democracy as part of the British war effort, an event which helped to fracture the Catholic intellectual community. As part of a summing up of "Bellocianism," he writes that, because of "Belloc's antipathy to parliamentary democracy and his advocacy of monarchy as the more desirable form of government . . . subsequent English Catholic writers . . . shared Belloc's enthusiasm for the authoritarian regimes in nations such as Italy, Austria, and Portugal. . . ." (70). When he specifically discusses Chesterton's views on Mussolini and Fascism (128–134), although Prof. Lothian seeks to present the nuances of Chesterton's thought, he seems to think that Chesterton committed the unpardonable sin in that "the tone of his *Resurrection of Rome* was that of moral equivalence" between Fascism and liberal democracy (132). A reading, however, of what Chesterton wrote in that book manifests his conviction that the facade of liberal democracy most often masked rule by the rich, who in fact controlled the government on their own behalf. Chesterton thought that the Fascist state at least had the power to curb the rich and that on occasion it seemed willing to do so. Even if Chesterton was utterly wrong in his judgment about Fascism and social justice, in the 1920s and 1930s Fascism and its associated movements, such as the Falange in Spain, did present a critique of capitalism and economic exploitation which is not without interest. *Fascist* has since become simply a synonym for *Bad Guy*, so that people actually took seriously the Bush administration's term *Islamo-Fascist*, a quite meaningless expression. In Chesterton's lifetime it was not a mark of moral depravity to see elements of the Fascist system as a reasonable alternative to both capitalism and communism. That Mussolini later brutally invaded Ethiopia and embraced the Nazi racial theories could hardly have been known in the 1920s, when Chesterton wrote. Belloc, moreover, as Prof. Lothian notes (325), specifically criticized Nazi anti-semitism and at least privately opposed the Italian invasion of Ethiopia (62).

Moreover, Belloc's criticism of parliamentary government and his advocacy of "monarchy" was not simply a brief for the dictators of continental Europe. His notion of "monarch" included any strong executive, such as the president of the United States and the governors of the separate American states. Belloc in fact met and was favorably impressed by President Franklin Roosevelt, whose economic policy, incidentally, especially the National Recovery Administration, was compared by critics with Mussolini's own Fascist economic programs.

After the chapters devoted to the "Bellocians," in chapter four, Prof. Lothian introduces Christopher Dawson and others more or less associated with him. These personages include Frank Sheed and Maisie Ward; Tom Burns; David Jones; and, in chapter five, Barbara Ward (no relation to Maisie). It is clear that Dawson did not especially like Belloc, writing in a letter to Maisie Ward that, as Lothian quotes, Belloc "is not only not a philosopher himself, he is definitely an anti-philosophic influence and has done a lot to make the younger generation of Catholics hostile and contemptuous toward modern thought" (289), and refusing to meet him, much to Frank Sheed's dismay (289–90). Prof. Lothian claims that Dawson influenced Sheed to publish continental theologians and philosophers, such as Karl Adam and Maritain, thereby making a partial break with the "Bellocians," who had been allegedly occupied solely with socio-political matters. I think that Prof. Lothian draws too great a contrast here, for in reality some of the "Bellocians" had strong interests in philosophy and theology, notably Chesterton, McNabb, and Gill. It is true, however, that there was a definite slant in the intellectual interests both of Belloc and of the "Bellocians" toward the social question. Although Prof. Lothian is clear that the unity of this intellectual community was not really broken by any differences in outlook or interest between Belloc and Dawson, he does try to make the most of whatever differences there were, titling this chapter, "The Dawsonite Challenge." One example of what seems to me to be Prof. Lothian's undue stress on differences between those whom he calls Bellocians and those whom he places in the Dawsonite camp is his comment about the "sustained criticism of Bellocianism in Tom Burns' Order" (372). In fact, Prof. Lothian cites only one article in *Order* specifically targeting Belloc (262), and his summary of that periodical's contents evinces little that could be called antipathetic to Belloc's thought (261–63). In the end he writes,

> Common agreement, despite Dawson's objections, still united Catholic writers in England, and there remained close personal bonds among them.... It would be remiss, indeed, not to acknowledge the similarities and personal links even between Dawson himself and the Bellocians.... Nor were Dawson's ideas entirely unrelated to those of the Bellocians. In fact, much of his diagnosis of the maladies of contemporary Europe were so similar to those of Belloc, Chesterton, and Gill that even the most orthodox Distributist greeted his work approvingly, passing over the differences.... Dawson was a valuable and frequent contributor to the *English Review* during Douglas Jerrold's

tenure as editor, and Jerrold believed that he and Dawson were of the same mind. (290–91)

In any case it was not any dislike of Belloc by Dawson nor any alleged lack of interest in philosophy among the "Bellocians" that led to the community's breakup, but rather the events of the Second World War. Here Prof. Lothian seems to be on surer ground, but also with a smaller cast of characters. Chesterton had been dead for several years by the time the war started; Belloc became incapacitated early in the war; Gill died in 1940; and McNabb died in 1943. Thus, most of the important "Bellocians" were out of the picture. However, there definitely was a conflict between Douglas Jerrold and Dawson. Briefly, as Prof. Lothian presents the affair, Jerrold was a proponent of the superficially interesting but actually stupid idea of the Latin Catholic bloc, a plan for the Latin Catholic countries to work together to rechristianize Europe, beginning apparently with their Nazi ally, and for Britain to make peace with Germany on distinctly unfavorable terms. Jerrold continued to promote this idea even up to and immediately after the fall of France in 1940. It was stupid, of course, in that Mussolini clearly never had any interest in rechristianizing anything; and Pétain, whatever his wishes might have been, was almost totally subservient to the Germans, whereas neither the Spanish nor the Portuguese governments, both neutral in the war and outwardly friendly to the Church, whatever they might have desired, could possibly have undertaken such an effort.

Dawson, meanwhile, at the instigation of Barbara Ward and with the enthusiastic approval of Cardinal Hinsley, Archbishop of Westminster, had become editor of *The Dublin Review* and one of the leaders of the Sword of the Spirit movement. The Sword movement was designed to rally Catholic support for Britain's war efforts and counter opinions that continued to hold out hope for detaching Italy from Germany as part of the Latin Catholic bloc idea. Even though Jerrold, as publisher of the *Dublin*, eventually succeeded in ousting Dawson as editor after Cardinal Hinsley's death, it was a hollow victory. For not only had Britain's position in the war improved with the entry of the Soviet Union and the United States, the end of the war also meant the end of whatever coherence the Catholic intellectual community had enjoyed up to then. Before I discuss that, however, I should note that any conflict between "Bellocianism" and the efforts of Christopher Dawson and Barbara Ward to promote liberal democracy was really a conflict just with Douglas Jerrold. Other "Bellocians," such as Douglas Woodruff, Christopher Hollis, Arnold Lunn, and Evelyn Waugh, supported the war effort whatever may have been their misgivings about parliamentary democracy then or earlier, whereas the only figure to support Jerrold, Michael de la

Bedoyère, editor of the *Catholic Herald*, is presented by Prof. Lothian as one of the Dawsonites. More fundamentally, one can question Prof. Lothian's judgment that "Bellocianism" was somehow disproven by the war's successful conclusion.

> Even the condemnations of parliamentary democracy for its weakness and corruption, the very hallmark of Bellocianism . . . had dissipated. . . . Above all, Britain's victory in the war had validated its parliamentary democracy. The very system that Belloc and his acolytes had dismissed as corrupt and ineffectual compared to its continental rivals had demonstrated that it remained functional. (369)

But in fact, Britain and the United States both functioned during the war under the types of strong men that Belloc and Chesterton had at times championed. Though Churchill and Roosevelt were hardly dictators, each certainly exploited the powers of his office to the full; and it is not fair to judge the ordinary performance of parliamentary democracy by them. In addition, one can hardly leave out the contribution of the U.S.S.R. to the victory over Germany, a contribution at least as great as that of the Atlantic powers, and achieved by a regime that hardly constituted a validation of any kind of democracy.

After his account of the dramatic events of the Second World War, Prof Lothian in his Epilogue both sums up his book and raises his most interesting questions. He writes, "A growing segment of Catholic intellectuals had begun to recognize the inadequacy of Bellocianism in the postwar world" (374). This change, however, was not so much because of any refutation of these ideas, but in large part because intellectual fashions had changed.

> In the end, it was World War II that had revealed Bellocianism to be an intellectual blind alley. The postwar realization that Catholic intellectuals had to transcend the Bellocian intellectual ghetto was built on the wartime ecumenism of Dawson and his friends at the *Dublin Review* and the Sword of the Spirit. (381)

Facts or experiences themselves, however, rarely teach anything without some framework by which to interpret them. Whether or how Catholic intellectuals before the war had lived in an intellectual ghetto, and what this meant and whether that was good or bad, depends on what view one holds on the proper relations of Catholics to those outside the Church. In fact, what had occurred after the war was one of those difficult-to-explain shifts in ideas and outlook, the kind of shift that leads people to talk about an idea whose time has come. At certain times certain ideas are eagerly greeted and welcomed, not usually because they have refuted their opposition but for reasons not always clear. Prof

Lothian, for example, writes of Bernard Wall, who as editor of the *Colosseum* before the war, had been typical of the extreme "Bellocians," increasingly hostile to liberal democracy and supportive of Franco and of Maurras's Action Francaise. After the war his whole intellectual outlook seems to have changed, not only on politics, but more importantly on the fundamental attitude that Catholics should take toward the world. Prof. Lothian notes his 1946 letter to Dawson on "the dilemma they faced after the war . . . whether to continue to separate themselves from the greater society or to 'collaborate.' The first option led in his estimation to 'sterility.' Where the second led Wall admitted he was not sure; but there was, he believed, no alternative" (381). All this, Lothian rightly remarks, had meaning beyond the English church.

> The postwar rejection of Bellocianism by the English Catholic intellectuals was thus part of a much more significant development. The reconciliation of English Catholic intellectuals with modern English society had been a step in the direction of the Church's subsequent advocation, in *Gaudium et Spes* . . . of active engagement in contemporary society, of dialogue with modernity rather than reflexive opposition to it. (383)

There is certainly truth here, but I must reiterate that it is false to refer to Belloc and his contemporaries and followers as proponents of a "'fortress' Catholicism," opposed to "active engagement in contemporary society." They engaged the world outside the Church at least as much as Catholics do now. Nor is it true that Catholics were having no effect on the world around them. Aside from the large numbers of converts, Prof. Lothian recounts the interesting incident that in 1932 the *Manchester Guardian* had taken note of the publishing house of Sheed & Ward and its role in "bringing the fruits of the intellectual renaissance among Catholics in Europe to the English public" (242). The main difference is that then there was agreement among Catholics on the purpose of such engagement with their contemporaries. Today there is little agreement on what is the purpose of engagement and dialog, whether conversion, mutual understanding and collaboration, or even an effort toward syncretism. "Bellocianism" had its defects, to be sure, especially as it was carried on by those who considered themselves Belloc's disciples, such as Woodruff, Jerrold, and Hollis, but who often took more extreme positions than did Belloc himself. Nevertheless, it was an intellectual view built around Catholic teaching and tradition and that sought to apply that teaching and tradition to the world, even if its judgments were sometimes skewed.

Thus, Prof. Lothian in his Epilogue raises the always pertinent question of what stance the Church should take toward the contemporary world outside her boundaries. He clearly thinks that what he calls "Bellocianism" was a mistake, but we shall judge Belloc, Chesterton, and the rest largely by what we think the Church is and what her bearing should be toward the world. Chesterton says somewhere that the Church is larger than the world. If we believe that—if we believe that the Church's classical understanding of her mission was largely correct—we shall favor engagement, but engagement that seeks in some fashion to apply what Christ mandated when he told his apostles to go out into the world and preach the Gospel to every creature. On the other hand, if we see the Church as a valuable institution no doubt, one among many probably equally valuable institutions, and not only with no monopoly on the truth but in fact with at least as much to learn from those outside her as to teach them, we shall want a very different kind of engagement and a dialog whose purpose is far from clear, except that it is definitely not the conversion of our interlocutors. Prof. Lothian's book is valuable in that it presents these alternative approaches to engagement in the context of an especially interesting group of writers. For all their short-comings, the "Bellocians" did try to apply Catholic teaching to the world around them and to present the Church in a fresh and attractive manner to the world. If conversions are any index of success, to a great extent they succeeded. But beginning after the war, and even more today, we do what Bernard Wall advocated: we "collaborate." And what that will achieve we appear to have no better idea than did Wall himself.

10

The World, Modernity, and the Church

FUNDAMENTALLY, the Church of God throughout all of her history has the same mission: to fulfill the commandment of Our Lord recorded in St. Matthew's Gospel, "Go therefore and make disciples of all nations, baptizing them in the name of the Father and of the Son and of the Holy Spirit, teaching them to observe all that I have commanded you" (28:19–20a). Because the Church exists in history, however, she

> carries the responsibility of reading the signs of the time and of inter-preting them in the light of the Gospel. . . . In language intelligible to every generation, she should be able to answer the ever recurring questions which men ask about the meaning of this present life and of the life to come, and how one is related to the other.[1]

To carry out that responsibility, the Church must attend to those to whom she has the duty of preaching the Gospel. The Apostles themselves provided the first model of this, for their method of preaching to Jews was different from their way of addressing gentiles. St. Paul gave a particularly striking example of how to address pagan intellectuals in his visit to Athens, as recorded in Acts, chapter 17.

It is possible, of course, to read the times in different ways, even to misread them. Long after an event there can still be debate on whether the right policy was pursued or not. Today's unresolved question concerns the future of the Church and her mission to the world. What should the Church's stance be toward modernity, or now perhaps to post-modernity? What is the best way of communicating the Gospel in this age? This question underlies most of the specific disputes about the liturgy, catechesis, Catholic education, and the like.

A rough sort of consensus, it seems, has arisen since the Council, a

---

1. Vatican Council II, Pastoral Constitution on the Church in the Modern World, *Gaudium et Spes*, no. 4 (Flannery translation).

consensus typified by Pope Benedict XVI in an address to the Roman Curia on December 22, 2005, in which he devoted part of his talk to the Second Vatican Council on the fortieth anniversary of its conclusion. Alluding to Pope Paul VI's closing address to the Council, he made the following remarks:

> In the great dispute about man which marks the modern epoch, the Council had to focus in particular on the theme of anthropology. It had to question the relationship between the Church and her faith on the one hand, and man and the contemporary world on the other. The question becomes even clearer if, instead of the generic term "contemporary world," we opt for another that is more precise: the Council had to determine in a new way the relationship between the Church and the modern era.

An attitude broadly in line with these remarks has underlain, I think, the programs of the last several pontificates, beginning with Paul VI or even perhaps John XXIII, and becoming more precise with John Paul II and his two successors. Looked at in historical context there is essential continuity between these various pontiffs; any differences are mostly in emphasis or personality, even though these are often magnified by the media and presented as fundamental differences or disagreements about policy or even doctrine. Before discussing this in more detail, however, let us look at another project to address modern man on behalf of the Church, a project that seemed to be in full swing only a few short years before the Council opened.

In 1954, the French philosopher Etienne Gilson, surely one of the pre-eminent Catholic intellectuals of the twentieth century, edited a volume entitled, *The Church Speaks to the Modern World: the Social Teachings of Leo XIII.* This book contains the text of twelve encyclical letters of Pope Leo, with a general introduction to Leo XIII, his life and teaching, as well as specific introductions and notes to each encyclical, all by Gilson. The words *Social Teachings* in the subtitle must be understood in a wide sense, for Gilson included encyclicals dealing with the revival of Thomistic philosophy, with the foundations of the political order, and with marriage, and included the famous Rerum Novarum. What is striking about this volume is that as late as 1954 the encyclicals of Leo could be presented as the Church's message to the modern world. A few years later they would be seen as embarrassing relics of the pre-modern papacy, no longer applicable to the Church's apostolate. But just a few years before the Council assembled, Leo's teachings were offered to the world as the Church's considered response to modernity and its problems. Let us briefly look at some of what Gilson wrote.

In his general introduction Gilson summarizes Leo's encyclical on philosophy,

> where the doctrines of St. Thomas on the divine origin of all authority, on laws, and on all the other fundamental notions in political philosophy are said to be, after the grace of God, the best means there is to introduce modern minds to a proper understanding and appreciation of Catholic institutions.[2]

On other points, Gilson notes that

> Practically all the positions rejected by Pope Leo XIII are so many varieties of one and the same error, namely, the refusal to recognize the existence of God, of a supernatural order, and of the duty we have to submit to it.[3]

Gilson speaks of Leo's teaching on "the domestic authority of husband over wife, of parents over children, or of masters over servants [which] not only takes its origin and force from God, but also derives from Him 'its nature and character.'"[4] He goes on to sketch the Pope's doctrine on "the natural relations created by God between human beings . . . in political societies, between the rulers and the ruled [which] follows from the natural inequalities which obtain between men."[5]

One of the most interesting parts of Gilson's introduction is the section entitled, *The Modern Liberties*. His summary of Leo's teaching on these liberties is apt to seem odd to a twenty-first-century reader in the age of Facebook and Twitter:

> There can be no such right as that of thinking anything, of saying anything, of writing anything, of teaching anything, and of maintaining every conceivable position about every possible subject. The true meaning of the criticisms of these so-called "modern liberties" is not that there are no such liberties; rather, it is that these liberties consist in the firm resolve only to think, to say, and to write that which is true, and only to will that which is good according to the prescriptions of the natural law, of the human law, and of their common source, which is the divine law.[6]

Briefly summarized, Gilson's account of Leo's teaching on Church and state is as follows: "when she acquiesces to certain situations in which

---

2. Etienne Gilson, ed., *The Church Speaks to the Modern World: the Social Teachings of Leo XIII* (Garden City, NY: Image, 1954), 7.

3. Ibid.

4. Ibid., 10.

5. Ibid., 11.

6. Ibid., 16.

the fullness of her rights are not recognized, the Church never gives up these rights; she simply waits for more favorable circumstances," and "in no case will she ever admit that Church and State should be kept separate."[7]

No doubt Leo's teaching strikes one as sufficiently bold and even confrontational to have been uttered in the age of Darwin, Nietzsche, and Freud; but to republish that teaching, with a commentary that makes no attempt to hide or water it down, in the age of Bertrand Russell and Sartre, might seem insane indeed. But regardless of the effect of such words on those outside the Church, do they represent a proper stance for communicating the Gospel today? Was it true that "the Council had to determine in a new way the relationship between the Church and the modern era?" To put the question in its strongest and most precise form: who was addressing modern man most effectively and most correctly, Leo XIII and Etienne Gilson or the post-Conciliar Church?

Although the nature of modernity can and has been hotly debated, I think one can make a case that the defining characteristic of modernity is the removal of the Church from her leading and official role as shaper of culture. All else about modernity flows from this fact, directly or indirectly. Before the modern era, the Church in varying degrees and ways informed culture and usually had an official or semi-official role in doing so. Whether by design or not, the Church realized well the aspiration of Pope Paul VI that "[t]he gospel must impregnate the culture and the whole way of life of man."[8] This synthesis broke down, sometimes dramatically, sometimes gradually, depending on time and place, between the early sixteenth century and the early nineteenth, so that the Church lost her leading position as shaper of culture and began a slow retreat into a perceived cultural and intellectual obscurity or even irrelevancy. Adherence to the Catholic faith now began to be fundamentally a personal choice; there was no longer an overriding Catholic cultural or intellectual framework within which nearly all individuals found meaning for their lives. That overarching framework was instead provided by liberal individualism, which offered a radically different mental blueprint for understanding reality. Modernity on this reading came about when adherence to the Faith became simply a personal choice and no longer rested on acquiescence in a socially accepted cultural frame of reference.

One can argue that because of this important cultural change, a radically new kind of apostolate is necessary. But when Leo XIII set forth his

---

7. Ibid., 17.

8. Paul VI, Apostolic Exhortation *Evangelii nuntiandi* (December 8, 1975), no. 20.

program of a deliberate restatement of fundamental Catholic positions concerning philosophy, the political and social order, and the family, modernity was already well entrenched throughout the Catholic world. Despite this, Leo did not hesitate to restate Catholic teaching in ways that without doubt were jarring to the dominant liberal mind of the nineteenth century. By the middle of the twentieth century, however, this approach no longer seemed sufficient to many even within the Church. Their reading of the signs of the times was that something new was necessary. Were they correct?

Whatever can be said for and against both Leo XIII's program and that of the Council and its aftermath, the best way, it seems to me, by which we can evaluate whether the new approach was a realistic reading of the times is by examining how it has contributed to the success of the Church's mission. Although it is often said, and rightly, that we are called to be faithful, not successful, nevertheless it is both natural and sensible to hope that the Church's apostolate will be both. The program that Leo XIII inaugurated, which was in the main a restatement of the Church's historic positions, did seem to be a success. The Catholic intellectual revival, which had begun under Pius IX or even earlier, received new energy and not only attracted converts of a high quality but also forced those outside the Church to take notice of Catholic positions on any number of questions. A chief feature of Leo's program was clarity about what the Church believed. That clarity had a twofold effect, an effect on those outside the Church and on her own members. As I noted above, it managed to attract numerous talented and learned people to the Faith, and it gave those already Catholics a sense of identity. Frank Sheed spoke about his youth in a provincial Australia, where a Catholic ghetto mentality prevailed, marked by the fear of intellectual contact with the outside world: people were "proud of being Catholics, but [with] an unstated feeling that while we had the Faith, the others had the arguments!" But then came his first contact as a young student with the Catholic intellectual revival in the writings of Chesterton and Belloc; they "turned my mental world upside down," he wrote.[9] When Pope Francis speaks with aplomb to the world, this likewise has the potential of increasing Catholic self-confidence; but unless Catholics can also recover clarity of doctrine, a sense of why being a Catholic matters, I fear that no program will have the success that Pope Leo's did, either on Catholics or those outside the Church.

Another objection may be raised, however. Both approaches, that of Pope Leo and that suggested by Pope Benedict, presuppose a church

9. *The Church and I* (Garden City, NY: Doubleday, 1974), 30–31, 33.

fully engaged with the world, including with the political powers of the world. Is that realistic today? Is it not better, perhaps, to emulate an earlier Benedict, who in his time retreated into the wilderness, whence his followers eventually emerged to till the soil of all Europe—both literally and figuratively? Saint Benedict fled the world to establish a *dominici schola servitii*, a school of the Lord's service, as he says in the Prologue of his *Rule*. But even while his monks sought God in the wilderness, the Church pursued her life at the center of things, interacting with emperors and the barbarian chiefs, who were rapidly becoming kings in their own right. Can the Church of God turn her back on the world, even if only temporarily? Will the world ignore us or forget us while we seek to recover the spiritual resources we seem to have squandered?

In my view, she cannot. Neither will the world allow us that leisure nor ought we even to seek it. For some individuals, certainly, it can and probably should be the path sought, for it can be an important part of any Catholic recovery. For the Church as a whole, however, I do not see it. The Church has been placed within the world since her beginning, and especially since Constantine ended the persecution. Pope Francis is certainly not shy about engaging the world, and this is to the good; but the entire post-conciliar "new way" for "the relationship between the Church and the modern era" has not proved itself. I regard it as beyond serious debate, moreover, that in the effort to delineate a "new way" the Church's apostolate was seriously weakened. Something at least of Pope Leo's program must become part of any successful Catholic engagement, in the modern era as in any other. No doubt his approach cannot simply be replicated, but if Pope Leo's program did seem at one time an adequate approach to modernity, we should not reject it merely because it does not seem up-to-date. History can never be merely slavishly imitated; if intelligently used, however, it can be an important guide for our present conduct. I suggest that we look seriously at Leo XIII's program and adopt its essentials as the best response we have to the situation today, which is fundamentally the situation that always faces God's Church in her pilgrimage through history toward eternity.

11

Christendom or Europe?

MR. FLEMMING ROSE, cultural editor of the Danish newspaper *Jyl-lands-Posten*, the man responsible for the publication of the Mohammad cartoons in the fall of 2005 that occasioned the protests and rioting in more than one Moslem country, published a few months ago both in English and German some reflections on the position of Moslem immigrants in Europe. Mr. Rose is rightly concerned about the growing numbers of Moslems in Europe and about the seeming inability or difficulty of many Moslems to accept and live by the liberal, tolerant culture of Europe. He is also critical of the multiculturalism of many on the European left who make every excuse for Moslem intolerance and even violence as long as it is directed against Europeans and European culture.

> [M]ulticulturalism ... has all too often become mere cultural relativism ... that often justifies reactionary and oppressive practices. Giving the same weight to the illiberal values of conservative Islam as to the liberal traditions of the European Enlightenment will, in time, destroy the very things that make Europe such a desirable target for migration.[1]

Rose realizes that a large and growing body of people who constitute an *imperium in imperio* is a danger to European culture, but he recognizes that the time is past for preventing large-scale Moslem immigration.

> Obviously, we can never return to the comfortable monocultures of old. A demographic revolution is changing the face, and look, of Europe. In an age of mass migration and the Internet, cheap air fares and cell phones everywhere, cultural pluralism is an irreversible fact, like it or not.[2]

---

1. Fleming Rose, "Why I Published the Muhammad Cartoons," in *Spiegel Online International*, May 31, 2006.
2. Ibid.

What then does he propose should be done? Rose's way of dealing with this situation is for Moslems to adapt to European culture and mores— at least in their public stance and participation in civic and political life. Just as Rose says that he would not hesitate to print cartoons of "any other Dane, whether the queen, the head of the Church, or the prime minister," Moslems must come to understand that the price of living in a liberal society is that their own sacred figures and symbols are subject to such satire. In fact, by doing so, Europeans will be treating the Moslems as equals:

> You are not strangers, you are here to stay, and we accept you as an integrated part of our life. And we will satirize you, too. It was an act of inclusion, not exclusion; an act of respect and recognition.[3]

So, "Europe must shed the straitjacket of political correctness, which makes it impossible to criticize minorities for anything," while Moslem immigrants must "not only learn the host language but also respect their new countries' political and cultural traditions. . . ."

There is certainly much to be said for Mr. Rose's proposals. They are certainly better than a status quo that is afraid even to point out failings in immigrants while equally afraid to defend anything that Europeans value. Nevertheless, I fear that at bottom his program is lacking. On what basis can Denmark or any other European nation make such demands of Moslems? What criteria of truth would such a demand be based on? If Moslems proclaim that the cartoons—and any similar kind of criticism or satire—constitute "a declaration of war against our religion, our faith and our civilization," as Mullah Krekar, a Norwegian Kurd stated, what is a European to say in reply? How is he to respond to the Moslem's proclamation of an absolute, to the notion that mockery of the sacred is blasphemy? Remember that Mr. Rose had justified cartoons of "the queen, the head of the Church, or the prime minister" and—I daresay—of Jesus Christ and of the Blessed Virgin as well. But the liberal tolerance that Rose calls upon Moslems to accept will never be able to stand up against the assertion of absolutes. The very European tolerance that Rose wants to preserve is the reason in the first place for the absurd refusal ever to point out the real faults of individual Moslems or of Islamic culture as a whole. A liberal Europe has at its heart only emptiness, the relativism that Pope Benedict XVI criticized. The assertion of absolutes can only be opposed with truth, not with an adherence to tolerance based on philosophical nihilism.

3. Ibid.

Rose in a sense gives himself away when he writes, "Europe today finds itself trapped in a posture of moral relativism that is undermining its liberal values." But is it not precisely those "liberal values" that have created that relativism? Indeed, could not Rose's sentence be rewritten with little change of meaning to read, "Europe today finds itself trapped in a posture of liberal values that is undermining its moral relativism"? Liberalism is precisely the refusal to adhere to an explicit religious or philosophical absolute. Its tolerance is grounded on an unwillingness to impose anything except relativism on the socio-political order, an unwillingness ultimately based on philosophical nihilism, a refusal to ground its way of life on religious or philosophical absolutes, even on a rejection of its own religious and cultural heritage, as in the refusal to mention Christianity in the preamble of the proposed European constitution. Unless European intellectual circles can say to Islam, "You are wrong and this is why," in the end they will have no logical answer to Islamic assertions and demands.

What then is the real method of dealing with the Moslem immigrants? Rose is undoubtedly correct—Europe "can never return to the comfortable monocultures of old." A new and restless population has moved into that continent whose culture historically developed along with the Faith. This, however, happened once before. At the time of the collapse of the Roman Empire in western Europe, large numbers of Germanic and other tribes—pagans—moved into all the old Roman lands. And what happened to these new peoples? Well, they were met by Europeans who valued something more than tolerance. They were met by a Church that was sure of herself, by courageous bishops and monks, by popes whose first concern was converting the world to the revelation of Jesus Christ. These barbarian nations eventually became Catholic; they entered the Church and underwent that long religious and cultural tutelage that resulted in the glories and achievements of medieval Europe. Is something like this still possible today? Surely it is if we who are Catholics return to that firmness of faith that our fathers had. Then Europeans could say to their new fellow citizens, "Forgive us for neglecting you; forgive us for not sharing with you the greatest gift we have—not prosperity, not freedom, not security—but the Gospel of Jesus Christ, the riches of the Faith, the sure way to eternal salvation." Is this ridiculous? No more ridiculous than to sit back and watch while Christianity withers away entirely and Islam—even if its adherents become mild-mannered and tolerant Europeans—becomes the principal religion of that continent. But if Europe is no longer willing to defend what is not just its own heritage but is the truth about the Incarnation of Jesus Christ into the world, I see little reason why Catholics should take sides between militant Moslems and militant secularists. Both doubtless have their good points, and probably the secularists will allow us more freedom for a longer time. In the end, however, neither corresponds to either the revelation of God or the real requirements of our human nature. Only in the Catholic Church, "the natural home of the human spirit" as Hilaire Belloc used to say, can European man, or any other man, find not only truth but peace and genuine freedom as well.

12

Christendom or the West?

RECENTLY in *The Wall Street Journal Online*,[1] Mark Steyn of *The New Criterion* wrote a perceptive article on the coming demographic extinction of Europe. He rightly points out the dismal statistics of Europe's birthrate: from Ireland with 1.87 children down to Spain at 1.1. The United States, at 2.07, is not much better. For 2.1, famously, is the break-even point at which a society will reproduce itself. Otherwise it will die, slowly or quickly. And without doubt a society on the way to demographic extinction is a society that no longer believes in itself. It is dying and its denizens do not care. Steyn quotes Arnold Toynbee, "Civilizations die from suicide, not murder." As Steyn says later, "A society that has no children has no future."

What is this dying Western world? Toward the beginning of his article, Steyn says, "The design flaw of the secular social-democratic state is that it requires a religious-society birthrate to sustain it." Secularists, chiefly occupied with material possessions and pleasures, do not want to bother with the babies necessary to sustain their own way of life. He notes how irrational all this is. If secular Europeans, attached to their affluence and freedom, allow their countries to be taken over by Moslem immigrants who are having more children than they are, then those very freedoms of which they are enamored, will be lost. "By prioritizing a 'woman's right to choose,' Western women are delivering their societies into the hands of fellows far more patriarchal than a 1950s sitcom dad." By spending their time focusing on what seem to them the egregious faults of the West—such as its "oppression" of women—they do not understand that their own civilization is much more to their taste, and allows them much more freedom, than anything likely to take its place.

1. Mark Steyn, "It's the Demography, Stupid," in *Wall Street Journal Online*, January 4, 2006.

I certainly agree with all of this. Whatever the immediate economic prospects of Europe or North America, no nation or culture that does not reproduce itself can possibly survive. Even more curious than the self-defeating behavior of Europeans and North Americans, however, are the presuppositions of Mr. Steyn himself. Although he recognizes that a secular society, in order to survive, requires behavior associated with a religious commitment, what does he offer, what in the end does he promote? What is his concept of the Western culture that he thinks worth saving?

Unfortunately, it would seem that for him Western culture is valuable only because of that very materialism which he recognizes as the cause of its own coming demise. "The Western world has delivered more wealth and more comfort to more of its citizens than any other civilization in history." Doubtless true, but one wonders if that is exactly a cause for celebration. Affluence and comfort are not exactly ideals calculated to rally people. Indeed, Mr. Steyn himself recognizes their corrosive effects. "The latter half of the decline and fall of great civilizations follows a familiar pattern: affluence, softness, decadence, extinction." Steyn wonders whether Japan or Germany can remain an "economic powerhouse" if overrun by immigrants; but if being an "economic powerhouse" leads to the slow death of a society, why would anyone want a nation to become one? Why would we want to encourage behavior that in the end will lead to the destruction of our society? More importantly, even if such behavior could be sustained, would that be a good thing? If the West has meaning only because it produces loads of goods, many of them useless or harmful, I for one do not care whether it survives or not.

In the end Steyn has nothing to offer except a society whose goals are to be a "pluralist, liberal democracy" and an "economic powerhouse." Yet he wants its inhabitants to engage in "religious society" behavior for secular reasons. He wants secular, agnostic Europeans and North Americans to adopt behavior calculated to ensure their society's future survival. But why should secularists, interested only in pluralism and affluence, care about the future? They will mostly be dead; and anyway, raising a good-sized family can be an irksome enterprise and certainly requires greater and more immediate motivation than a vague concern about the future of Western secular civilization or the material prospects of one's grandchildren.

A religious society will have a healthy birthrate because religious people respect the law of God, because they have confidence in God's fatherly care for mankind, because they are not so focused on affluence that they neglect the obvious duty of a married couple to procreate.

Very few secularists will have sufficient motivation to set aside their immediate selfish happiness for a general benevolence toward future generations. It is not rational to expect them to do so.

This brings us back to the question in my title: "Christendom or the West?" Does the culture of Europe and its daughter societies represent affluence, liberal democracy, and the maximum amount of personal freedom or does it historically represent Christendom, the embodiment of a Christian social order, not a theocracy to be sure, but a society in which concern for our eternal salvation and communicating the Gospel to all of mankind are not only goals of individual believers, but are properly the concern also of society as a whole? I realize that today the Western world is far from its Christian roots, but that is not the point. The point is how we see ourselves, whether we eagerly embrace a Western world with roots no deeper than its commercial activity or whether we at least aspire to become a "civilization of love," to use the phrase popularized by St. John Paul II.

If we want the first, we must be content with the behavior that accompanies it. If we want the second, we must want it for its own sake, for the glory of God and the truth of the Gospel, not as a means to an end. Hardly anyone will choose religious behavior for the sake of secular ends. God must be chosen for Himself, and the Catholic Faith must be embraced because it is true, not because it leads to outcomes desired for other reasons. God cannot be a means to an end.

Mr. Steyn, then, is as much a part of the Western world's extincting behavior as the, admittedly stupid, Europeans who are allowing their nations to disappear. If we want to save the West because it embodies liberal pluralism, I am afraid that we want the impossible. We must want God and then all else may follow. Otherwise, not only are we doomed to extinction, but we also deserve to be.

13

Post-Modernism
and the End of an Age

AS THE HUMAN RACE enters the third millennium of the Christian era, there is a widespread feeling that more than a mere chronological mark on the calendar has passed. Very often it is said that the modern age, that great edifice which like a colossus bestrode first the Western world and then the entire globe, has ended and that we are entering, or have entered, the post-modern era. What exactly the post-modern era is, and whether it is something Catholics ought to welcome or deplore, will be the subject of this chapter.

In the first place I must say a word about terminology. The word *modern* often denotes simply *today, now, present-day.*[1] So, one could argue that it is as absurd to speak of the post-modern as of the post-today or the post-now. When tomorrow comes we shall call it simply *today.* But long usage has termed the historical era that began sometime between the fifteenth and the eighteenth centuries as the modern age, and no matter what any descendants of ours might call their times, since we have used modern to denote such a specific period of time, I suppose that it was inevitable that people would begin to speak of the end of the modern age and the beginning of the post-modern. In any case, conventional usage has now sanctioned *post-modern,* and it seems vain to resist it, at least for the time being.

Part of the reason the term *post-modern* seems appropriate is that the characteristics of the post-modern era are usually framed in contrast

---

1. The first recorded use of modern, in Latin *modernus,* meaning new or present-day, was in about A.D. 495 (Peter Henrici, "Modernity and Christianity," in *Communio* 17, no. 2 (summer 1990): 141). It was used widely from the end of the Middle Ages in this sense. Henrici gives other examples in both Latin and English; more can be found in the Oxford English Dictionary.

with those features that are considered as distinguishing the modern age. If the modern age has ended, something that is not modern has taken its place, whose meaning can only be understood as a reaction against modernity and that could only have come into being as a result of modernity. Thus, our task must be to set out what are the distinguishing marks of the modern age in order to understand the post-modern. In fact, since the modern age itself is a development of or successor to what came before, namely the pre-modern, we shall have to start with an account of what came before modernity. However, in labeling ages as pre-modern, modern, or post-modern, it does not mean that we are taking the modern age as the standard and valuing other ages only in relation to modern times. It is simply a linguistic convention, and I shall later suggest other terms that seem to me to describe more accurately what has really occurred in these great historical cultural shifts.

The development of rational thought, of philosophy, took place only in one place on the earth: Greece.

> In Greece, alone in the ancient world, the wisdom of man found the right path, and as the result of a fortunate harmony of the soul's powers and of a long effort to achieve mental order and discipline human reason attained its full vigour and maturity.[2]

As Western philosophy developed from the Greeks, different philosophers took different paths; but at its best, especially in the thought of Aristotle and St. Thomas, pre-modern philosophy had certain characteristics that are important to note. In the first place, such philosophers did not generally attempt to build philosophical systems; rather they strove to provide a philosophical description of reality. Nor did each philosopher feel he must create his own original and unique philosophy, but was usually content to build upon the work of his predecessors. In contrast, the modern age has been marked by the proliferation of philosophical systems. Each philosopher has elaborated his own philosophy, very often in marked disagreement with those who came before him; indeed, the hallmark of a philosopher has been that he advances his own unique brand of thought. Thus, a long parade of individual geniuses has stridden the Western world: Descartes, Spinoza, Leibniz, Newton, Locke, Rousseau, Adam Smith, Kant, Hegel, Marx, Freud, and many others, each of whom created his own intellectual edifice, his own personal system.

What do I mean by a system? As I am using the term, a *system* is a body of thought with the following characteristics: it usually denies the

---

2. Jacques Maritain, *An Introduction to Philosophy* (London: Sheed & Ward, 1947), 33.

ordinary experience of our senses or thought processes; it is in contact with reality at only one or a few points; and it claims to be the one, true, all-encompassing explanation of everything. These characteristics can be illustrated by the philosophy of René Descartes (1596–1650). In his *Meditations on First Philosophy*, Descartes resolved to doubt the reality of

> the sky, the earth, colors, shapes, sounds and all external things.... I shall consider myself as having no hands, no eyes, no flesh, no blood, nor any senses, but as falsely opining myself to possess all these things.[3]

Uttering his famous *Cogito ergo sum*—I think therefore I am—Descartes first proves his own existence. Thereupon, by analyzing his thoughts he arrives at a knowledge of God; only from that does he come to acknowledge the material world around him, including his own body. Here we see the marks of the modern system builders: first, Descartes denies the ordinary experience of our senses and our common-sense knowledge that not only we ourselves exist but also the world around us. This procedure contrasts with pre-modern philosophers, who did not doubt such ordinary knowledge even when, as in Plato, they argued that it essentially masked deeper and greater realities.

Secondly, Descartes' philosophy is in contact with reality at only one or a few points. Descartes is correct when he says that he thinks, but he is wrong when he pretends to deduce his existence from that fact, for one surely is as obvious as the other. By basing all his knowledge—the knowledge of his own existence, of God, of the material world—on that one narrow point of contact with reality, the recognition of his own thinking, he constructs a veritable castle in the air.

Thirdly, Descartes' system strives to be the one, true, and all-encompassing explanation of reality. Though naive people might think they see a world about them and though even some philosophers might claim to prove God's existence from the created world, those who have adopted Descartes' outlook know that all this is mere illusion and that reality must be based on his *Cogito*, the key to knowledge.

Much of the same could be said of the other great modern system builders. In the case of Freud, for example, though a person might think that he desired such and such thing for such and such reason, upon accepting the theories of Freud he would learn that, no, in reality his desires are prompted by deep, unconscious urges, probably related to sex. So again, we have the attempted explanation of all reality, the denial

---

3. René Descartes, *Meditations on First Philosophy*, "Meditation I," trans. Donald A. Cress (Indianapolis: Hackett Publishing Co., 1993).

of ordinary experience, and contact with the real world at only a few points.

The modern age has been characterized by such grand gnostic myths propagated by powerful, *sui generis* thinkers. As a result of their systems, other myths equally or more fundamental and far reaching have come to have almost universal influence over the population at least of the Western world—myths such as progress, science, democracy, the emancipation of mankind from ignorance by modern enlightenment and education. These myths are sometimes called meta-narratives by post-modernists, because they attempt to provide an explanation for everything.[4] To a greater extent than they realize, Catholics have grown comfortable with the myths of modernism, even when they directly contravene the tenets of the Faith. As we shall see, we must be grateful to post-modernism if only for exploding the modernist myths.

The modern age, then, battened on such meta-narratives, but even in the midst of such systems the first stirrings of post-modernism began to be heard. When did post-modernism begin? That is difficult to say. Perhaps one can discern some proto-post-modernists with the invention of non-Euclidean geometries in the mid-nineteenth century, the geometries that by denying or ignoring the fifth or parallel postulate of Euclid—the postulate that states (in effect) that parallel lines will never meet—conjured up a world in which truth seemed manufactured at the whim of the thinker, the world having no firm reality of its own. Others have seen in the artistic movements of the 1920s, such as dada and surrealism and James Joyce's novel *Finnegans Wake* (1939), the beginnings of post-modernism. Whatever may have been the early signs of this cultural shift, it was after the Second World War that the first unmistakable evidences of post-modernism can be discerned.

The first manifestations of what is universally agreed to be post-modernism were literary and artistic; only later was this movement embodied as a philosophy. In fact, the philosophical expression has been seen as largely an *ex post facto* attempt to justify the literary movement. "When the mood of a period is looking for an ideology it finds philosophical contradictions and objections no barrier. . . ."[5] And a major part of this new "mood" in literature was an attack on humanism,

---

4. It is necessary to distinguish between something held as a myth and the same thing otherwise conceived. Thus, there is nothing wrong with democracy conceived as simply one among the various legitimate forms of government, but this is a far cry from democracy looked upon as the only valid form of government and the key to solving all the problems of nations. This latter is what I mean by the myth of democracy.

5. Jean-Marie Domenach, "The Attack on Humanism in Contemporary Culture," in *Humanism and Christianity*, ed. Claude Geffré (New York: Herder & Herder, 1973), 19.

indeed, an attack on man himself. Modernism had sought to exalt man, in fact, had erroneously thought that it must deny God in order to do so. Post-modernism began by denying man, who was seen as simply a substitute for God in humanist thinking.[6]

One of the earliest and most important of these literary representatives was the French novelist, short-story writer, and film writer and director, Alain Robbe-Grillet, who "claimed that the novel ought to describe man as an object, at the most as an insect among insects."[7] Robbe-Grillet embodied this technique in his own works, beginning with *Les Gommes* (*The Erasers*) in 1953. Even more important would seem to be the calling into question of objective reality, which also occurs in many of his works of fiction. For example, in his short story, "The Secret Room," it is said of a man who has just committed a murder that "near the top of the stairway, a black silhouette is seen fleeing, a man wrapped in a long floating cape, ascending the last steps without turning around. . . ." Then, a few paragraphs later it is said of the same man that he "is now on the first steps of the stairs, ready to go up," and later again that he "is still standing about a yard away" from the murder victim, "half leaning over her."[8] In fact the whole atmosphere of the story has more than a hint of the unreal about it, suggesting that reality is not a stable thing.

This literary movement soon conjured up a similar movement in philosophy, though as a philosophy post-modernism does not teach an exact or coherent set of doctrines. As one commentator has noted,

> They do not form a school of thought, nor even a movement. Indeed, even the word "trend" gives them too much unity, a unity which they would be the first to reject. Nevertheless, however broad, loose and flexible they are, they have introduced into philosophy what I will call

---

6. Michel Foucault, "echoing Nietzsche's prophecy of the death of God," had in 1967 announced the death of man in his book, *Les mots et les choses* (Louis Marin, "The Disappearance of Man in the Humane Sciences—A Linguistic Model and Signifying Subject," in *Humanism and Christianity*, ed. Claude Geffré, 29). Moreover, "if deconstruction seems to oppose Humanism, it is because Humanism operates by substituting the concept 'man' for the concept 'God' . . . and so placing 'man' as the unproblematic ground of meaningfulness for human life" (John Lye, "Deconstruction, Some Assumptions," Brock University, English 4F70, Contemporary Literary Theory [1996; updated April 30, 2008]), accessed November 11, 2014, http://www.brocku.ca/english/courses/4F70/deconstruction.php.

7. Jean-Marie Domenach, "The Attack on Humanism in Contemporary Culture," in *Humanism and Christianity*, ed. Claude Geffré, 25.

8. In *The Short Story: Fiction in Transition*, ed. J. Chesley Taylor (New York: Scribner's, 1969), 608–613.

a distinctive atmosphere, a tonality that already announced their arrival in the 1950s.[9]

Nonetheless, the doctrines of post-modernism, however hard they may be to define, do have some things in common.

> What we have is a broad and elusive movement of thought that is as differentiated internally as it is generalizable externally as a new philosophical development. Indeed, deconstruction, which might be presented as an extreme form of postmodernism, is explicitly an anti-definition theory of thought.[10]

This anti-philosophy philosophy was presented in an increasing number of books and articles in the 1960s, the 1970s, and thereafter. Most of its leading writers were French philosophers and literary critics, including Jacques Derrida, Michel Foucault, Jean-Francois Lyotard, and others.

Post-modernist philosophy took its origin from the novels and short stories of the 1950s and early 1960s. As a philosophy it has attacked man chiefly on the level of his rationality. Post-modernism has attacked modernism's grand schemes or meta-narratives *because* post-modernism has called into question the idea that man is capable of seeing the truth enough to construct such intellectual edifices;[11] it is deeply hostile to systems or schemes that purport to *describe* reality, as they are seen as attempts to *prescribe* or *circumscribe* reality, to exercise power, to control others by setting the bounds of reality and thus of behavior. Not only the statement of grand meta-narratives, but also "any claim to the theoretical pursuit of truth will raise the question: What is *really* behind this claim?"[12] As Mr. Slavoj Žižek wrote regarding cultural studies, one of the academic disciplines most influenced by such an approach,

> Cultural Studies, as a rule, involves [sic] the stance of cognitive suspension characteristic of historicist relativism: cinema theorists in Cultural Studies, for instance, no longer ask basic questions like "What is the nature of cinematic perception?", they simply tend to reduce such

9. Kenneth L. Schmitz, "Postmodernism and the Catholic Tradition," in *American Catholic Philosophical Quarterly* 73, no. 2 (spring 1999): 233–34.

10. William Grassie, "Postmodernism: What One Needs to Know," in *Zygon, Journal of Religion and Science*, March 1997.

11. Jean-Francois Lyotard (in his *The Postmodern Condition*, 1979) gave "incredulity toward metanarratives" as a kind of definition of post-modernism. Quoted from Huston Smith, "Postmodernism and the World's Religions," in *The Truth About the Truth*, ed. Walter Truett Anderson (New York: G. P. Putnam's, 1995), 206.

12. Kenneth L. Schmitz, "Postmodern or Modern-plus?" in *Communio, International Catholic Review* 17, no. 2 (summer 1990): 163.

questions to the historicist reflection upon conditions in which certain notions emerged as the result of historically specific power relations. In other words, we are dealing with the historicist abandonment of the very question of the inherent "truth-value" of a theory under consideration: when a typical Cultural Studies theorist deals with a philosophical or psychoanalytic edifice, the analysis focuses exclusively on unearthing its hidden patriarchal, Eurocentric, identitarian, etc., "bias", without even asking the naive but none the less [sic] necessary question: OK, but what *is* the structure of the universe? How *does* the human psyche "really" work?[13]

In fact, post-modernism goes so far as to reject the truth of nature, for example, the natural distinction of mankind into two sexes, regarding it as an unwarranted restriction on our behavior—another instance of asserting control. An article in *The Chronicle of Higher Education*[14] about a young male college student who announces to his parents that he is really a girl and begins to wear dresses and asks his parents to refer to him as their daughter, captures well this radical assault on nature. This unfortunate young man asserts, "I'm a girl. I want to wear dresses, makeup and challenge the whole patriarchal, bourgeois idea of gender." To this way of thinking, male and female are only two of many possible stopping points on the sexuality spectrum; and indeed, by trying to separate sex from what is called gender, the social and cultural expression of one's sexuality, they make the expression of one's sexuality something utterly separable from one's biological sex.

Another feature that may be considered central to post-modern thought is the technique of *deconstruction*, or what is sometimes called the decentering of the text. This involves what is known as *working at the margins* and proceeds to take away both the author and the meaning of the written text. Deconstruction, moreover, is connected with the attack on man that I mentioned above, for it rids the world of both author and even the ability to communicate with others. Let us look in some detail at how this works, first with regard to the deconstruction of the author, then of the text itself.

Since no error, however bizarre, can make headway without some shadow of truth, post-modernism proceeds by attacking the exaggerations of modernism on the question of authorship. For example, Prof.

---

13. Slavoj Žižek, "Da Capo senza Fine," in Judith Butler, Ernesto Laclau, and Slavoj Žižek, *Contingency, Hegemony, Universality: Contemporary Dialogues on the Left* (London: Verso, 2000), 230–31.

14. Lennard J. Davis, "Gaining a Daughter: a Father's Transgendered Tale," March 24, 2000, B4.

Martha Woodmansee, a post-modernist critic and professor of English, attempts to dissolve authorship into the many people responsible for the production of the physical book. She begins by quoting a typical modernist pronouncement about original genius by the English poet, William Wordsworth (1770–1850).

> Of genius the only proof is, the act of doing well what is worthy to be done, and what was never done before: Of genius in the fine arts, the only infallible sign is the widening the sphere of human sensibility, for the delight, honor, and benefit of human nature. Genius is the introduction of a new element into the intellectual universe: or, if that be not allowed, it is the application of powers to objects on which they had not before been exercised, or the employment of them in such a manner as to produce effects hitherto unknown.[15]

To this she contrasts a passage from St. Bonaventure (1221–1274):

> A man might write the works of others, adding and changing nothing, in which case he is simply called a "scribe" (*scriptor*). Another writes the work of others with additions which are not his own; and he is called a "compiler" (*compilator*). Another writes both others' work and his own, but with others' work in principal place, adding his own for purposes of explanation; and he is called a "commentator" (*commentator*).... Another writes both his own work and others' but with his own work in principal place adding others' for purposes of confirmation; and such a man should be called an "author" (*auctor*).[16]

Now, there is certainly a difference between the passage from Wordsworth and that of St. Bonaventure. Wordsworth emphasizes the uniqueness of the artistic creator, whereas Bonaventure puts the true author in a kind of gradation with the simple scribe. In the pre-modern period there was generally much less concern about authorship and whether a writer had introduced precisely a "new element into the intellectual universe" and, if so, by whom exactly was it introduced. Several works of Thomas Aquinas, for example, were not completed by the saint, but by colleagues or students or others; and exactly where the pen of St. Thomas stopped and the pen of someone else took over we do not always know. But the modernist approach to literature and art has been preoccupied with such questions. Who collaborated with Shakespeare, exactly which lines were written by the Bard and which by his collabora-

---

15. William Wordsworth, Essay, Supplementary to the Preface, quoted in Martha Woodmansee, "On the Author Effect: Recovering Collectivity," in *Cardozo Arts & Entertainment Law Journal* 10, no. 2 (1992): 280.

16. Quoted in ibid., 281.

tors? In fact, in sixteenth-century drama there was a fluidity about the text and about authorship that reveals a fundamentally different attitude from that of the modern age. Often the director or the actors would add, subtract, or change lines, depending on the audience or other factors. Readers might recall that in Shakespeare's *Hamlet* exactly this takes place, as Hamlet asks the players to add a few lines of his own composition as part of his plot against the king.[17] In general, pre-modern writers, composers, and other artists worked more collaboratively, borrowed freely from one another and from their own works, and seemed to care less that every work of their own would be attributed to their own unique genius. Of course, this occurs even today: in speech writing, ghost writing, editing, and other kinds of cooperative or assisted writing. Granting all this as true, however, we can still very obviously make a distinction, and an important distinction, between a scribe and an author, even though we might well agree that authorship frequently depends on the efforts of others as well. The post-modernists, however, go far beyond this and attempt to dissolve authorship altogether. For example, Prof. Woodmansee comments as follows on the passage from St. Bonaventure that I quoted above:

> While Bonaventura's *auctor* seems to be making a substantial (original) contribution of his own, he does so as part of an enterprise conceived collaboratively. Nor is *this* mode of book production privileged over the other three—over transcription, compilation, and commentary.[18]

This is surely not the case. Just because Bonaventure sees authorship as in a series ranging from transcription does not mean that he does not see the obvious differences between the two. Probably most ancient and medieval writers were in the habit of using a scribe or secretary to whom they dictated their works; but clearly these scribes are largely unknown, and no one credits them with the importance that the author himself has. Often we do not even know their names.

Simply because most pre-modern writers cared less about who was the unique and original author and readily accepted the fact that often the final text was the result of many different writers' and editors' pens, we need not acquiesce in the post-modern destruction or deconstruction of authorship. So, although it is certainly the case that we assume the model of the solitary author too often and forget that much of the

---

17. "You could, for a need, study a speech of some dozen or sixteen lines which I would set down and insert in't, could you not?" (Act II, scene 3).

18. Woodmansee, "On the Author Effect: Recovering Collectivity," 281.

writing in the world is the result of some sort of collaboration, it is too much to suggest that because of this authors and authorship somehow disappear entirely.

Let us next consider how post-modernists dissolve the meaning of the text itself; then we shall see what use they make of their deconstruction of both writer and text.

The destruction or deconstruction of text begins in the text itself.

> The strategy is not to bring some alien force against the text, but rather to exploit the text's own resources against itself. It is meant to probe its blind spots, to do 'violence' to the text, but from within the text itself, to expose the moments of inner stress. That is why Derrida can claim that he does not go beyond the text, but rather that he simply puts it to the test. The strategy is to catch whatever there is in the text that cannot quite be brought to rational concepts, and then to worry the text until the central meaning gives way to a plurality of different possible meanings.[19]

That is, anything in a text that does not quite seem to fit—something on the "margins"—is pounced upon, and the critic then seeks to show how this one bit could be understood differently from the presumed message of the entire text; then, little by little, the text and its meaning begins to fall apart.

> It does not attempt to contradict the argument of the text; it merely saps its strength. The deconstructionist fights somewhat in the Parthian manner; if not exactly by fleeing from the main argument, still by striking side-glancing blows. The strategy, especially Derrida's, is to put an accepted interpretation off balance, and once tilted, to put it out of play.[20]

Now, a text takes its meaning both from its unity in the author's mind and intention and from the meaning of the words themselves. If the author, however, has been dissolved and the actual meaning of the words called into question, obviously the dissolution of meaning results. As we saw above, post-modernism is hostile to truth claims, but hostile not by making counter arguments but by attempting to destroy argument itself. Thence comes the celebration of contradiction and of play or parody in the post-modern. What the following quotation says about image can also be taken to apply to text and meaning:

> The role of the image in post-modern culture is essentially one of *parody*. By this is meant that the image no longer refers primarily to some

19. Schmitz, "Postmodern or Modern-plus?," 159.
20. Ibid., 161.

'original', situated outside of itself in the 'real' world or inside of human consciousness. Devoid of any fixed reference to an origin, the image appears to refer only to other images. The post-modern image circulates in a seemingly endless play of imitation. Each image becomes a parody of another which precedes it . . . and so on.[21]

So, we end up with the situation in which a "message is now no longer a unique expression sent from an author to a reader."[22] A text is no longer about the world outside the mind of the author or even about the thoughts inside the mind of the author. Texts are simply about other texts.

> Hence we note that the pre-modern model of the image as *mirror* . . . and the modern model as *lamp* . . . give way to the post-modern model of a *circle of looking glasses*—each one reproducing the surface images of the other in a play of infinite multiplication.[23]

Clearly, we have here something like the death of reason. Texts are no longer arguments made to convince someone of some point of view; for, as we saw, post-modernism suspects every such argument to be a covert attempt to grab power. Instead, an argument is play; argument becomes trivial. Although modernism very often espoused error and made wrong arguments, it was very much, indeed passionately, interested in truth whereas post-modernism is not interested in making an argument. Rather it seeks to destroy every argument, even every possibility of argument.

The negative aspects of post-modernism are obvious. Above I suggested that, since modernism itself was inimical to Catholic thought and faith, we should be grateful to a certain extent to the post-modernists for dissolving the modernist worldview. In fact, there are certain features of post-modern thought and art that somewhat approximate pre-modern thought and practice. Beginning in the 1960s, for example, post-modern practice in the theater duplicated certain features of the medieval theater, such as direct interaction between actor and audience and experimenting with different arrangements of the stage rather than simply using the proscenium stage so typical of the modern era, which induced the spectator to gaze into the make-believe world of the play, a world kept strictly separate from the real world of the audience.

---

21. Richard Kearney, "The Crisis of the Post-modern Image," in *Contemporary French Philosophy*, ed. A. Phillips Griffiths (Cambridge: Cambridge University Press, 1987), 113.

22. Ibid., 115.

23. Ibid., 113.

More fundamentally, since post-modernists both claim that the text is everything[24] and then set about to subvert it, we might ask whether the role of writing and purely rational thought has differed in modern times from their pre-modern role. In the Middle Ages books were very often heavily decorated, exhibiting pictures in the margins and various other kinds of designs and illustrations. A variety of colors were used for letters, so that in the medieval book the text danced, as it were, amid a sea of beauty. The text existed within a context, but with the invention of printing this state of affairs soon changed. The medieval face of the book eventually vanished; and the modern book, in which text is everything or almost everything, became the rule. Text came to rule the modern world. This predominance can be seen especially in Protestantism, which erected a text, Sacred Scripture, into a rule it was never meant to be. In general, the modern world has seen the tyranny of the text because our world has lost the sense of approaching man on every level of his being, rational and non-rational. At the very beginning of the modern era, Descartes had stamped modern thought with the notion that man was only a mind, and the body merely an appendage. But medieval Catholicism approached man through all his five senses: with music, the smell of incense, pictures and statues, even the taste of salt at baptism. One wonders if the modern age had not distorted text and made it supreme, the post-modernists would have felt the need to overthrow this tyranny of words and wordy systems.

I said above that the terms *pre-modern*, *modern*, and *post-modern* were not the best terms to describe the great cultural shifts that have occurred in our civilization. In pre-modern times the Catholic faith approached man according to his entire nature, the best foundation on which grace can build. With Descartes and his successors all this changed, so perhaps one could call modernity and all that has followed simply the post-human. For modernism and post-modernism have both essentially refused to look at man as he is and have in one way or another persisted in distorting man and indeed all of reality.

Naturally, post-modernism as a reaction against modernism was bound to discover some truths rejected by modernism; but, as we have seen, it also embraced many new errors, especially the view that all assertions of truth are attempts to dominate, and the accompanying deconstruction of meaning and even of man himself. Although Catholics can take some legitimate pleasure, after the long journey through

---

24. Derrida famously wrote (in *Of Grammatology*): "Il n'y a pas de hors-texte," that is, there is nothing outside the text.

the desert of modernism, in some facets of post-modernism, in reality it provides us an opportunity, or rather two opportunities. In the first place, post-modernism gives us the opportunity of looking at our own thoughts and seeing to what extent we have compromised with modernism in our own understanding of things. Modernism has been around for so long that we Catholics have grown too comfortable with it and sometimes even defend modernist theses against post-modernism. We ought, however, to purge our minds of both these sorts of error as we look toward St. Thomas as the philosopher able to cope with both modernism and post-modernism.

The second opportunity that post-modernism gives us is directed not at ourselves, but rather *ad extra*. That is, post-modernism demands that we look at our methods of apostolate and see to what extent the post-modern worldview indicates a different approach, an approach that may seem new but that in reality is old. It is the approach that includes the creation of atmosphere—in the liturgy, for example, an atmosphere that reflects man in his essential nature, not just as thinker but on every level of his being as a rational animal having body and soul, senses, affections, loves, and hates. Here again, since St. Thomas deals with man in all these ways, by a true recovery of his philosophy we may more easily not only see through and refute post-modernist nonsense but also appeal to the post-modern man, that man for whom Christ our God lived, suffered, and died as much as He did for medieval man and modern man.

Our methods of evangelization ought therefore to reflect a world that feels itself stifled under texts and that is looking, in its confused way, for something different. It may be that if we can offer this world the pre-modern in a way that is fresh, not simply offer a tame and stale compromise with modernism, what is old will indeed seem very new. As Chesterton wrote in a very different era in the life of the Church and of the world,

> The Catholic faith used to be called the Old Religion; but at the present moment it has a recognized place among the New Religions. This has nothing to do with its truth or falsehood; but it is a fact that has a great deal to do with the understanding of the modern world.
>
> It would be very undesirable that modern man should accept Catholicism merely as a novelty; but it is a novelty. It does act upon its existing environment with the peculiar force and freshness of a novelty.... The worthy merchant of the middle class, the worthy farmer of the Middle West, when he sends his son to college, does now feel a faint alarm lest the boy should fall among thieves, in the sense of

Communists; but he has the same sort of fear lest he should fall among Catholics.[25]

If we are to have an apostolate to the post-modern age that has hope of any success, it is in such a manner that we must proceed. We must show that the Faith is the one exciting thing in the universe; the one thing that can appeal to man in soul and body; the thing that does not repress, but offers him, his true fulfillment and imports a beauty not just from another age but from outside our world altogether.

25. *The Catholic Church and Conversion*, in *The Collected Works of G.K. Chesterton*, vol. 3 (San Francisco: Ignatius Press, 1990), 64–65.

14

The Catholic Vocations of the Americas

IT IS A CURIOUS FACT that the two nations that left the greatest mark on the New World of the Americas were the two nations at perhaps the farthest extremes of European culture, Spain and England. Spain, after centuries of crusading zeal in recovering lands seized by Muslim invaders, became by default the leading political and cultural defender of the Church and of Catholic civilization in the face of apostasy in so much of northern Europe. England, on the other hand, although preserving some of the medieval Catholic ethos in the Anglican liturgy, became culturally and especially politically the bulwark of Protestant civilization and even of the most extreme form of Protestantism, Calvinism. Neither the remote kingdoms of Scandinavia nor the divided and weak Protestant states of Germany could have engaged in a worldwide war against Catholic interests as did the English, with some assistance from the Protestant Dutch, to be sure. But if we admit this fact, what conclusions can we draw from it?

It is of doubtful value to speculate on the actions of God as embodied in history, but to some extent it seems that we can discern them, at least dimly, after the fact. For example, many have remarked on how the wide extent of the Roman Empire allowed the rapid diffusion of the Gospel in the early centuries of the Church and how the cultures of Greece and Rome seemed to have reached their apogee and begun a decline at about the time the Church began preaching the message of salvation. Is there, then, anything we can say about the fact that the New World has been mostly shaped by the chief upholder of Catholic civilization and by the most bitter enemy of that civilization?

Although God never wills sin, He is always able to bring some good out of it. The defection of England from the Faith is a sin that has affected the entire subsequent history of the world; and, so far at least, we look in vain for some compensating good. Christopher Dawson commented on the crucial role of England as follows:

The religious wars in which first Germany, then France, and finally Germany again, were plunged, left Continental Protestantism maimed and weakened, whereas English Protestantism became all the stronger in spite of the civil wars and revolutions in which it was involved. Hence it has been argued by some historians that the English Reformation was one of the most important events in the history of Christendom since the great Schism in the East. For it produced a new form of culture, and indeed a new type of Christianity, which was subsequently diffused all over the world, and especially in North America, so that it became one of the great forces that have shaped the modern world.[1]

Given that we must deplore that defection and the immense influence it has had throughout the world, what can we say of the situation that has resulted from that disaster? In particular, can we discern what might be the task of Catholics in the Americas? Here we must talk separately about two groups of Catholics: those inhabiting the Anglo-Saxon portions and those inhabiting the Iberian portions of that region.

As to the regions of Anglo-Saxon culture, the northern regions of the Americas, the United States and English-speaking Canada, are unequivocally Protestant lands despite the large numbers of Catholics who have immigrated there. Numerous witnesses have noted the lack of influence of these immigrants on the culture of the United States. One of these, the historian and Catholic convert Carlton J.H. Hayes said in 1922, "Nevertheless, in spite of the Church's amazing growth, American Catholics have had no such influence upon the thought and life of the whole nation as their numbers would lead us to expect."[2]

The reasons for this would seem to be threefold. First, the culture of the United States, "the essential character of the American states," was already fundamentally formed "in politics, culture and in philosophical thought" before the beginnings of the mass Catholic immigration beginning around the middle of the nineteenth century.[3] Secondly, most of these immigrants were too poor, too necessarily fixed on simply

1. Christopher Dawson, *The Dividing of Christendom* (Garden City, NY: Image, 1967), 104.

2. *American Catholicism and the Intellectual Ideal*, Frank L. Christ and Gerard E. Sherry, eds. (New York: Appleton-Century-Crofts, 1961), 72–73.

3. "Der Katholizismus der späteren Einwanderung, vor allem aus Südeuropa, kam erst zu einem Zeitpunkt, als sich die wesentlichen Charakteristika dieses amerikanischen Staates bereits herauskristallisiert hatten.

"Die amerikanischen Kolonien waren in Politik, Kuktur und auch im philosophischen Denken überwiegend angelsächsisch ausgerichtet." Constantin von Barloewen, *Werte in der Kulturphilosophie Nord- und Lateinamerikas* (Frankfurt am Main: Athenäum, 1989), 51.

surviving and making a living, to take much of an interest in converting American or Canadian culture. Those who might have done something—the clergy—were in turn forced to concentrate on providing the essential elements of the Faith, the sacraments and catechesis, to their rapidly growing flocks. Thirdly, few Catholics of the time understood what was at stake, that unless American culture was transformed, it would instead transform the manner of thinking and acting of those Catholics who had come to dwell within that culture. The desire to convert the nation was often admirably stated, as when in 1850 Archbishop John Hughes of New York proclaimed in a sermon,

> Everyone should know that we have for our mission to convert the world—including the inhabitants of the United States,—the people of the cities, and the people of the country, the officers of the navy and the marines, commanders of the army, the Legislatures, the Senate, the Cabinet, the President, and all.[4]

Until sometime around 1960, almost all Catholics in this country would probably have given at least verbal agreement to Archbishop Hughes's understanding of their mission even if, as time went on, enthusiasm for this goal faded. To some extent our forebears in the Faith did make efforts to convert their non-Catholic fellow citizens. They did not realize, however, that the patterns of thinking and acting in North America were so infused with Protestantism that these also had to be converted; that they themselves were hardly immune from being influenced by the surrounding Protestant ethos; and that therefore simple adherence to the Faith as set forth in the catechism, though obviously essential, was not sufficient to safeguard their spiritual health. In fact, many Catholics of that era, as now, outdid themselves in aping Protestant ways of thinking and acting owing to an unhealthy sense of cultural inferiority. Thus, because the matter of cultural conversion was little addressed, we have today the situation that the former Archbishop of Chicago, Francis George, correctly appraised when he stated during the Synod of Bishops for the Americas in November of 1997 that U.S. citizens "are culturally Calvinist, even those who profess the Catholic faith" and that American society "is the civil counterpart of a faith based on private interpretation of Scripture and private experience of God."

Among Catholic immigrant groups, German Catholics exhibited a greater realization of the dangers associated with uncritical assimilation

---

4. Quoted in Theodore Maynard, *The Story of American Catholicism* (New York: Macmillan, 1941), 298.

into a Protestant culture. One of the most eloquent and persistent advocates for this point of view was Arthur Preuss (1871–1934), a long-time editor and writer. His biographer sums up Preuss's work thus:

> ... the position that Arthur Preuss took on *the* question of American Catholicism, that is, 'how are we to be both Catholic and American,' is as germane today as it was in his lifetime. Preuss believed that Catholicism must work to counter the skepticism, materialism, and excessive individualism of American society, and that this requires that one's loyalty to America not stifle the 'subversive' character of Christianity.
>
> To be successful in such a struggle Preuss believed that the Catholic Church in America had to survive as a distinctive community and to do this it must propagate a 'Catholic world view' or culture. This world view could only be sustained if Catholics of the twentieth century, like their immigrant ancestors, continued to look to the Church as the central locus of their daily lives. . . . It was only by maintaining this transnational loyalty that Catholics in America would elude the double-edged threat of Americanism; this included the myth of American providentialism of the Americanists and the notion of American Catholic 'particularism' within the universal Church. . . . Through the maintenance of their distinctive identity the Catholics of the United States could make a positive contribution to American society by being a 'sign of contradiction' to the prevailing culture and a viable alternative to it.[5]

German Catholics were even concerned that the premature use of the English language would have a deleterious effect on the faith and spiritual health of immigrant Catholics; if one looks at the claims of some proponents of English, this concern does not seem misplaced.

> Consider, again, the great work of the English language in the American Continent—the countless millions drawn from the middle or working classes of all parts of Europe who have been persuaded or penetrated by a more or less characteristic English civilization . . . which . . . teaches to other peoples certain principles of honesty, tolerance, justice, and respect for the sanctity of law and contract which are the ideals of all English-speaking lands. . . . In art, religion, and literature it is moderation, compromise and humanity, that prevail with [the Englishman]. . . .
>
> In the modern world the English language expresses modern habits of thought more adequately than any other and therefore, . . . we

should try to preserve and extend to other nations, hitherto less pene-
trated by those ideals, her linguistic expression as the vehicle of her
practical, tolerant, sporting, easy-going, concrete, and democratic
point of view.[6]

Of course, by no means are all the qualities the author associates with
England and the English language evils, nor is it impossible to use that
language to promote Catholic faith and culture; but a discerning reader
will grasp that he is in fact proposing a way of thought and life different
from, and in important ways, hostile to that of Catholic culture, but
usually hostile in a quiet and gentle manner, a manner that subtly rather
than violently undermines Catholic identity.

As I pointed out above, Christopher Dawson maintained that English
Protestantism "produced a new form of culture, and indeed a new type
of Christianity, which was subsequently diffused all over the world, and
especially in North America, so that it became one of the great forces
that have shaped the modern world." When Anglo-Saxon North America, the United States especially, is looked at in its historical, or perhaps
meta-historical role, it is obvious that it has been the chief proponent of
Protestant culture for some time, probably since the second half of the
nineteenth century. The United States has funded large numbers of
Protestant missionaries, including missionaries to traditionally Catholic
regions, particularly Latin America; at times destabilized Catholic governments and supported anti-clerical regimes in Latin America; conquered parts of Latin American Catholic territory; and, perhaps most
importantly, exported Protestant culture in many spheres of human life,
such as economics, education, and law. This cultural export, it is true,
has lately been devoid of any explicit theological content, but it is Protestant nonetheless and inimical to the social life of Catholic communities.

Before we can consider what might be the task for Catholics who live
in those areas of the Americas shaped by Anglo-Saxon Protestant culture, we must briefly look at the situation in the other part of the Americas, those regions originally evangelized by Catholics and formed by
the Faith. Although much of what I say here could apply not only to
Spanish or Portuguese-speaking areas of the Americas but also to the
Catholics of Quebec, it will be concerned almost entirely with the
former. I will note, however, that it is a catastrophe that Quebec, whose
Catholics at one time were singularly conscious of their position as
Catholics in a non-Catholic environment and zealous in guarding their

6. Harold Goad, *Language in History* (Harmondsworth, England: Penguin, 1958),
237, 239–42.

faith, has in the last several decades largely lost its faith and Catholic culture. This remarkably rapid apostasy has removed a potentially very important element from the Americas, an element that could have contributed considerable intellectual leadership for both Anglo-Saxon and Iberian Catholics and perhaps helped form a bridge between those two parts of the Americas.

When we turn to Latin America, the chief problem in any rational discussion is that most Americans of Anglo-Saxon culture, unfortunately even most Catholics it seems, regard our southern brethren as backward, ignorant, corrupt, and lazy—in fact, as lacking all the virtues, real or imagined, that the Anglo-Saxon world likes to confer upon itself. To attempt to refute this view would require more space than I have here, nor do I want to be understood as denying the genuine defects in those societies. To a great extent, however, this viewpoint, when not founded on a mere stupid assumption of some kind of racial or ethnic superiority in the peoples of northern Europe or on ignorance of the actual conditions in Latin America, rests on the error of *economism*, which St. John Paul condemned in his encyclical *Laborem Exercens* (no. 13). Economism is *"an error of materialism* [that] directly or indirectly includes a conviction of the primacy and superiority of the material, and directly or indirectly places the spiritual and the personal . . . in a position of subordination to material reality." Economism evaluates every nation solely or primarily by its quantity of production. My high school chemistry textbook stated that we could judge the level of civilization in a country by the amount of sulphuric acid used. In fact, the common term *third world* groups nations only according to the level of goods produced, and even merely according to goods that can be measured and are offered on the market for sale. This is simply a kind of practical materialism.

> Some countries or parts of countries in Latin America may have per-capita incomes as low as any in Africa or Asia. But Latin America differs from them in that its basic social, political, and economic values come from the European tradition. Three hundred years of colonization by Spain and Portugal, more than one hundred and fifty years of independent life inspired by European and American ideals, and the important contributions by European immigrants, have produced a continent of many races unified by a common set of values inspired by Western Christian culture.[7]

7. Horacio H. Godoy, "Latin American Culture and Its Transformation," in *Cultural Factors in Inter-American Relations*, ed. Samuel Shapiro (Notre Dame, IN: Notre Dame University Press, 1968), 167.

Thus, the first fact to be grasped is that Latin America is an integral part of Western culture; and, if Western culture is simply the secularized remains of Christendom, then Latin America has a greater right to be regarded as a survival of Christendom than those lands colonized and formed by Protestants. No doubt most Latin-American Catholics are imperfect in their beliefs or their practice of the Faith, but unfortunately the same may be said of every other part of the Catholic world. My point is not that I claim them all to be exemplary Catholics, but that any sensible discussion of Latin America must begin with a recognition that not only are they our co-religionists, but that their culture and its institutions also derive from Europe, equally with ours; and unlike ours, they derive from Catholic Europe. That the Spanish in particular consciously sought not merely to transplant European civilization but also to found a new province of Christendom incorporating much of Indian traditions and styles does not detract from its essentially Western character; it also shows how a successful evangelization of a radically different culture should be conducted.

> A new product developed, bred from the encounter between imported Western European Christian culture and the local populations.... It really speaks much for the Iberian Church of that imperial day that its churchmen were able to admit a kind of blending of Western and local forms of expression which can be seen across the continent, as far south as Jujuy and Catamarca in Argentina, and sometimes as far north as Sonora, Mexico.[8]

Indeed, it can be seen even farther north in what is now the United States.

Obviously, especially since independence from Spain, the states of Spanish America have departed in various ways and various degrees from the militant Catholic civilization the Spanish established. Their intellectual and culture elites are very often estranged from the Faith. In the nineteenth century they began to take many of their leading ideas from the latest French or German philosophers, and today some of them even try to hark back to pre-Columbian paganism as part of their rejection of everything that followed from Columbus's discovery.

With this brief sketch of both parts of the Americas, we must now address the question of the task that is set before Catholics in each of them. That task is the same in each part, but in different ways. The com-

---

8. Jorge Mejia, "Church and Culture in Latin America," in *Cultural Factors in Inter-American Relations*, ed. Samuel Shapiro (Notre Dame, IN: Notre Dame University Press, 1968), 215.

mon task—indeed, the task of Catholics everywhere—is to adhere to the Faith as taught by the Church's magisterium and to seek to shape both our individual lives and the thought and life of our societies according to Catholic tradition, rejecting the various ideologies that undermine the Catholic mind. We Catholics living in areas formed by Anglo-Saxon culture have a more difficult task, since we must come to recognize that many of the patterns of thought and life that we have grown up with and accept as a matter of course are in fact profoundly at odds with Catholic faith and tradition. But this difficulty can confer an advantage also. Some of the Catholics most aware of the cultural divide between Protestants and Catholics, such as Christopher Dawson and Hilaire Belloc, were aware precisely because they lived and worked within Protestant culture. We are in a unique position to understand it from within and thus interpret it to the rest of the Church, not by promoting "the notion of American Catholic 'particularism' within the universal Church" but by pointing out social and cultural paths that Catholics must avoid.

An important matter that cannot be passed over is the question of immigration to the United States from Latin America, much of it illegal, to be sure. Here I would suggest that American Catholics must avoid the temptation to look at this primarily as a juridical matter and instead consider the long-term interests of the Church and of Catholic culture. Insofar as aspects of Catholic life still exist founded on the Catholic immigration of the nineteenth century, whether Irish, German, Italian, Polish, or whatever other kind, these aspects are certainly worthy of esteem and preservation. I do not think, however, that a Catholic need regard the preservation of the Protestant way of life in North America as especially worthy of his efforts. No doubt there are goods that have come from it; but if we take seriously Our Lord's command to evangelize the world and if we recognize that evangelization has to be of cultures as well as of individuals, it would seem that we should welcome an opportunity to fundamentally change the culture of Anglo-Saxon America, a change that was never seriously attempted before. This would be a benefit to ourselves, even to our Protestant fellow citizens, and to the immigrants themselves.

Right now most of the new Catholic immigrants are relatively poor and uneducated. What sense of Catholic faith and culture they hold is inherited and largely unreflective. If there is any possibility of actually converting America, that sense of faith and culture must be preserved and strengthened; but already some of these immigrants, or their children, are becoming educated, growing richer, and rising in American society. As they do, it is almost certain that even if they do not cease to identify themselves as Catholics, they will become acculturated into

Protestant Anglo-Saxon culture just as our own immigrant ancestors largely did. Thus, to prevent this, efforts must somehow be made to educate the immigrants and their children in an authentically Catholic manner and to work to preserve and strengthen their cultures.

This, however, is not the ultimate goal we should hope for. Although it was probably impossible for the Protestant culture of North America, while remaining Protestant, to be significantly altered by the presence of so many Catholics—for it was like mixing oil with water—in principle it should not be impossible to mix two Catholic cultures. Thus, Catholics of the United States might do well to remember and look to their own immigrant ancestors and their cultures and languages to find some common bond or identity themselves with the new Catholic immigrants. If we remember that we once seemed alien to American Protestants, we shall be more likely not only to have sympathy with our brethren but also to find common cultural ground with them.

In 1932, Herbert Bolton, President of the American Historical Association, delivered to its annual meeting an address entitled, "The Epic of Greater America." He called for a broader view of American history that would encompass the whole of the Americas; their common heritage as colonies; their struggles for independence; and their efforts "for national solidarity, political stability, and economic well being, and . . . for a satisfactory adjustment of relations with each other and with the rest of the world."[9] Although Bolton was surely correct in his call for greater attention to the rest of the Americas by historians from the United States, his reasons for doing so might seem somewhat shallow to a Catholic. A Catholic should see history *sub specie aeternitatis* and thus as an attempt on the part of the Church to carry out Our Lord's commission to preach the Gospel everywhere, not just to individuals but also to nations, creating those cultural supports for Catholic life that are necessary if it is to have any depth and stability. We need to find a bond greater than simply the kind of political and economic measures that Bolton named and that in fact are common to all nations. This greater bond we have been providentially given in Our Lady of Guadalupe, Empress and Mother of all the Americas.

> How can we fail to emphasize the role which belongs to the Virgin Mary in relation to the pilgrim church in America journeying toward its encounter with the Lord? Indeed, the most Blessed Virgin "is linked

9. Herbert Bolton, "The Epic of Greater America," in *Do the Americas Have a Common History? A Critique of the Bolton Theory,* ed. Lewis Hanke (New York: Alfred A. Knopf, 1963), 69.

in a special way to the birth of the church in the history . . . of the peoples of America; through Mary they came to encounter the Lord."[10]

The genuine unity of the two Americas, "so different in origin and history,"[11] must be a Catholic unity, one that recognizes Mary's appearance to Juan Diego as its foundation. No other kind takes seriously the fundamental mission given by Our Lord to His Church, a mission that it is our task to accomplish in the New World. No other kind takes seriously the action of God in history, an action whose purpose often transcends our ability to comprehend. We do, however, know our simple duty, which I expressed before as fidelity to God's revelation as taught by His Church, fidelity lived out both in our individual lives and in our cultures. If we achieve this to any degree, we can be sure that we are cooperating with His will, however dimly we may discern it.

10. Pope John Paul II, Apostolic Exhortation, *Ecclesia in America*, no. 11 (January 22, 1999).

11. Pope John Paul II, Apostolic Letter, *Tertio Millennio Adveniente*, no. 38 (November 10, 1994).

15

Government, Society, and the Common Good

Authority in the State, which resides in the public authorities, is indispensable because, among other things, citizens may misuse their natural freedom and work against the public purpose. Therefore, what is needed is a principle of internal unity which obligates the citizens to orderly living together, and which can keep the conduct of the individual in harmony with the purposes of the whole community.

—Heinrich Pesch[1]

"IF MEN WERE ANGELS," wrote James Madison[2] in *Federalist* no. 51, "no government would be necessary." I suppose that this statement seems as self-evident to most Americans today as it did to its original readers. It is, however, neither obvious nor necessarily true. In fact, St. Thomas Aquinas did not share this opinion; rather, he explicitly defended the opposite view. The difference of viewpoint here is expressive, I think, of a fundamental difference in approach to the necessity and role of government and even to the nature of man. So, beginning with this seemingly arcane question about angels and men, we can examine two very different ways of looking at government and its place in human society.

St. Thomas did indeed teach the existence of a hierarchy of superior and inferior angels, the superior angels illuminating and instructing

---

1. *Lehrbuch der Nationalökonomie/Teaching Guide to Economics*, vol. I, book 1, trans. Rupert Ederer (Lewiston, NY: Edwin Mellen Press, 2002), 233.
2. Madison was most probably the author of no. 51, although Alexander Hamilton claimed authorship in a list he drew up shortly before his death. For my purpose here the question is not important.

their inferiors;[3] but it is not really angels with whom we are concerned. When Madison said if "men were angels," he meant if men were without sin or without evil passions, such as ambition. He was of course not interested in the question of how men would behave if they were pure spirits like angels. We might paraphrase him by saying, "If humanity had no sinful tendencies, no government would be necessary." But even if we accept that emendation, we still find St. Thomas disagreeing. In the *Summa Theologiae*, part one, question 96, article 4, he asks whether there would be subordination of man to man in the state of innocence, i.e., without Adam's fall into sin.[4] He answers clearly in the affirmative. Although there would not have been the domination (*dominium*) characteristic of the slave, who is "ordered to another," there would still have been the kind of subjection proper to the free man, as when someone directs him to his own good or to the common good. Aquinas gives two reasons: first, because man is "naturally a social animal" and "social life cannot exist unless someone presides who aims at the common good"; secondly, because it would be unfitting for someone who had "supereminence in knowledge or justice" unless he could use it for the good of others. In other words, even if our first parents had never sinned and lost the state of original justice, we should still have required a sort of government, one that would not have involved punishing anyone but that would still have been there to coordinate and direct our efforts toward the common good or even one's individual good.

Thomas thus distinguishes between two sorts of governmental authority, one kind, as we saw, concerning the government's function of directing people toward the good, the other, which would not have existed in the state of innocence, being the result of sin. Although Aquinas does not explicitly include the police powers of government or national defense in this latter category, implicitly he does; for this kind of *dominium* results from and governs all those human relationships that are the effect of sin. Thomas looks at the result of sin in a more comprehensive sense than simply as necessitating a police force and jails, for he sees in it the origin of all domination that he calls *servitude*, a term with a much wider meaning here than simply slavery or serfdom

---

3. *Summa Theologiae* I, q. 106, a. 1 and 3, q. 107, a. 2, and q. 108, a. 4. This opinion, incidentally, was shared by Locke's "judicious Hooker." See Richard Hooker, *Of the Laws of Ecclesiastical Polity. A Critical Edition with Modern Spelling*, book I, IV, [2], ed. Arthur Stephen McGrade (Oxford, England: Oxford University Press, 2013).

4. All further quotations from or references to St. Thomas not otherwise attributed are from this question and article from the Summa.

and that includes all forms of human domination that are effects of sin, including coercive power of the governing authorities.[5] Broadly, then, we can say that for Thomas there exist two sorts of *dominium*; one we may call positive, which directs men toward the good, and the other we may call negative, which is the result of sin and includes all the familiar restraining, coercive, and punitive powers of the state.

Now, I submit that this difference of opinion between Madison and Aquinas is of the highest importance for our political and social life. Of course this question does not necessitate any particular belief or opinion about angels or about the origins of the human race or sin. Fundamentally it is a question of whether we think that government is natural to man as such or whether it stems only from a defect in man, from his proclivity to selfish conduct, however we may suppose that tendency to have originally arisen. Whether we hold the first opinion about government or the second will affect many of our political and social views and behaviors. A person holding the latter opinion will necessarily see government as at best a necessary evil and tend to be suspicious of every undertaking that limits, or appears to limit, his freedom whereas a person who embraces the former opinion will generally understand the need for state action on behalf of the common good, even if he might disagree with some particular instance of it.

The view expressed by Madison sees government fundamentally as merely a restraining or punishing force, not a positive force in human society. It is the myriad of private individual choices and motivations of individual free men that are the necessary mainspring of social action. Only because men are driven by passions—because they are apt to use force and fraud against their fellows—is government necessary. The only positive force moving human society is the sum total of individual choices and acts made by the many individuals who make up society, each pursuing his own notion of happiness in his own way. Aristotle had noted that people differ radically in what they think is happiness;[6] but it follows from Madison's perspective that, whatever subjective idea of happiness or the good an individual has, it is none of the government's business. So long as each individual's pursuit of what he regards as his good does not infringe upon his neighbor's like pursuit, one ought generally to be free of governmental restraint. As a present-day adherent of this view, Fr. Robert Sirico, puts it: "So long as individuals

---

5. Cf. *Summa Theologiae*, I-II q. 94, a. 5, ad 3, and q. 96, a. 2.
6. *Nicomachean Ethics*, I, 4.

avoid forceful or fraudulent actions in their dealings with one another, government is to stay out of their business."[7]

The other attitude, that of St. Thomas, supposes that, "because man naturally is a social animal," the kind of *dominium* that directs citizens toward the good is always appropriate to mankind; it is not only the *common* good of which he speaks but likewise one's particular good (*proprium bonum ejus qui dirigitur*). In other words, not only does society as a whole need to be directed toward its common good but also, at least in some cases, individual men need to be directed toward their own good. This opinion seems connected with Aquinas's second reason for his teaching cited above, that it would be unfitting if someone who had "supereminence in knowledge or justice" were prevented from exercising that superiority for the good of others. In Aquinas therefore it is the objective good both of the whole and of individuals on which the necessity of *dominium* in a state of innocence is based, and it is the state's responsibility to direct people toward their authentic good, a responsibility that, as we shall see, was not fundamentally altered when human sin entered the picture.

The practical consequences of this difference of opinion about the purposes of government are clear when we examine the differences in public opinion—and even clearer differences in legislation and public policy—between the United States and most other Western nations on such matters as environmental regulation, the possession of guns, national healthcare, and taxation. Because of the almost universal acceptance in the United States of the liberal viewpoint, the usual attitude in the United States is one of suspicion of the government's ability to do anything positive, in fact, the attitude that government is not the solution but is part of the problem.[8] Of course, this does not mean that in other Western countries there is a robust Thomistic understanding of man and the state; there is an echo, even if distorted, in social democratic and even socialist conceptions of political authority of the earlier classical and medieval outlook, as Michael Novak noted with regard to Latin American socialists.[9]

---

7. *Acton Notes* 8, no. 1 (January 1998): 1. Accessed May 7, 2015. http://www.acton.org/pub/religion-liberty/volume-8-number-1.

8. Although there have been periods of time in American history during which a positive role for government has enjoyed wide acceptance, the attitude engendered by Madison's statement seems by far the more fundamental one, an attitude easily stirred into life and that in many people's minds is pretty much self-evident.

9. "In many respects, a socialist order is closer to their own past. It is less pluralistic and more centralized, and it allows for a more intense union of church and state than

From this difference also come some fundamentally different ideas about justice.[10] Although commutative justice is the fundamental form of justice, in the United States it is apt to be taken as the only form. The other kinds of justice—distributive, legal, and social—struggle for recognition because of the constant tendency to regard the state or even society as simply a collection of individuals and having no sort of real existence.

> The individualist's criticism would be that there are in reality only individuals, and that, when an individual confronts the social totality, *one* individual confronts *many* individuals. For him the social whole is not a reality of a special order. Therefore he admits of only one single type of justice—commutative justice—because individuals always have to do with other individuals. Every phase of man's communal life, in the family as well as in the state, is a compromise between the interests of individuals with equal rights.[11]

If political and social thought in the United States does not always reach such an extreme, it tends toward it; and it is difficult for many people to make the case for the existence of the other forms of justice or for the rights of the social whole as such. Our customary political vocabulary and discourse often lack the appropriate terms. It requires an effort to make a case for the social viewpoint, whereas it is simply second nature for Americans to see the individualist viewpoint as the only and obvious one.

Can it not be said, however, regardless of how anyone looks at the Christian account of the Fall of Man, that historically the family came first, then the village, then finally what can be called political society in the proper sense and that therefore the state or the political community is simply a contrivance for safeguarding the fundamental human society of the family, merely a convenience for the sake of the fundamental and natural unit of mankind? Aristotle himself had traced the rise of the political community in this manner.[12] Clearly for him the family was temporally prior to the state. Does that mean that he supported a view

does democratic capitalism of the North American type.... In a socialist system, a unitary authority governs the political system, the economic system, and the moral-cultural system. Socialism entails less of a structural break with the past than does democratic capitalism." "Introduction," in *Liberation South, Liberation North*, ed. Michael Novak (Washington: American Enterprise Institute, 1981), 4.

10. On the different forms of justice, see the *Catechism of the Catholic Church*, no. 2411.

11. Josef Pieper, *The Four Cardinal Virtues* (Notre Dame, IN: University of Notre Dame Press, 1966), 73–74.

12. *Politics*, I, 1–2.

something like that of Madison's? Though it is true that for Aristotle the family was temporally prior, it does not follow that he held anything like the liberal viewpoint. He states, "it is evident that the state is a creation of nature, and that man is by nature a political animal" and "the state is by nature clearly prior to the family and to the individual, since the whole is of necessity prior to the part. . . ."[13] The implications of this relationship, in which the family is temporally prior while the state is logically prior, is explained by Josef Pieper as follows:

> The state, we may note, occupies a unique place in the scale that extends from the individual to the whole of mankind; more than any-thing else, it represents the 'social whole.' The idea of the common good is its distinctive attribute. A nation (in the midst of other nations) ordered in a state is the proper, historically concrete image of man's communal life. *Communitas politica est communitas principalissima*— Political community is community in the highest degree. In the fullest sense the state alone incorporates, realizes, and administers the *bonum commune*. That does not mean, however, that the family, the commu-nity, free associations, and the Church are not important for the real-ization of the common good, too. But it means that the harmonizing and integration of nearly all men's functions occurs only in the political community.[14]

If man is a social or political animal, it is proper to his nature to live in a political community. He is incomplete without it; and that community, although obviously made up of individuals, is more than simply a col-lection of individuals but has in itself an essential function to pursue and realize the good, a function that no other entity has. Of course, the political community exists for the sake of something else; it is not an end in itself. But it is still both natural and necessary since "the harmo-nizing and integration of nearly all men's functions occurs only in the political community."[15]

One very important difference between the view expressed by Madi-son and St. Thomas's opinion concerns the proper level at which dis-course concerning the good for man ought to take place. I noted above

---

13. Ibid., I, 2.

14. *The Four Cardinal Virtues*, 85.

15. It might be objected that, when Aristotle speaks of the polis, it is an error to equate it with the modern nation-state and assume that the characteristics and func-tions that Aristotle or St. Thomas attributed to the essential human political community can rightly be transferred to the modern state. I think, however, that this objection rests on a misapprehension. Aristotle indeed seems to have thought that a large-sized polis was hardly the ideal (see *Politics*, VII, 4). The question is not whether or not a large nation-state is an example of an ideal polity, but rather whether or not such a state must

that one consequence of Madison's opinion is that the motive force of human society is the totality of the many individual choices and acts made by the multitude of individual persons who make up society, each one pursuing his own notion of happiness in his own unique way. The result of this is that discourse about the good for man, both collectively and individually, must be merely private discourse, that is, discourse conducted below the level of the political community's conversation about its proper acts and purposes. This is so because the state, and society as constituted thereby, have no concern with individuals beyond restraining them from harming others. Each individual's conception of the good is his own business; and, although he is no doubt free to argue for his own idea of the good, it necessarily remains private no matter how many others he might convince to share his view. The state as such has no opinion on it. The political community's concern is necessarily limited to questions of public order, and the community has no interest in whether there is a good for man that is knowable. This kind of thinking lies behind the religion clauses in the First Amendment to the U.S. Constitution. No matter how many Americans might become convinced of the truth of any particular religious faith, it would be no business of the government *qua* government. Religion, like all concern with the genuine human good, remains always a private matter.[16]

This does not mean that in St. Thomas's conception of political authority the state would act after the manner of a totalitarian regime. Above I quoted Pieper to the effect that, although "the state alone incorporates, realizes, and administers the *bonum commune* [this] does not mean, however, that the family, the community, free associations, and the Church are not important for the realization of the common good, too." In fact they are crucial, since the state as such is not the source of morality; rather the state, as constituted and governed by persons who

be understood as a polis, even if a bloated one. In other words, if human social life necessarily has a political character, then wherever the human race lives there will be a political community of some sort, even if far from the ideal. The same argument applies to primitive peoples, in whose attenuated political institutions one recognizes with difficulty the outline of a polis. But in each case, that of modern and of tribal organization, the key to understanding them is to regard them as types of a polis, even if far from the ideal type. Aristotle himself referred matter-of-factly to the Persian empire along with Athens when discussing the behavior of different states (*Politics*, III, 13). For Aristotle's view on the size of polities, see as well *Politics*, III, 3.

16. But in a curious and indirect way, the liberal notion of governmental authority does propose a model of the good; for by privatizing all explicit discussion of what is the transcendent good for man, it implicitly teaches that only the things of this world, that with which government deals, are what really matter.

have learned the good precisely from "the family, the community, free associations, and the Church," reasonably incorporates that knowledge into the conduct of its affairs. It is unnatural to draw a line between the affairs of the individual and the affairs of the community such that the community qua community cannot acknowledge the entire range of human concerns, including the genuine human good. If the political community is natural to man, it is hardly logical to exclude from its concern the good for man or to artificially relegate that to the private sphere on the plea that not all citizens agree on what is the good.

Although Madison and St. Thomas differ on whether political authority would exist if man were without his disruptive passions and his tendency to defraud or rob his fellows, both thinkers recognize the ubiquity of human evil in the world as it now is. Indeed, at one point Thomas even goes so far as to say that human law ought principally to prohibit those sins "which are harmful to others, without the prohibition of which human society cannot be preserved; as murder, theft and the like are prohibited by human law."[17] Does this mean then that because man is now in a fallen state—however we understand that theologically—the primary purpose of government for Thomas is altered? Does it mean that restraining evildoers rather than pursuing the good is now the main function of the state authority? More than once Aquinas affirms that the original purpose of society, and hence of the state, is still the primary one. In his *De Regimine Principum* he writes, "It seems moreover to be the purpose of the multitude joined together to live according to virtue ... the virtuous life therefore is the purpose of the human community," and even adds that "the ultimate end of the multitude joined together is not to live according to virtue, but through virtuous living to attain to enjoyment of God,"[18] while in the *Summa Theologiae* he states that "human law aims to lead men to virtue...."[19] So, even though in the present state of the human race it is obviously necessary to deal not only with the promotion of the good but also with restraining and punishing evil, still the essential and fundamental task of government for St. Thomas is to promote the good.

We can see this expressed in the writings of two of Aquinas's modern followers, both Roman pontiffs. Pope Pius XI, in his 1931 encyclical *Quadragesimo Anno*, discussing the earlier encyclical of Leo XIII, *Rerum*

---

17. *Summa Theologiae*, I-II, q. 96, a. 2.

18. I, 14. This work is also known as *De Regno*. Most of book II is probably not the work of St. Thomas.

19. I-II, q. 96, a. 2, ad 2.

Novarum, explicitly rejects the view that limits governmental authority to those matters only that are occasioned by human wickedness.

> With regard to the civil power, Leo XIII boldly passed beyond the restrictions imposed by liberalism, and fearlessly proclaimed the doctrine that the civil power is more than the mere guardian of law and order, and that it must strive with all zeal "to make sure that the laws and institutions, the general character and administration of the commonwealth, should be such as of themselves to realize public well-being and private prosperity." (no. 25)

More recently, Pope Paul VI in his Apostolic Letter *Octogesima Adveniens* of May 1971 wrote,

> Political power, which is the natural and necessary link for ensuring the cohesion of the social body, must have as its aim the achievement of the common good. While respecting the legitimate liberties of individuals, families and subsidiary groups, it acts in such a way as to create, effectively and for the well-being of all, the conditions required for attaining man's true and complete good, including his spiritual end. (no. 46)

If it is the case that the promotion of the good remains the essential task of government, a task unchanged by the human propensity to fraud and violence, does this propensity in any way affect our notion of political prudence? After all, much of the *Federalist* is concerned with how to prevent, limit, or circumvent the damage that the flawed individuals who perforce must administer the government might be tempted to inflict in the furtherance of their ambition or greed. One must admit that the question presents a real difficulty. Though the authors of the *Federalist* framed the question wrongly and unnecessarily restricted the scope of public authority, still they are correct that some means must be devised to prevent or at least inhibit the establishment of tyranny and other evils on the part of rulers. It is in this question that there can be some convergence of these two traditions of political thought, for many of the practical means written in the U.S. Constitution and stressed in the *Federalist* are by no means alien to the school of political thought originated by Aristotle and refined by St. Thomas. In several chapters of the *De Regimine Principum*, Aquinas deals with ways of preventing rulers from becoming tyrants and discusses which kind of governmental structure is least likely to degenerate into tyranny, a question of course that Plato had examined at length in books VIII and IX of the *Republic*. That Thomas's suggestions are not always the same as those of the American Founders is not the point; the point rather is that each recognized the importance of the question. Although St. Thomas taught both the goodness and naturalness of the state, he was not blind to the fact that any government would always be administered by sinful men who could not simply be trusted always to do the right thing.

Nevertheless, the many differences in attitudes toward governmental authority between the United States and most other Western countries do show that there exist real differences between Thomas and the liberal tradition as represented by James Madison's statement. Government, as Aquinas understands it, does have a positive role that is essential and primary. The complicating factor of human sin does not change that, but only shows that the rulers of the state can never be absolutely trusted. That St. Thomas believed that "tyranny more often occurs in the rule of the many than in the rule of one" and that therefore the "rule of one is better"[20] and that James Madison would have dissented violently from this judgment does not mean that both men were not trying to think intelligently about the question. It does mean, however, that we can go beyond Madison's limited understanding of the nature and purpose of political authority without leaving the door open to tyranny. Anything done in human affairs is liable to degenerate or to overreach itself, and government is no exception. We do no favor to mankind, however, by forgetting the most important part and purpose of public authority and simply leaving the shaping of society to the multifarious passions of individuals.

Excursus: The Question of State Religious Establishments

At the time the U.S. Constitution was adopted, a few of the states had individually established churches or otherwise provided public support for religious worship and instruction, a situation that obtained in Massachusetts, the last state to have such an arrangement, until its constitution was amended in 1833. This fact is often held to prove that, in the minds of the American Founders, discourse about the ultimate good for man was not privatized but rather was simply left to the individual states, since the federal government was seen as dealing with only a limited number of enumerated concerns. Although in a formal sense this may be true, we must ask whether the cultural, economic, and political trends were not such that these local particulars were bound to be eliminated eventually. The fundamental question is whether the people of that time conceived the United States as one country, one political community, or many. If it is the case that it was regarded as a single nation, it

---

20. *De Regimine Principum*, chap. 5. Elsewhere, though, Thomas speaks favorably of a mixed regime incorporating elements of monarchy, aristocracy, and democracy. See, e.g., *Summa Theologiae*, I-II, q. 105, a. 1.

is hard to see how in one part of the country the authority of the state could recognize God as the ultimate good for both individuals and society, while other parts of the same polity could be officially agnostic on that point. My own view is that, despite some ambiguity in the text of the Constitution and likely some confusion in the public mind, the cultural, economic, and political forces pushing for an essentially unitary state, with only minor concessions to state sovereignty, were overwhelming and that only a determined and principled opposition could have halted or modified these trends. If this is true, the privatizing of religion at the federal level effectively doomed both the state churches that still remained and any attempt to insert religious discourse into the national political conversation. If the United States was one national community or fast becoming such, discourse at the level of the political community necessarily prescinded from religious questions, as the Constitution requires.

16

John Locke, Liberal Totalitarianism, and the Trivialization of Religion

[N]o society will long survive if in its public structure it is built agnostically and materialistically and wishes to permit anything else to exist only below the threshold of the public.

—Joseph Cardinal Ratzinger[1]

ON APRIL 17, 1990, the United States Supreme Court, speaking through Justice Antonin Scalia, decided the case of Employment Division v. Smith.[2] In this case, two men, Alfred Smith and Galen Black,

> were fired from their jobs with a private drug rehabilitation organization because they ingested peyote for sacramental purposes at a ceremony of the Native American Church, of which both are members. When [Smith and Black] applied to [the Oregon] Employment Division ... for unemployment compensation, they were determined to be ineligible for benefits because they had been discharged for work-related "misconduct."[3]

On appeal from the Supreme Court of Oregon, the U.S. Supreme Court ruled against Smith and Black, because it determined that "neutral, generally applicable" laws, which are directed to some secular purpose, and only incidentally infringe on religious practice, may be enforced even though religious believers are thereby inconvenienced. Oregon's laws against drug, and specifically peyote, use were not directed against members of the Native American Church as such but were general prohibitions against any use. The Court stated, "We have never held that an

---

1. *A Turning Point for Europe?* (San Francisco: Ignatius Press, 1994), 171.
2. 494 U.S. 872.
3. Ibid., 874.

individual's religious beliefs excuse him from compliance with an otherwise valid law prohibiting conduct that the State is free to regulate."[4] Moreover,

> the right of free exercise does not relieve an individual of the obligation to comply with a "valid and neutral law of general applicability on the ground that the law proscribes (or prescribes) conduct that his religion prescribes (or proscribes)."[5]

The Smith decision provoked considerable protest. A concurring opinion by Justice O'Connor and a dissent by justices Brennan, Marshall, and Blackmun, strongly criticized the basis of the Court's opinion, charging that it departed from established jurisprudence that forbade governmental infringement of religious freedom "unless required by clear and compelling governmental interests 'of the highest order.'"[6] The Smith decision spurred Congress to pass the Religious Freedom Restoration Act, Public Law 103–141, which was signed by President Clinton in November 1993. Although this law has since been judged in part as unconstitutional by the Supreme Court, it is an important example of the "compelling governmental interest" approach to regulating religious conduct. I shall discuss the law further below.

One should note, however, that although many criticized the Court's opinion in the Smith case, those criticisms were within definite limits. For example, Justice O'Connor in her concurring opinion states plainly, "Under our established First Amendment jurisprudence, we have recognized that the freedom to act, unlike the freedom to believe, cannot be absolute."[7] Practically no one challenged the notion that government had the ultimate say over conduct, even when religiously based and motivated.

A few years later, on June 11, 1993, the Supreme Court decided another free-exercise-of-religion case, Church of Lukumi Babalu Aye v. City of Hialeah.[8] This case involved adherents of the Santeria religion, which includes animal sacrifices in its rituals. The city of Hialeah, Florida, had proscribed such animal sacrifices in a series of measures that singled out only the religious slaughter of animals and exempted other animal killings. The Supreme Court found that these laws were indeed unconstitutional, because they were obviously targeted at *religious* practices per se, not simply that they happened to burden religious behavior

---

4. Ibid., 878–79.
5. Ibid., 879.
6. Ibid., 895.
7. Ibid., 894.
8. 508 U.S. 520.

incidentally. "It is a necessary conclusion that almost the only conduct subject to [the] Ordinances . . . is the religious exercise of Santeria church members. The texts show that they were drafted . . . to achieve this result."[9] The Court in this case, however, also expressly reaffirmed the central and controversial point of Smith, ". . . that a law that is neutral and of general applicability need not be justified by a compelling governmental interest even if the law has the incidental effect of burdening a particular religious practice."[10]

The history of the treatment of the free-exercise clause[11] of the First Amendment by the U.S. judicial system, and in particular by the Supreme Court, varies; but as we shall see, it varies only within certain definite limits. In what seems to have been the first free-exercise case, the 1878 case of Reynolds v. United States,[12] which upheld the law criminalizing the Mormon practice of polygamy, the Supreme Court took the view that there was no reason why government need hesitate about restricting religious conduct by general and neutral laws. The Court in Reynolds said, "Congress was deprived of all legislative power over mere opinion, but was left free to reach actions which were in violation of social duties or subversive of good order"[13] and "Laws are made for the government of actions, and while they cannot interfere with mere religious belief and opinions, they may with practices."[14]

In later cases the Supreme Court seemed to take a softer line. For example, in the 1940 case of Cantwell v. Connecticut,[15] a case involving the selling of religious literature and soliciting of donations by two Jehovah's Witnesses, contrary to state law, the Court sided with the Witnesses although it stated that the Constitution's requirements for the protection of religious behavior were nevertheless not absolute.

> The constitutional inhibition of legislation on the subject of religion has a double aspect. On the one hand, it forestalls compulsion by law of the acceptance of any creed or the practice of any form of worship. Freedom of conscience and freedom to adhere to such religious organization or form of worship as the individual may choose cannot be restricted by law. On the other hand, it safeguards the free exercise of

9. Ibid., 535.

10. Ibid., 531.

11. This is the second clause of the First Amendment to the U.S. Constitution, "Congress shall make no law respecting an establishment of religion, *or prohibiting the free exercise thereof. . . .*" (emphasis added)

12. 98 U.S. 145.

13. Ibid., 164.

14. Ibid., 166.

15. 310 U.S. 296.

the chosen form of religion. Thus the [first] Amendment embraces two concepts,—freedom to believe and freedom to act. The first is absolute but, in the nature of things, the second cannot be. Conduct remains subject to regulation for the protection of society.[16]

Thus the Court did not give up the government's stated right to regulate or restrict religious conduct in at least some cases. But generally, since then, the Court has shown more concern and deference toward believers who because of their religion either were denied some governmental benefit or became subject to some governmental penalty. It has often stated, for example, that in order to abridge someone's religious freedom the government must show that it has a "compelling state interest" that "no alternative form of regulation" could accomplish.[17] The case in which it seems to have given the most latitude toward religious conduct was the 1972 case of Wisconsin v. Yoder,[18] the Amish school case. Here the Court said,

> But to agree that religiously grounded conduct must often be subject to the broad police power of the State is not to deny that there are areas of conduct protected by the Free Exercise Clause of the First Amendment and thus beyond the power of the State to control, even under regulations of general applicability.[19]

This represents the outer bounds that the Supreme Court has approached, for in this case the Court appears to take the position that some religiously inspired conduct is entirely "beyond the power to the State to control" regardless of what state interests may exist. Generally, however, it has not proceeded this far. More often the question is presented as one of balancing the religious interests of the individual against the proclaimed interests of the authorities. When Congress legislatively attempted to overturn the Smith decision by passing the Religious Freedom Restoration Act, this balancing test was enacted as law. Section 3, subsection (b) of the law states as follows:

> Government may substantially burden a person's exercise of religion only if it demonstrates that application of the burden to the person—
>   (1) is in furtherance of a compelling governmental interest; and
>   (2) is the least restrictive means of furthering that compelling governmental interest.[20]

16. Ibid., 303–4.
17. From Sherbert v. Verner, 374 U.S. 398 (1963).
18. 406 U.S. 205.
19. Ibid. 220.
20. 107 Stat. 1488 and 1489.

This attempt by Congress to establish a "compelling governmental interest" standard for regulating religious conduct succeeded only to a limited degree, however; for the Supreme Court overturned this act in part.[21] In recent decisions, including both Smith and Church of Lukumi Babalu Aye, the Court seems to have returned to a standard more similar to Reynolds than to Yoder and other post-Second World War cases. Obviously one cannot say which way future decisions will go, but I think that one can confidently predict that they will fall within an area bounded on the one hand by Yoder and on the other by Reynolds and Smith. Although it might seem that these two extremes of opinion differ fundamentally, I will contend that in principle the differences between Yoder and Smith are simply differences of degree.

What can be said, then, of the differences between the attitude toward free exercise of religion contained in Reynolds and Smith and that contained in the other cases and in the Religious Freedom Restoration Act itself? Reynolds and Smith claim that in making general and neutral laws that deal with matters under its competence, a government need not bother about the fact that some persons' exercise of religion is thereby burdened. To allow exemptions from law on account of religious belief "would be to make the professed doctrines of religious belief superior to the law of the land, and in effect to permit every citizen to become a law unto himself."[22] As Smith put it,

> The government's ability to enforce generally applicable prohibitions of socially harmful conduct, like its ability to carry out other aspects of public policy, "cannot depend on measuring the effects of a governmental action on a religious objector's spiritual development."[23]

But the other approach, with the possible exception of some passages in the Yoder opinion,[24] also asserts the government's supremacy over all religious conduct—except that such regulation must justify itself by, as the Religious Freedom Restoration Act states, "a compelling governmen-

---

21. In City of Boerne v. Flores (521 U.S. 507), decided June 25, 1997, the Court overturned the RFRA, but only with regard to action by the several states. It should be remembered, however, that most religious liberty legislation has involved state or local, not federal, law.

22. Reynolds, 167.

23. Smith, 885.

24. Yoder is not always clear or consistent. On an earlier page (215), the Court wrote, "The essence of all that has been said and written on the subject [i.e., on free exercise of religion] is that only those interests of the highest order and those not otherwise served can overbalance legitimate claims to the free exercise of religion." This appears to be the balancing test again, the approach Congress attempted to consolidate by the Religious Freedom Restoration Act.

tal interest." However, we should remember that it is the same government that enacts the statute restricting religious behavior and that also asserts its "compelling interest" in seeing the statute obeyed. It is true that it must justify itself before an independent judicial branch, but is it that difficult to imagine circumstances in which all the branches of government would be united in the same, to them self-evident, opinion? What the government considers its compelling interest depends much on the cultural or intellectual milieu in which, not only congressmen and judges but also the entire body of persons whom congressmen and judges regard as their peers and fellows, live. Even within the short history of our own country, we can see striking changes of opinion about the most important subjects—religion, slavery, sexuality, the place of women in society, and many other matters. Who would doubt that what seemed self-evident to most judges of 1800 would differ considerably from what seems self-evident to most judges of today? Not many years ago it seemed clear to most Americans that the prohibition of "intoxicating liquors" was socially desirable.[25] Although the use of wine for Christian sacramental purposes was exempted from the law, does it require much imagination to think that the society of that time might have deemed even religious use of wine contrary to a "compelling governmental interest" and thus outlawed Catholic, Eastern Orthodox, Episcopal, and other religious rituals, as some states do with peyote in the Native American Church? Justice O'Connor, in her concurring opinion in Smith, reached the same result as the Court's majority although she applied the "compelling interest test" in doing so.[26]

The point, then, as I see it, is that U.S. jurisprudence unhesitatingly regards all religious conduct, even in religious rituals themselves, as subject to at least any important law that is passed only provided that this law have a neutral and secular purpose and burden the religious actions only incidentally. Is this something to be troubled about, or is it simply a common sense approach to governing? After all, as the Court said in Reynolds,

> Suppose one believed that human sacrifices were a necessary part of religious worship, would it be seriously contended that the civil gov-

25. Section 1 of the Eighteenth Amendment to the U.S. Constitution states, "After one year from the ratification of this article the manufacture, sale, or transportation of intoxicating liquors within, the importation thereof into, or the exportation thereof from the United States and all territory subject to the jurisdiction thereof for beverage purposes is hereby prohibited." This amendment was ratified in 1919 and repealed in 1933 by the Twenty-First Amendment.

26. Smith, 903–7.

ernment under which he lived could not interfere to prevent a sacrifice?[27]

I think, though, that before one evaluates the Supreme Court's jurisprudence, it is necessary to see the background and context of the Court's opinions, which can be found in none other than John Locke's (first) *Letter Concerning Toleration* of 1689.[28]

The kinds of situations our Supreme Court has had to confront in free-exercise litigation were discussed some 300 years earlier by Locke, except that, instead of the Santeria sacrifices of "chickens, pigeons, doves, ducks, guinea pigs, goats, sheep and turtles,"[29] Locke only spoke of calves. Before considering Locke's example further, we should begin by examining his entire argument.

Locke's *Letter Concerning Toleration* would seem to have been written to further mutual toleration among Christians. He says in the very beginning that "I esteem that toleration to be the chief characteristic mark of the true Church."[30] Following on this genial statement, Locke continues in the same vein. He says, "If the Gospel and the apostles may be credited, no man can be a Christian without charity and without that faith which works, not by force, but by love."[31] He writes also,

> The toleration of those that differ from others in matters of religion is so agreeable to the Gospel of Jesus Christ, and to the genuine reason of mankind, that it seems monstrous for men to be so blind as not to perceive the necessity and advantage of it in so clear a light.[32]

Locke, however, is not seeking simply to denounce those whom he esteems as cruel to other Christians; he is also going to "distinguish exactly the business of civil government from that of religion" so that there can be an "end put to the controversies that will be always arising between those that have, . . . on the one side, a concernment for the interest of men's souls, and, on the other side, a care of the commonwealth."[33]

With this, Locke begins his arguments for his well-known position that governments exist "only for the procuring, preserving, and

27. Reynolds, 166.

28. Locke later published a *Second* (1690) and a *Third Letter Concerning Toleration* (1692).

29. Church of Lukumi Babalu Aye, 525.

30. Page 1. All references to the *Letter* are to the edition published in the *Encyclopaedia Britannica Great Books* series (Chicago: Encyclopaedia Britannica, 1952), vol. 35.

31. Ibid.

32. Ibid., 2.

33. Ibid., 2–3.

advancing . . . civil interests." What are these civil interests? "Civil interests I call life, liberty, health, and indolency of body; and the possession of outward things, such as money, lands, houses, furniture, and the like." Thus, the state's duty is "by the impartial execution of equal laws, to secure unto all the people . . . the just possession of these things belonging to this life" and "neither can nor ought in any manner to be extended to the salvation of souls. . . ."[34]

Since he has limited the concerns of men when coming together into a political society to material affairs, all the laws and power of the state will likewise concern only material matters. Thus a fellow citizen's religious opinions would seem to have nothing to do with how well he will obey the laws of the commonwealth and are thus of no concern to his neighbor.

> If a heathen doubt of both Testaments, he is not therefore to be punished as a pernicious citizen. The power of the magistrate and the estates of the people may be equally secure whether any man believe these things or no.[35]

For "the business of laws is not to provide for the truth of opinions, but for the safety and security of the commonwealth and of every particular man's goods and person."[36]

Since the power of the ruler extends only to material things, he therefore "has no power to impose by his laws the use of any rites and ceremonies in any Church" nor "any power to forbid the use of such rites and ceremonies as are . . . practiced by any Church."[37] It would seem, then, that Locke has established a regime of the utmost religious freedom in which each and every man may worship God or gods in any manner of his choosing. Locke, however, has to deal with an obvious objection, and his answer closely parallels the reasoning of our own Supreme Court.

The objection that naturally arises is that, if entire freedom is granted to every religion, what if some religion performs outrageous rites in its worship—"if some congregations should have a mind to sacrifice infants, or . . . lustfully pollute themselves in promiscuous uncleanness"—should this be permitted on the grounds that the state may not meddle in spiritual matters? Locke answers thus: "No. These things are not lawful in the ordinary course of life, nor in any private house; and

---

34. Ibid., 3.
35. Ibid., 15.
36. Ibid.
37. Ibid., 12.

therefore neither are they so in the worship of God, or in any religious meeting."[38]

One might think that this is indeed a reasonable response, since, after all, could anyone really expect that murder would be permitted under color of religious worship? Locke immediately makes it clear that he is speaking not only of what lawyers call *malum in se* but also of what they call *malum prohibitum*.[39]

> But, indeed, if any people congregated upon account of religion should be desirous to sacrifice a calf, I deny that they ought to be prohibited by a law. Meliboeus, whose calf it is, may lawfully kill his calf at home, and burn any part of it that he thinks fit. For no injury is thereby done to any one, no prejudice to another man's goods. And for the same reason he may kill his calf also in a religious meeting.

Almost immediately, however, he goes on to say,

> But if peradventure such were the state of things that the interest of the commonwealth required all slaughter of beasts should be forborne for some while, in order to the increasing of the stock of cattle that had been destroyed by some extraordinary murrain, who sees not that the magistrate, in such a case, may forbid all his subjects to kill any calves for any use whatsoever? Only it is to be observed that, in this case, the law is not made about a religious, but a political matter. . . .[40]

In other words, "The mere possession of religious convictions which contradict the relevant concerns of a political society does not relieve the citizen from the discharge of political responsibilities."[41] Whenever Locke's established-only-for-the-sake-of-property government decides about some this-worldly matter, the fact that it requires believers to abstain from, or perform, some act contrary to their religious beliefs, matters not at all. Locke himself opines that "this will seldom happen"; but in answer to his question, "What if the magistrate should enjoin anything by his authority that appears unlawful to the conscience of a private person?" he replies,

> that such a private person is to abstain from the action that he judges unlawful, and he is to undergo the punishment. . . . For the private judgement of any person concerning a law enacted in political matters,

---

38. Ibid.
39. *Malum in se*, of course, is something evil in itself whereas *malum prohibitum* is something evil merely because some governmental enactment has made it such.
40. Locke, *Letter*, 12–13.
41. Smith v. Employment Division, 879.

for the public good, does not take away the obligation of that law, nor deserve a dispensation.[42]

I think one can see that the frameworks within which both Locke's jurisprudence and our own First Amendment jurisprudence exist are identical.[43] Legislative enactments within either framework would not deal with religious belief itself. Locke has no explicit prohibition, such as our First Amendment has, of government legislating on religious belief. He does not need one; for since his government is limited only to "civil interests" in its enactments, it can never touch religious belief itself. As to religious *conduct*, both assert their right to prohibit or regulate it whenever some "civil interest" of sufficient importance makes this necessary.

This method of dealing with conflict between civil and religious prescriptions, especially when applied using the "compelling governmental interest" standard sometimes used by the Supreme Court, might seem to establish a reasonable *modus vivendi*. In a country such as the United States, where we have every kind of religion from Appalachian snake handlers to Zen Buddhists, there would surely be chaos if everyone were allowed to ignore any law that conflicted with his sincere religious beliefs. Nevertheless, I suggest that present in Locke's doctrine, and our own, is a latent totalitarianism. In a liberal society, whenever there is an overwhelming consensus about, if not *belief*, at least about what kinds of *conduct* are reasonable or customary, these totalitarian implications are not likely to come to the fore. Almost all the religious liberty cases that have come before our courts, for example, have involved minority religions, whose adherents do things like sacrifice animals, marry more than one wife, fail to salute the flag,[44] observe Saturday as their day of

---

42. *Letter*, 16.

43. Many historians have remarked on the pervasive influence of John Locke in the United States. For example, Louis Hartz says that in America Locke is a "massive national cliché" and that he "dominates American political thought, as no thinker anywhere dominates the political thought of a nation." *The Liberal Tradition in America* (New York: Harcourt, Brace & World, 1955), 140. Moreover, it is most interesting to note the following from the concurring opinion by Justice Scalia in City of Boerne v. Flores, the decision striking down the Religious Freedom Restoration Act:

> This limitation upon the scope of religious exercise would have been in accord with the background political philosophy of the age (*associated most prominently with John Locke*), which regarded freedom as the right "to do only what was not lawfully prohibited." (540, emphasis mine)

Justice Scalia is at least clear about what he thinks and why.

44. The two flag salute cases were Minersville School District Board of Education v. Gobitis, 310 U.S. 586 (1940) and West Virginia State Board of Education v. Barnette, 319 U.S. 624 (1943). Both involved Jehovah's Witnesses.

rest,[45] or take peyote—things not part of the way most Americans have traditionally behaved. It is easy to see how any one of these unusual practices is more likely to fall afoul of "generally applicable and otherwise valid" laws even if the laws are not aimed at religious conduct in particular. For since general laws that deal with secular matters naturally are framed to apply to the way most citizens live or to how they have traditionally lived, whenever minority religions depart from this way of life there is a possibility that one of their religiously mandated norms of conduct will come into conflict with these laws.

It should be clear, however, that this approach to the question subordinates potentially *all* religious conduct to policy decisions of legislatures and courts. It is not difficult to imagine, given the right climate of opinion, a general law's being passed prohibiting almost any act that any religion might mandate. Thus, in the 1920s, the State of Oregon sought by general laws to prohibit all but public school education. Although in Pierce v. Society of Sisters the U.S. Supreme Court decided against the State of Oregon,[46] the Court asserted in the Smith opinion that the only reason the Pierce case was decided in that way was because the religious freedom claim was "in conjunction with other constitutional protections, such as . . . the right of parents . . . to direct the education of their children. . . ."[47] Although the Supreme Court has often invalidated legislation held to violate the free-exercise clause, it is not hard to imagine a unanimity of opinion between both the legislature and the courts.[48]

However problematical this may be, I think the root of the matter lies deeper still. It is not simply a question of the asserted right to regulate potentially any religious conduct whatsoever. It is that both Locke and American jurisprudence render religion entirely irrelevant to the real concerns of the political community. This irrelevance is most strikingly stated in Reynolds v. United States. There the Court quotes as follows from the preamble to the Virginia statute of 1785, written by Thomas Jefferson, establishing religious freedom: "to suffer the civil magistrate

---

45. There have been several cases involving those who observe Saturday as the weekly holy day. They include Braunfeld v. Brown, 366 U.S. 599 (1961), which concerned Orthodox Jews, and Sherbert v. Verner, 374 U.S. 398 (1963), and Hobbie v. Unemployment Appeals Commission of Florida, 480 U.S. 136 (1987), both of which concerned Seventh-Day Adventists.

46. Pierce v. Society of Sisters, 268 U.S. 510.

47. Smith, 881.

48. See the excursus on the government's persecution of the Mormons at the end of this chapter.

to intrude his powers into the field of opinion ... is a dangerous fallacy...."[49] On the next page, commenting on the adoption of the First Amendment to the U.S. Constitution, the Court says, "Congress was deprived of all legislative power over mere opinion...." The reason why the Lockean state, both on paper and as realized in the United States, can so calmly assert its right to regulate religious conduct when it comes into conflict with its secular laws is because at bottom it considers religion not only a private affair, and hence subject to the political order, but also merely a matter of *opinion*. Locke's political community is concerned exclusively with such weighty matters as "life, liberty, health, and indolency of body; ... money, lands, houses, furniture, and the like." To it religion, both belief and practice, is at best something to be benignly tolerated so long as it does not get in the way of the state's business. The state itself is either atheistic or agnostic. How could it not be when it regards religious beliefs as so many "opinions," and officially removes itself from any consideration of them?[50]

Locke's example of the magistrate who may prohibit the sacrifice of calves when "some extraordinary murrain" makes it necessary that "all slaughter of beasts should be forborne for some while" and the real-life example of the prohibition of peyote use by the State of Oregon illustrate this well. If God were really pleased by the sacrifice of calves, or by the use of peyote, then clearly the secular purposes that were held to justify these respective prohibitions would count as nothing—that is, provided that the governmental authorities believed and acknowledged this fact. But in fact neither Locke's putative magistrate nor the Supreme Court has the slightest interest in whether or not God is propitiated by the sacrifice of calves or the use of peyote or by men marrying more

---

49. Reynolds, 163.

50. One might take issue with what I have just said by pointing out that Congress, many state legislatures, the armed services, and many courts employ chaplains or have official opening prayers. Presidents have often invoked the name of God in their official addresses and proclamations. Indeed, the U.S. Supreme Court in Zorach v. Clauson, 343 U.S. 306 (1952), wrote as follows: "We are a religious people whose institutions presuppose a Supreme Being" (313). But the real meaning of this becomes clear a few sentences later. "When the state encourages religious instruction or cooperates with religious authorities by adjusting the schedule of public events to sectarian needs, it follows the best of our traditions. For it then respects the religious nature of our people and accommodates the public service to their spiritual needs" (313–14). Any benign governmental acts toward religion are based on the private, but pervasive, religious beliefs of the people. The government as such is not interested in whether the prayers that open legislative sessions actually are pleasing to God, any more than whether sacrifices of animals would be, but "accommodates" its actions to popular belief.

than one wife[51] or by any of the other kinds of conduct at issue in the course of free exercise-clause litigation. These religious behaviors are permitted, regulated, or prohibited (as the case may be) only according to how they fit in with the secular purposes that alone are held to be proper to government. Religion is simply not part of the serious business of the state. The political community is secular, not only in the sense that its legislative concerns are exclusively secular but more importantly because it is wholly uninterested either in the truth of any of the religions that its laws regulate or in the very question of whether there is any religious truth at all. Surely, if in fact we could please God by the sacrifice of "chickens, pigeons, doves, ducks, guinea pigs, goats, sheep and turtles," or even of mere calves, would not a regime that wanted even secular prosperity be interested in promoting such acts in order to gain the blessing of God upon itself? Though the Supreme Court allowed the Santeria sacrifices to continue, it did not do so because it thought those sacrifices might be potent tools in the fight against budget deficits or illegal drug use or political corruption. It was only because the City of Hialeah singled out the Santeria sacrifices and failed to demonstrate any "compelling governmental interest" in its prohibitions that the Court prevented it from proscribing them.

We should note further that, since religion is not part of the serious business with which the political authorities are occupied, neither is it part of the real business of society either, as society is ultimately governed and shaped by the political.[52] It is not simply that the government will not officially sponsor the sacrifices of animals or investigate whether or not such sacrifices are pleasing to God but that, since the government permits or prohibits such acts based on its own secular criteria, society is only able to engage in such acts based on whether they satisfy the secular criteria employed by the authorities. I and my co-religionists might be convinced that it is our duty to perform one of the acts that are held to violate some "compelling governmental interest," and we might not care about the alleged interest asserted by the state.

51. At his trial George Reynolds offered evidence that according to the doctrine of the Mormon Church, of which he was a member, "the failing or refusing to practise polygamy by...male members of said church, when circumstances would admit, would be punished, and that the penalty for such failure and refusal would be damnation in the life to come" (Reynolds v. United States, 161).

52. There are exceptions to this rule, as when the political order is controlled by an occupying power whose way of life is at odds with that of the population. Thus, Ireland under English domination and Poland under Communist largely preserved their own cultures, but not without suffering damage, as for example, the loss of the Irish language.

Nonetheless, according to the methods of the Lockean state and of the U.S. Constitution, we too are compelled to live and act according to secular criteria. The fact that we are permitted to *believe* whatever we like would seem to have little meaning if our external acts are forced to conform to secularist standards. Thus, it is society as much as the political order that is rendered secular. The obvious retort that there is in fact much religious activity taking place in our society undisturbed by the police or the courts is actually neither here nor there. Potentially any and all of this religious activity could be stopped if the state declared it had a sufficient interest in doing so. In theory, all religious activity exists simply because it does not interfere with any important—and necessarily secular—state purpose. If it does not, the state can safely ignore it. It is like children playing—as long as their noise and commotion is below a certain level, the parents will ignore it; but in principle it exists simply by their sufferance.

Moreover, if the political community has no interest in religion, it is hard to see why any private person should have. If religion cannot play any role in the political or public life of a nation, why should it be important to the individual either, except perhaps as a psychological crutch or a merely subjective aid to personal rectitude? A God whom our rulers can officially ignore would hardly be a God that private citizens need worry much about. It is surely an odd kind of religion that must be put into one's pocket whenever one ventures into the political realm, just as it is surely odd to have to defend religious activity, not on the ground that it is pleasing to God, but on the ground that it fits in with the secular interests of the state. Is there anything wrong with this? Is there any reason why a government should not ignore the question of religious truth? Has not America's history been sufficient justification for its philosophy? Is not the large amount of freedom allowed to the Christian and to other believers by a Lockean regime adequate in most circumstances? Perhaps our state is not ideal, so it is argued, but it is surely better than incessant strife, or worse still, a situation in which one religious party has gained the upper hand and actually persecutes its opponents.

These are the types of arguments raised by defenders of the Lockean state. Americans are all too ready to assent to them without much thought; for as soon as the specter of religious strife or religious persecution is raised, most of us are only too happy to embrace Locke as an escape from these difficulties. This is done, however, without much considering the assumptions and implications of the Lockean program. It would seem that if there is a God and if it is possible to know anything about what is pleasing to Him, it would be a matter of interest to mankind. For just that reason people have been interested in religious questions. It is difficult to understand why the government they form would not likewise be interested in these questions; for, unless God has no concern with human affairs, knowledge of His will would seem to be one of the best means of obtaining his blessing on all our human undertakings.

It is no doubt true, as I said above, that Locke and the Founding Fathers strove to sequester religion from state concern at least partly because of their memory of two hundred years of religious warfare in Europe. Confessional states and official religions seemed to them to invite strife and persecution and to work against prosperity in human affairs. To say, however, that men subject to a government may legitimately be concerned about religious truth does not mean that there need be an established church or the persecution of dissenters. The thirteen colonies that became the United States contained a plurality of religions nearly from their beginning, and whatever arrangements the Founding Fathers made would have had to have taken that into account. Nevertheless, to adopt the Lockean solution to the problem of religious pluralism makes religion forever after merely a private hobby, worthy of being protected perhaps but not because it makes any truth claims to be taken seriously in the political or intellectual arena. The First Amendment bars religion from ever being a relevant factor at the level of political life.

I am not, of course, suggesting here the opposite solution, that of the confessional state, an obvious absurdity in this country. I simply want to point out to those who have unthinkingly accepted Locke's version of the correct relations between religion and society that it is not the self-evident truth it is usually imagined to be. The Lockean solution to the problem of religious pluralism seems so obvious to most Americans as to need little or no defense. But in reality this is not so. The assumptions and implications of such a means of dealing with religion are rarely brought out and not readily perceived in the United States; if they were to be, perhaps then a new debate on the Lockean doctrine itself and on other possible roles for religion could begin. Then, regardless of the practical steps that might be taken to allow diverse religious believers (and non-believers) to live together in peace, Americans could see that claims to religious truth, if really taken seriously, might have implications even for the political and public order. At the very least, regardless of what changes we might or might not make, we should understand that the Lockean solution is not the only method of dealing with pluralism and that it involves a definite relegation of religion to a private and inconsequential role. We should be able to ask ourselves whether we truly desire a public order that deliberately excludes religion. It is not just "money, lands, houses, furniture, and the like" that men seek when they join together in a community; it is the good and how to achieve that elusive goal.

Excursus: Persecution of the Mormons by the United States Government

To discover how a liberal government might proceed against an unpopular religion, one ought to look at the federal government's campaign against the Mormons during the nineteenth century. The antipathy toward the Mormons was shared by all branches of government, so that the courts readily sanctioned each new anti-Mormon action of Congress and the territorial legislatures.

Congress in 1862 prohibited polygamy in the territories, of which Utah was then one. In Reynolds v. United States the Supreme Court more than upheld the action of Congress: its opinion makes clear that it was far from neutral in this matter. The Court stated that

> Polygamy has always been odious among the northern and western nations of Europe, and, until the establishment of the Mormon Church, was almost exclusively a feature of the life of Asiatic and of African people.[53]

The Court then went on to say,

> In fact, according as monogamous or polygamous marriages are allowed, do we find the principles on which the government of the people, to a greater or less extent, rests. Professor Lieber says, polygamy leads to the patriarchal principle, and which, when applied to large communities, fetters the people in stationary despotism, while that principle cannot long exist in connection with monogamy.[54]

The Court also refused to find any judicial error in the instructions to the jury given by the trial judge in Utah, which included the sentence, "I think it not improper, in the discharge of your duties in this case, that you should consider what are to be the consequences to the innocent victims of this delusion."[55]

In 1882, Congress made it an offense in the territories to cohabit with more than one woman (an act easier to prove than the fact of plural marriage), deprived polygamists or "any person cohabiting with more than one woman" of the right to vote, barred them from public office,

53. Reynolds, 164.
54. Ibid., 165–66.
55. Ibid., 167.

and excluded them and anyone who "believes it right for a man to have more than one living and undivorced wife at the same time, or to live in the practice of cohabiting with more than one woman" from juries in trials for these offenses. This was upheld by the Supreme Court.[56]

In Davis v. Beason[57] the Court unanimously upheld a law of the Territory of Idaho forbidding not merely actual polygamists, but

> any person ... who teaches, advises, counsels, or encourages any person or persons to become bigamists or polygamists ... or who is a member of any order, organization, or association which teaches, advises, counsels, or encourages its members ... to commit the crime of bigamy or polygamy

from voting or holding public office.[58] This of course prevented any Mormon from voting, although according to an authoritative judicial estimate not more than "twenty per cent of the marriageable members, male and female, were engaged in the actual practice of polygamy. ..."[59]

Finally, Congress, by an act of 1887, dissolved the legal corporation of the Mormon church and confiscated all its property, except for a portion actually used for religious worship. This act was upheld six to three by the Supreme Court in The Late Corporation of the Church of Jesus Christ of Latter-Day Saints v. United States.[60]

I am not, of course, suggesting that the practice of polygamy is right or is merely a *malum prohibitum*; rather, I am pointing out that the extremes of the government's actions against the Mormon church could, in other circumstances, be directed against any religion, given the right climate of opinion.[61]

56. See Murphy v. Ramsey, 114 U.S. 15 (1885).

57. 133 U.S. 333 (1890).

58. Ibid., 335–36.

59. Cited in Late Corporation of the Church of Jesus Christ of Latter-Day Saints v. United States, 136 U.S. 1, at 27.

60. 136 U.S. 1 (1890).

61. Does it take much imagination to see possible dangers to the Catholic Church over either the ordination of women or approval of homosexual conduct?

17

The Catholic Failure to Change America

Nevertheless, in spite of the Church's amazing growth, American Catholics have had no such influence upon the thought and life of the whole nation as their numbers would lead us to expect.

—Carlton J.H. Hayes[1]

Important as are the contributions of individual members of the Church to the life of the United States, it is yet worthy of note how small the part is that the Roman Catholic Church has taken in the formation of the general culture.

—Thomas C. Hall[2]

IN THE NINETEENTH and first third of the twentieth century, there was a sometimes bitter controversy over how many Catholic immigrants to the United States after arriving in their new homeland had lost their faith as a result of the shortage of priests or simply the unsettling conditions of a country in which Catholicism was not taken for granted in the public culture. Many commentators, often German Catholics, argued for massive losses well into the late nineteenth century. Even the optimists admitted a huge number of defections, at least during the colonial era. Their most noteworthy contribution to the debate, the 1925 book, *Has the Immigrant Kept the Faith?*, by Fr. (later bishop of Seattle) Gerald Shaughnessy, held that in colonial times "the Church had suffered here a loss of 240,000 members or possible members by the year 1790"[3]—leaving an estimated Catholic population of merely 35,000 for

1. *American Catholicism and the Intellectual Ideal*, eds. Frank L. Christ and Gerard E. Sherry (New York: Appleton-Century-Crofts, 1961), 72–73.

2. Ibid., 92.

3. Quoted in John Tracy Ellis, *American Catholicism* (Garden City, NY: Image, 1965), 153.

that same year. Whatever might be the truth about eighteenth- or nineteenth-century defections from the Faith in the United States, for our own time we have harder numbers in the Pew survey of a few years ago.

> Overall, 2.6% of the U.S. adult population has switched their affiliation to Catholic after being raised in another faith or in no faith at all. But nearly four times as many people (10.1% of the adult population overall) were raised in the Catholic Church but have since left for another faith or for no faith at all.[4]

That means, according to the Pew survey, that although 31.4% of Americans were raised Catholic and 2.6% converted to the Faith, only 23.9% now identify as Catholic. I am sure that all my readers have lapsed Catholics of their acquaintance, whose children and grandchildren in turn, whether baptized or not, are hardly aware that they have a Catholic heritage and may not show up in such surveys as losses to the Church. Thus, the loss of actual members translates over generations to an even greater loss in their descendants.

Although the question of Catholic influence on American culture is separate from the question of mere Catholic numbers, they are not unrelated. Had Catholics simply maintained strength of numbers, it is probable that at some point merely the increasingly overwhelming size of the Church would have resulted in some significant "influence upon the thought and life of the whole nation." But that was not to be; Catholics did not have much influence "in the formation of the general culture," in part certainly because they were a minority group and the general culture was too overwhelming to influence. Even if deficient in numbers, we have not had the influence that we might have had if we had understood the situation better, if we had grasped the task that was set before us. To convert individuals—yes, many laudably sought that. To convert American ideas, ways of thinking, institutions—all of which were thoroughly imbued with Protestant and Enlightenment principles—this, it seems, was rarely seen as part of the Church's apostolic mission in this country. To the Protestant charge that Catholics could not be good Americans, our ancestors were all too apt to cry, "Yes we can, better than you in fact!" Many it seems did not see that the term "good American" could mean two things: on the one hand, simply an

---

4. Pew Research Center, Religion & Public Life, "Chapter 2: Changes in Americans' Religious Affiliation," in U.S. Religious Landscape Survey: Religious Affiliation, accessed August 15, 2014, http://www.pewforum.org/2008/02/01/chapter-2-changes-in-americans -religious-affiliation/.

inhabitant and citizen of this country, but on the other, someone who wholeheartedly accepted the country's founding principles and spirit; hence, the ambiguity in Archbishop John Ireland's statement that "Catholicism and Americanism are in complete agreement." Although one can hardly criticize Ireland for his desire to adopt apostolic methods suited to the conditions of this country, he and his like seem to have imagined that the United States was in some way a realization on the natural level of Catholic principles. In his preface to Fr. Walter Elliott's *Life of Father Hecker*, Ireland wrote, "the Church ought to love a polity which is the offspring of her own spirit" and "[a]n honest ballot and social decorum among Catholics will do more for God's glory and the salvation of souls than midnight flagellations or Compostellan pilgrimages."[5] A quasi-mystical idealization of the United States and the institutions of democracy lay behind Ireland's ecclesiastical and political views, for example his at-best lukewarm support of parochial schools, and suggests that he thought the Church had as much to gain from America as vice versa.

Be that as it may, the controversy over Catholic losses in the United States is related to the question of Catholic influence in another way. Generally those holding to minimal losses maintained that there was nothing in American culture that was especially unfriendly to the Faith, whereas those, such as German Catholics, who believed that losses had been huge attributed this in part at least to the Protestant and secular atmosphere of this country. For example, Fr. Anton Walburg, a German-born Cincinnati priest, wrote as follows in his 1889 book, *The Question of Nationality in its Relation to the Catholic Church*:

> The ideal set before every American youth is money. Money is not only needful, but is the one thing needful. Money is a power everywhere, but here it is the supreme power. . . . In Europe, a man enjoys his competence; but here, no one has enough. . . .
>
> The Anglo-Saxon nationality has always been in England and in this country the bulwark of Protestantism and the mainstay of the enemies of the faith. It is so puffed up with spiritual pride, so steeped in materialism, that it is callous, and impervious to the spirit and the doctrines of the Catholic religion.[6]

This divide among American Catholics vis-à-vis American culture continues to this day. Some of the responses to Patrick J. Deneen's online

---

5. (New York: Columbia Press, 1891).

6. *American Catholic Thought on Social Questions*, ed. Aaron Abell (Indianapolis: Bobbs-Merrill, 1968), 40, 41, and 43.

article of last year, "A Catholic Showdown Worth Watching,"[7] could have been written by Archbishop Ireland himself. Peter Lawler, for example, charges that Deneen "is repulsively lacking in gratitude."[8] Gratitude to America, he means. And for what? For freedom, "in some respects an unprecedented freedom." Evidently, Lawler is unaware that religious freedom under the First Amendment is merely a freedom of belief, not necessarily of conduct, even religiously motivated conduct. One need only read Justice Antonin Scalia's majority opinion in the 1990 case of Employment Division v. Smith to see this.[9] "We have never held that an individual's religious beliefs excuse him from compliance with an otherwise valid law prohibiting conduct that the State is free to regulate."[10] And he continued,

> the right of free exercise does not relieve an individual of the obligation to comply with a "valid and neutral law of general applicability on the ground that the law proscribes (or prescribes) conduct that his religion prescribes (or proscribes)."[11]

This understanding of religious freedom, rooted in John Locke, informs the whole tradition of American jurisprudence. The 1779 Virginia Statute for Religious Freedom, for example, written by Thomas Jefferson, gave freedom only to belief, what it called "religious opinion." Moreover, even with regard to belief this freedom is not so absolute as is supposed, and one might take note of the fact that in the 1890 case of Davis v. Beason[12] the Supreme Court unanimously upheld a law of the Territory of Idaho that denied the right to vote or hold public office not merely to polygamists, but to

> any person ... who teaches, advises, counsels, or encourages any person or persons to become bigamists or polygamists ... or who is a member of any order, organization, or association which teaches, advises, counsels, or encourages its members ... to commit the crime of bigamy or polygamy.[13]

7. "A Catholic Showdown Worth Watching," in *The American Conservative* (February 6, 2014), accessed on August 15, 2014, www.theamericanconservative.com/a-catholic-showdown-worth-watching/.

8. "Catholic and American (and Quirky About It)," in *First Things* (February 8, 2014), accessed August 15, 2014, www.firstthings.com/blogs/firstthoughts/2014/02/catholic-and-ambiguous-pro-american-and-quirky-about-it.

9. 494 U.S. 872.

10. Ibid., 878–79.

11. Ibid., 879.

12. 133 U.S. 333 (1890).

13. Ibid., 335–36.

If at some point this more-than-century-old legal dictum is used against Catholics, shall we still be so ready to speak of the "unprecedented freedom" we are said to enjoy here?

Despite the largely hostile culture, had Catholics, even in their reduced numbers, understood our apostolate in its totality, we might have been able to influence American culture, at least to some degree. Probably the root defect of that culture is its individualism, based both on a philosophical reductionism and on Protestantism. This individualism affects in the first place our fundamental attitudes toward government and authority and economic life. The effects of individualism on our economic life are often recognized, but less understood are the ways that the mores of a "commercial republic" corrupt nearly every aspect of life, public and private—for example, education and sports. Had the Church combined her efforts at making individual conversions with an intelligent critique of the fundamental cultural situation in the United States, she might have exerted an influence well beyond her visible boundaries. When efforts were made to influence the culture, as with the Legion of Decency, they were too often merely negative and *ad hoc*. It is entirely legitimate to stigmatize bad movies, but our criticism seemed to be mostly of obvious offenses against the sixth and ninth commandments rather than of the deeper thematic faults of American cinema, which were connected with the philosophical reductionism, individualism, and materialism already mentioned. This made our critique seem one-sided, directed against only a narrow range of moral failings, and unconcerned with other cultural and moral errors of American society. One critic, writing in the late 1950s, expressed his view of American Catholic culture with a trenchant severity, as follows:

> Outside the narrow moral sphere which American Catholicism has taken as its central province, the American Catholic is assimilated to the materialistic society about him in some of its most pernicious aspects. It is for this reason that middle-class Catholic ideals so often appear to be false, shallow and derivative.... Catholics in sermons and editorials often decry the "materialism" of our age, but it is not always clear what they consider that "materialism" to be. Indeed, the hypothesis proposed here is that outside a specifically religious, and often quite closed-off, sphere of consciousness which we may designate as "sacred," American Catholic middle-class life often tends to be more materialistic than is that of many Protestant and secularist groups.[14]

14. Thomas F. O'Dea, *American Catholic Dilemma: An Inquiry Into the Intellectual Life* (New York: Sheed & Ward, 1958), 117–18.

The only important area in which Catholic thought did have positive influence outside the boundaries of the Church was Catholic social doctrine. Here the Church presented more than a critique of specific injustices and social ills: it offered a vision of a more just society, a vision that found sympathy and support among politicians, union leaders, and publicists. But the Church did not offer a comprehensive, positive program that combined an intelligent evaluation of American culture as a whole with a presentation of Catholic principles in their fullness and beauty. Had this been done it would have been a spiritual work of mercy and a signal act of piety toward our country. This, rather than vain boasting of America's achievements, real or imagined, or uncritical support of every American military adventure, would have been a truly patriotic deed—an attempt to make one's country better. Instead, however, of trying to point out that it was Catholic principles that were the best remedy for the failings in American culture which even many non-Catholics perceived, and instead of assiduously working to make Catholic life embody those principles in their fullness, we largely copied Protestant and secular American manners when they did not obviously and directly contravene Catholic morals. This was the point of Robert M. Hutchins's 1937 address to the National Catholic Educational Association Midwest Regional Meeting, in which he charged that Catholic education in the United States had "imitated the worst features of secular education," namely "athleticism and collegiatism," the latter being "the production of well-tubbed young Americans." Hutchins was not a Catholic, but he used our own principles against us. "What I say," he continued,

> is that Catholic education is not Catholic enough. The Catholic Church has the longest intellectual tradition of any institution in the contemporary world, the only uninterrupted tradition and the only explicit tradition. . . . What I say is that this tradition must not be merely an ideal, but must be practiced.[15]

Sadly, the same might have been said of all too many other areas of Catholic life. Instead of holding up an attractive vision of something fundamentally different and better, the Church in the United States has in practice conducted her apostolate by making individual piety and rectitude, critical though these obviously are, the only goal of Catholic life and by seeking to influence society if at all only in a negative manner—by seeking to prohibit certain discrete evils. Now, of course, the

---

15. *American Catholicism and the Intellectual Ideal*, eds. Frank L. Christ and Gerard E. Sherry (New York: Appleton-Century-Crofts, 1961), 109, 111.

hour is late. It is no doubt harder to convince people today to calmly consider either the claims of the Catholic Church or the beauty of Catholic thought and life than it may have been in the past. But though many will consider such an effort quixotic if not foolish, it would be more likely to yield genuine success, it seems to me, than a frantic preoccupation with largely futile political activity in pursuit of goals that are not always even consistent with Catholic doctrine.

The divide among Catholics today that Deneen portrays has its roots in the nineteenth-century Catholic debate about immigration. For some, such as Archbishop Ireland, America was the place where the Church would flourish—flourish by adopting American principles. To discerning Catholics, however, the way of life offered by the Protestant colossus of the New World had to be carefully weighed and judged. What was good or indifferent could be accepted; what was not had to be discerned and either reformed or rejected. Although many of us are remote in time from our immigrant ancestors, this necessary process of discernment in light of Catholic principles and history remains still largely undone. Though it is late, while we are again experiencing a new Catholic immigration and the principles latent in American thought from the beginning are more evident than ever, it is nevertheless not too late to begin.

18

The End of the New Deal Coalition
and the Transformation of
American Politics

DISSATISFACTION with American politics is common right now, shown in sometimes surprisingly similar ways by both the Tea Party movement and Occupy Wall Street. Americans disapprove by large majorities of the job that Congress is doing; and, apart from Democratic and Republican stalwarts, not many are enthusiastic about either President Obama or any likely Republican candidate. In fact, there seems to be considerable recognition that American politics are at an impasse.

When we consider the policies advocated by the two major parties today, we also see some strange things—strange at least for those of us old enough to remember another era. For example, if we compare the platforms of the Republican candidates with the policies of the Republican Richard Nixon only some forty years ago, we might be amazed by the environmental legislation sponsored or supported by Nixon: the Clean Air Act, the Clear Water Act, the establishment of the Environmental Protection Agency—legislation that certainly would never be supported by today's Republicans and possibly not by Democrats either. On the other hand, who would ever have thought that the Democratic Party of Hubert Humphrey would support same-sex marriage or abortion or, as lately, go out of its way to pick a fight with the Catholic Church? The explanation for much of this state of affairs can be found, I think, if we take a historically longer look at American politics than is usually done and try to understand what has happened since the end of the Second World War.

The period beginning with the first Franklin Roosevelt administration in 1933 until the mid or late 1970s was largely dominated by the

New Deal coalition. Although Democrats did not control either the Presidency or Congress for all of that time, they almost always controlled either one or the other and frequently both. This coalition set a kind of political and social tone that, for those of us old enough to remember any of it, seems almost like another world.

The New Deal coalition was just that—a coalition. It included urban and academic liberals, some agrarian populists, blacks, some Southern Democrats, and largely urban Catholics. Although by European standards the economic and social legislation the coalition supported was hardly radical, it did take a stance on behalf of ordinary Americans, workers, and the poor. While the coalition was in the ascendant, the middle and lower classes did increase their share of the national income. For most of this period, social policy, as we should call it nowadays, was traditional, assuming the two-parent family, with fathers earning enough by their work so that their wives could stay at home and care for children and household. In fact, the legislative enactments of the New Deal coalition mostly aimed at strengthening this two-parent, one-earner family. Allan Carlson summed up as follows the thinking of those, chiefly women, responsible for shaping New Deal family policy:

> They . . . wanted social policy to recognize the centrality of the home and the primary power of the breadwinner/homemaker/child-rich family. Most major New Deal initiatives would build on these assumptions.[1]

Although it is certainly the case that this coalition was not a perfect representation of Catholic politics, it generally gave Catholics a political home without any obvious conflict with the teaching of the Church, at least as far as domestic policy went. When this coalition fell apart after 1970, it did so in large part because of the loss of one important component in the coalition: Catholics. All through her history, but more explicitly since Leo XIII's 1891 encyclical, *Rerum Novarum*, the Catholic Church has taught that there are demands of economic justice that cannot be simply left to the free play of market forces. The application of these principles to modern capitalism by both popes and various bishops' conferences resulted in what is usually called Catholic social teaching. In 1919, for example, the American bishops issued the Bishops' Program of Social Reconstruction, which called for numerous measures that did not become law until the New Deal—some of them we are still awaiting. In the former category were minimum-wage legislation,

---

1. Allan Carlson, *The "American Way": Family and Community in the Shaping of the American Identity* (Wilmington: ISI Books, 2003), 56–57.

unemployment insurance, labor's right to organize, and public housing. Among the latter are "prevention of excessive profits and incomes," worker participation in management, and control of monopolies "even by the method of government competition if that should prove necessary." Meanwhile in Rome, the popes were issuing similarly radical social encyclicals, especially Pius XI, supreme pontiff from 1922 to 1939. As the twentieth century progressed this teaching gradually became better known by the Catholic laity; and a general knowledge and acceptance of it, though unfortunately never universal, persisted through the 1970s and even beyond. Something happened, however, that deflected many American Catholics' attention away from an active interest in economic justice and brought about the end of the New Deal coalition.

Beginning in the 1970s the Democratic party began to repudiate the delicate balance of the New Deal coalition by embracing ideas that could only drive Catholics out of it. Chief among these was abortion. At the same time, Republicans began to use opposition to abortion and later other issues, such as same-sex marriage, to lure many working class Catholics out of the Democratic party—the so-called Reagan Democrats. Even though many of these are hardly died-in-the-wool conservatives, enough of them became regular or occasional Republican voters so as to give the Republicans a big boost in elections. Although those who control the conservative movement and the Republican party have no serious interest in putting a stop to abortions, the issue is convenient to attract politically naive Catholics. Even more serious, in my view, is that many Catholic publicists have identified themselves uncritically with the conservative political/cultural movement that assumed such importance with the election of Ronald Reagan in 1980. Some of these publicists have been bought by corporate money, it would appear, but others are sincerely confused. People are right to see abortion as a very serious crime, but as the example of all recent popes shows, the fact that abortion is a flagrant moral injustice should not prevent us from focusing on the entire range of moral issues, including economic justice, war and nuclear disarmament, and the environment. Unfortunately, however, the legacy of Catholic socio-economic teaching has been largely forgotten here in the United States. Some openly deny it and thus contradict the official doctrine of their Church; others water it down, reinterpreting it according to conservative free-market ideas; and others ignore it on the ground that now only one or a few issues matter. It is true that those who want to take part in the straitjacket of the two-party system will find neither party espousing a political agenda that corresponds to Catholic teaching, but one gets the impression that many Catholics today simply have no interest in the Church's social doctrine.

For them it is not a calculated decision to cooperate with Republicans, but rather a sellout of their own heritage.

So, if this is what happened, can anything be done? Can the New Deal coalition be revived in any form? Unfortunately, it does not seem likely and that for many reasons. The Democrats are unlikely to repudiate important parts of their current coalition: supporters of abortion, of legalized same-sex marriage, and the like; nor are there many Democratic politicians who would even feel comfortable with the economic priorities of the New Deal. On economic issues today's Democratic party is largely a tool of corporate control, little better than the Republicans; nor is the present state of Catholics in America encouraging for such a prospect. As I noted, many articulate Catholics now identify themselves as conservatives and Republicans, while the mass of Catholic voters do not seem to vote as Catholics at all. Their religious affiliation seems to have little or no influence on their political views and behavior.

The recent activities of the Occupy movement appeared to offer some hope that a new coalition could be formed that might address economic injustices without committing itself on what are today called the "social issues." Some leftwing spokesmen have explicitly advocated this approach in the hope of building a new coalition strong enough to fight the corporate control of the nation's economy, media, and political parties. However, I do not see how the Occupy movement will be able to translate its energy and numbers into political activity, at least in time for the 2012 elections; and the recent emergence of a new and unexpected conflict between the Catholic Church and the government has complicated things even more.

The attempt by the Obama administration to impose contraceptives and abortifacients as part of mandated health care coverage is surely a surprising development, for either the administration has entirely miscalculated and mismanaged the affair or the level of strident anti-Catholic secularism in the Democratic party is much greater than one might have suspected. Unfortunately, the record of Supreme Court jurisprudence on the matter does not seem especially favorable to the Church. Since the Mormon polygamy cases beginning in the 1870s, the Supreme Court has never held that religious belief necessarily exempts one from obeying general laws. As Justice Scalia wrote in the majority opinion in Employment Division v. Smith in 1990, "We have never held that an individual's religious beliefs excuse him from compliance with an otherwise valid law prohibiting conduct that the State is free to regulate" and "the right of free exercise does not relieve an individual of the obligation to comply with a 'valid and neutral law of general applicability on the ground that the law proscribes (or prescribes) conduct that his religion prescribes (or proscribes)." This approach to regulating religious conduct, which has its intellectual background in John Locke, is perhaps inevitable in a polity that has relegated theological arguments and reasons to the sphere of private life. As various minority religions—including Mormons, Jehovah's Witnesses, Seventh Day Adventists, and the Native American Church—have experienced, when the general society is hostile or indifferent one's free-exercise rights usually count for little. What is surprising about the current conflict, however, is that, although the Church is asking for an accommodation that by historical standards of American law is quite reasonable, the administration is unwilling to offer a real compromise. This suggests that the memory of the New Deal coalition has completely faded from our historical consciousness or else that the Obama administration is trying to distract attention from its dismal economic and foreign policy failures by attacking an institution unpopular with so many on the left.

Even though many in the Occupy movement have little but disdain for the Obama administration, there seems to be so much hostility on the left to the Catholic Church that any hope of sustained cooperation is remote. The left seems to have completely forgotten Catholic participation in the labor movement, the constant support by the bishops of national health care, and the criticisms of neo-liberal economics made both in Rome and here by popes and bishops. Apparently, for many on the left the politics of sex trump pretty much everything.

If the left has forgotten the New Deal coalition, it hardly behooves Catholics to do the same, not because it was perfect but because it was a reasonable vehicle for Catholic participation in American electoral politics, something that today does not exist. What then is the best Catholic strategy for the present? In 2004 I wrote an article for the *New Oxford Review* arguing that if we Catholics really wanted to have an effect on U.S. politics, the best means would be a strategy selectively to abstain from voting so as to serve notice to politicians that, until they come to us with a platform reasonably in conformity with the entire range of Catholic teaching, they could not expect our votes. Play hard to get and let them come courting, I argued. There are enough of us to make them earn our votes; we need not be running after one politician or another who mouths agreement with Catholic teaching on this or that issue.

Is this still our best hope of influencing American politics? Much depends, I think, on whether any of the current legal or political efforts to overturn the administration's health care mandate will succeed. If they do not, if there are not enough active and faithful Catholics to make this politically feasible, perhaps the best strategy for the Church is to forget about electoral politics entirely for the time being and simply preach the whole Gospel, both those parts that resonate with the left and those that resonate with the right. After all, was this not the mission given to the Church at her origins? At any rate, no compromise with either political bloc will serve the interests of the Church in the long run, interests ultimately indeed not of this world; her interests are the sanctification and salvation of souls.

19

What Happened in the 1960s

SOMETIME IN THE 1960s the movement or way of life that became known as the counterculture began. Though certainly related to the more political New Left, the counterculture was distinct in that it was more interested in cultural than political change. Speaking in the most general way, one can say that the burden of the counterculture's challenge to the establishment culture was that in North America and most of the Western world it had misused social organization and technology to create a civilization that was estranged from nature, both human nature and the natures of the various created things we need to live our lives and that make up our earth. Even though the counterculture gave way to the New Age, a movement less admirable in every way than its predecessor, still I think that a discussion of the connection between the counterculture and Western culture, and particularly the traditional religion of the West, Catholicism, could be useful.

Now, adherents of the counterculture usually assumed that their ideals bore absolutely no relationship with anything in Western civilization. They tended to look to the civilizations of India or to Native Americans for affinities with what they held. The defenders of contemporary Western culture, the establishment culture, agreed with that assessment. One of the strangest things, however, about any consideration of this question is that both the defenders of the establishment and the adherents to the counterculture were to a great extent mistaken about what each was committed to. Members of the establishment often loudly proclaimed that they were preserving eternal verities whereas quite often the ideals they embraced were of relatively recent origin. Capitalism is one case in point. Far from being traditional in Western culture, it was developed fairly recently on the ruins of all that is really native to our civilization.

On the other hand, although members of the counterculture assumed that the ideals they accepted were radically opposed to everything that Western culture had ever stood for, in many cases they had simply rediscovered Western traditions that had been lost or obscured for the previous one hundred or even three hundred years.

One example of this is our attitude toward nature. Since the triumph of the philosophy of René Descartes and Francis Bacon, which occurred about three hundred years ago, Western man has too often taken a ruthless, mechanistic view of nature. The earth has been seen as something not simply to be enjoyed by man but changed and twisted until it is no longer recognizable. We have not tried to work with the earth and all created natures but merely to change what is inconvenient to us. Men have imagined that any other attitude is foreign to Western civilization. They have not realized that Aristotle, who for centuries dominated Western philosophy and education, took a very different view of our relationship to nature—a view that in many ways approximates that of the counterculture. As Henry Veatch wrote in the early 1970s, when it was not yet apparent that the counterculture was about to run out of steam,

> For is it not a singular coincidence that in the confusion worse confounded of what we might call our contemporary youth culture, any number of young people today have begun to insist that they are "turned off" by the entire range of modern science and technology? Not only that, but they would not hesitate to throw out, along with science, the whole philosophical and cultural superstructure that has been erected over our increasingly frenzied and uncritical cults of science and technology as they have been developing over the last three hundred years. Now the irony is that the very rise of so-called modern science and modern philosophy was originally associated—certainly in the minds of men like Galileo and Descartes—with a determined repudiation of Aristotle: it was precisely his influence which it was thought necessary to destroy, root and branch, before what we now know as science and philosophy in the modern mode could get off the ground. Accordingly, could it be that as so many of us today are turning our backs so bitterly on all the heretofore boasted achievements of modern culture, we might find ourselves inclined, perhaps even compelled, to return to the Aristotelianism that both antedated and was considered antithetical to the whole modern experiment in knowledge and living?[1]

If the devotees of 1960s counterculture had known enough to look to their own past, they would have found a surer guide in Aristotle and his

---

1. Henry B. Veatch, *Aristotle: A Contemporary Appreciation* (Bloomington: Indiana University Press, 1974), 4.

tradition to recovering a better kind of culture than anything in the philosophies of Asia.

Many other instances of this sort could be cited, but the most interesting is the relationship of the counterculture to Catholicism, the religion that has shaped so much that is typical of Western culture. It is largely unknown that the Catholic religion and the culture it fosters exhibit striking similarities to much that characterized the counterculture. For example, in the Catholic literary and intellectual revival of the first half of the twentieth century, a number of the most famous Catholic writers, such as Hilaire Belloc, G.K. Chesterton, and Christopher Dawson, explicitly opposed industrial capitalism and recommended a return to small, craft-oriented enterprises in rural settings. E. F. Schumacher, author of *Small Is Beautiful* and a convert to Catholicism, advocated many of these same Catholic proposals in his own excellent works on economics. Another writer, Fr. Denis Fahey, was well aware years ago of the harm done to our diets by highly processed foods. Many of these writers also warned of pollution and environmental damage long before there was an organized environmental movement. In fact, the reason there was no concerted Catholic effort to influence society on these issues was because most Catholics were not Catholic enough; they were ignorant of the rich tradition of Catholic thought and the implications of their own Faith.

On another important issue, Catholic faith and tradition have always championed the concept of the organic community, bound by family and similar ties, rather than the atomistic, striving mass of individuals that modern society has created. The teaching of the Catholic Church is that there is a natural unity in society. Each person and each group have a natural part to play, and harmony will arise when each part is fulfilled. The relationship between different groups or classes must be based on a recognition that every person has needs because he is human, and the community must see to it that he is able to live in a manner worthy of a human being. The popes have specifically rejected the notion that the so-called laws of economics can ever override one's right to live with human dignity. This teaching of the Church has been updated and adapted to modern conditions, beginning with Pope Leo XIII in 1891 and continuing to the present.

In regard to specifics, the popes and other Catholic writers have advocated such things as employee-owned or managed industries, labor unions, cooperatives, the family farm, and a living wage for all workers. Catholicism also has affinities with the counterculture in areas other than economics. Most people are aware that the Catholic Church promotes natural family planning and condemns unnatural forms of birth control, a position also taken by some within the countercultural movement. In addition, however, Catholic writers have also promoted the breastfeeding of babies; even during the 1940s and 1950s, when very few mothers nursed their babies, manuals written for Catholic parents consistently recommended breastfeeding. La Leche League, the well-known organization that supports breastfeeding and a general way of life more in harmony with nature, was founded by a group of Catholic mothers and named after a shrine of the Blessed Virgin Mary in St. Augustine, Florida.

Catholicism has also always taken account of man's need for festivity and celebration. The word *holiday* comes from *holy day*; Catholic religious celebrations are both religious and festive, as can especially be seen in places such as southern Europe or Latin America, where Catholic culture has traditionally flourished. Although Catholics greatly respect Sunday, the day of the Lord's Resurrection, as a weekly holy day, we have never taken the Puritan view that it need be dour and boring. Religious services, yes, but also festivity, games, and plenty of human interaction.

It must be admitted that most Catholics are unaware of this heritage of ours and fail to live it fully. Even so, in the families and lives of many ethnic Catholics in this country, one can see an emphasis on community, manifested by large families, the extended family, and a concomitant rejection of the atomistic striving that unfortunately characterizes America and much of the modern world. Family and community first is a quite different motto from self first.

Despite these scattered survivals from our rich Catholic past, a vast project of education has to be undertaken within the Church. Catholics must be taught not only the truths of the Faith but also the implications of these truths for our lives and culture. No one should entertain illusions that this undertaking will be easy, but there is no other way we can promote the full flowering of the Faith, a faith that was meant to transform not only our personal conduct and our families but also our nations and cultures and the entire world. The job is simply to establish the social reign of Jesus Christ the King, and it is our primary task and duty after the conversion of our own lives and the salvation of our own souls.

20

Toward a Biblical Theology of History

IN MANY WAYS philosophy is about sorting things out. Philosophers, when confronted by a mass of observable or knowable facts, naturally want to order and make sense of what they perceive. Ever since the pre-Socratic philosophers attempted to account for the fact of change and of the physical composition of things, philosophy has had an honorable history as the highest exercise of pure human reason and later also as the handmaid of theology. There is one thing, however, that philosophers have attempted to understand by the light of human reason that has not yielded much success. This is the multiplicity of deeds that constitute mankind's history. Long ago Aristotle recognized that history is not very apt for philosophical understanding; unlike the fictional events described in poetry or other literature, historical events are unique and their significance is by no means apparent to us since they happen only once. "Hence poetry is something more philosophic and of graver import than history, since its statements are of the nature rather of universals, whereas those of history are singulars."[1]

However, this difficulty has not hindered either historians or philosophers from trying to use human reason to make sense of history. Thus, some ancient thinkers saw human history as an endless cycle of rise and decline, followed by more rise and decline; much later there came the first attempt, by Hegel, at creating a comprehensive philosophy of history. Sometimes the attempt is more or less a joke, as in the remark (perhaps not seriously intended) by Karl Marx that "all facts and personages of great importance in world history occur ... twice ... the first time as tragedy, the second as farce."[2] Even authors such as Oswald

1. *Poetics*, 9 (Oxford translation).
2. In "The Eighteenth Brumaire of Louis Bonaparte" (1852), in Karl Marx and Friedrich Engels, *Basic Writings on Politics and Philosophy*, ed. Lewis Feuer (Garden City, NY: Doubleday, 1959), 320.

Spengler[3] and Arnold Toynbee,[4] who constructed vast systems attempting to make sense of all of history, did little more than note certain similarities in the rise and fall of nations and cultures; but as to the final meaning of this flux, neither could say anything definite. Essentially, all these writers were simply speculating, making better or worse guesses about what, if any, pattern or meaning mankind's history offers. Human reason by its own light is simply unable to penetrate beyond the multitude of unique facts and individuals to discover their ultimate significance. Even if at times patterns can be discovered, they cannot tell us the meaning of the historical process as a whole.

To understand history, then, we must turn to its Author, that is, to God himself, the Lord of history, Who sees its beginning and its end, and Who controls events, both large and small (*Catechism of the Catholic Church* [*CCC*], nos. 269 and 302–3). Thus, we must seek not a philosophy of history but a *theology* of history, a knowledge of the meaning of man's deeds rooted not in human speculation but in divine revelation.[5] The first place we must look to discover a theology of history is in the Bible itself.

Sacred Scripture, especially the Old Testament, contains a vast historical narrative, beginning with the creation of the world and ending shortly before the Incarnation of Our Lord. Beginning at no. 55, the *Catechism of the Catholic Church* distills these historical accounts into what we may call the raw material for a theology of history. The *Catechism* sketches the history of the human race from the Fall of Adam and Eve to the Flood of Noah and its subsequent "division into many nations [which] is at once cosmic, social, and religious" (*CCC*, no. 57). It then speaks of the covenant made with Noah after the end of the Flood and the call of Abraham, whose descendants "would be the trustees of the promise made to the patriarchs, the chosen people, called to prepare for that day when God would gather all his children into the unity of the Church" (*CCC*, no. 60). This is the germ or framework of a correct understanding of history as revealed by God in His written Scriptures. To see its import we must flesh out, as it were, each of these separate parts.

---

3. *Der Untergang des Abendlandes* [The Decline of the West] (1918, 1922).

4. *A Study of History* (Oxford University Press, 1934–1961).

5. As Christopher Dawson wrote, "Hence there is no Christian 'philosophy of history' in the strict sense of the word. There is, instead, a Christian history and a Christian theology of history, and it is not too much to say that without them there would be no such thing as Christianity." "The Christian View of History," in *Dynamics of World History* (La Salle, IL: Sherwood Sugden, 1978), 234.

Before doing so, let us look at some of the general truths that we can acquire from this view of history. In the first place, this account gives us the certainty of the *unity* of human history (*CCC*, no. 360). The many different deeds of mankind are not simply so many separate actions of men in their various civilizations, with their many religions and languages, cultural achievements, and political acts, having nothing but an accidental relationship with one another. Although we do not fully understand the mysterious events that surrounded the attempt to build the Tower of Babel and mankind's subsequent "division into many nations" (*CCC*, no. 57), I suspect that if we knew more of what actually happened at Babel and immediately afterwards, we should understand more clearly the unity of the human race, not simply in that we are all descended from our first parents; we should discern better the unity of human cultures, as evidenced for example by myths that in some cases seem to contain parts of the original revelation made to Adam and Eve.[6]

Secondly, these texts assure us that history has a purpose. Apart from divine revelation we have no sure way of knowing where humanity is headed and whether the individual events or their totality have any meaning. If life on earth will simply die out when the sun grows cold, we might rightly ask what is the meaning of human achievement—of the undeniably great works of philosophy, literature, music, and architecture that mankind has produced. We might admire all this, we might admire truly saintly men and truly wise thinkers, but in the end do they signify anything? Might not all this lead a cynic to exclaim, "Then I considered all that my hands had done and the toil I had spent in doing it, and behold, all was vanity and a striving after wind, and there was nothing to be gained under the sun" (Ecclesiastes 2:11)? Revelation, however, assures us that the cynic is wrong. Human life, and thus human history, do have a purpose and will end with "the appearing of our great God and Savior Jesus Christ" (Titus 1:13), with the completion and fulfillment of the common life of mankind and of the life of each individual who is in a state of grace at the time of his death.

When we turn from these general considerations to the specific historical themes that Scripture narrates and that the Catechism notes, we see first the world from its creation until the Flood. In the Flood account humanity was again narrowed down to a few persons, the family of Noah, and had, as it were, a new beginning. Afterwards, God made

---

6. See Fr. Anthony Zimmerman, *The Primeval Revelation in Myths and in Genesis* (Lanham, MD: University Press of America, 1999); also (with reservations) Bill Cooper, *After the Flood: the Early Post-Flood History of Europe* (Chichester, England: New Wine Press, 1995).

a covenant with all of mankind, in fact repeating some of the same commands made originally to Adam and Eve.[7] But despite these signal notes of God's power and providence, the effects of original sin again asserted themselves; and in the mysterious events involving the tower of Babel, man again revolted against God and was punished this time with a confusion of tongues that brought about a dispersion throughout the earth. We must keep in mind, of course, that although these scriptural narratives recount real historical events, they do so "in simple and figurative language, adapted to the understanding of a less developed people."[8]

Even though the various nations were thus dispersed, it was God's intention that they should be governed by the covenant with Noah. "The covenant with Noah remains in force during the times of the Gentiles, until the universal proclamation of the Gospel" (*CCC*, no. 58). But as we know, this covenant was most often forgotten. Although the gentile nations did retain some notion of the moral law, in their behavior they very often descended into the darkness of idolatry and polytheism, even to the depths of human sacrifice, sexual perversion, slavery, and other kinds of political and economic oppression (*CCC*, no, 57).

While the gentiles were thus deviating from the plan and purposes of God, He was preparing an even greater work that began with the call of Abraham and was to lead to the Incarnation of God himself into the human race. "In order to gather together scattered humanity God calls Abram from his country, his kindred, and his father's house, and makes him Abraham, that is, 'the father of a multitude of nations'" (*CCC*, no. 59). "The people descended from Abraham would be the trustees of the promise made to the patriarchs. . . . They would be the root onto which the Gentiles would be grafted, once they came to believe" (*CCC*, no. 60).

The Old Testament, especially the historical and prophetic books, are mostly the record of this special relationship of God with the chosen people, of the repeated infidelities of the Jews and of God's many efforts to recall them to the covenant by means of the prophets, righteous kings, and even national disasters and conquests, culminating in the Babylonian exile. The Old Testament, however, also contains another theme, that of the bringing of the worship of the one true God to the gentile nations, to the ends of the earth, in fact.

The prophecies of the Anointed One or Messiah and His connection with the gentiles form one of the most interesting and astonishing

---

7. *Catechism of the Catholic Church*, no. 56. Genesis 8:20–9:17.

8. Response of the Pontifical Biblical Commission to Emmanuel Cardinal Suhard, Archbishop of Paris, concerning the time of documents of the Pentateuch and concerning the literary form of the [first] eleven chapters of Genesis; January 16, 1948.

motifs of the Old Testament. Even from the beginning with Abraham's call (Genesis 12:1–3), the rest of mankind is seen as an integral part of Abraham's vocation—"in you all the families of the earth shall be blessed." This becomes increasingly clear as the figure of the Messiah is more clearly adumbrated until in the prophets, especially Isaiah, and in some of the Psalms it becomes evident that in some manner the gentiles are to share in the covenant and worship of the God of Israel, Who is proclaimed as the one true God of the entire earth.[9] The gentile nations, however, are not to be incorporated into the Israel of the old covenant; rather, Israel herself is to be transformed into a community not based on race or ancestry but open to all: the Catholic Church, which is the New Israel. The task of this new community is to bring the Gospel of Jesus Christ to all the nations, thus fulfilling the prophecies made under the old covenant by making the God of Israel known to all peoples.

While God was forming and fostering the people of Israel, He was also preparing in various ways the rest of the human race for the preaching of the Gospel. St. Paul's words to the Athenians (Acts 17:22–31) make clear that amidst the poetry and myths of the gentiles there was some dim knowledge of the one true God. This was the case generally throughout the world; however, in one particular and special case, God used a gentile people to aid in the spread of the Gospel.

Although most of the human race had fallen into various systems of philosophical and intellectual error, there was one partial exception, doubtless caused by an exceptional divine grace that served as a preparation for the preaching of the Gospel and for the Church and her theology. God established among the Greeks alone a knowledge of philosophy, properly speaking, against the time when His revelation to mankind was to be universalized and leave the particularizing framework of Hebrew thought.

> In *Greece*, alone in the ancient world, the wisdom of man found the right path, and as the result of a fortunate harmony of the soul's powers and of a long effort to achieve mental order and discipline human reason attained its full vigour and maturity. In consequence, the small Hellenic race appears among the great empires of the East like a man amidst gigantic children, and may be truly termed the organ of the reason and word of man as the Jewish people was the organ of the revelation and word of God.[10]

---

9. Some of the most striking passages in this respect are Isaiah 11:10, 45:20–23, 56:6–8, and Malachi 1:11.

10. Jacques Maritain, *An Introduction to Philosophy* (London: Sheed and Ward, 1947), 33.

The proximity of Greece to Palestine meant that, even before the Incarnation, there would begin a fruitful contact between divine revelation and Greek culture, for example in the Septuagint—the Greek translation of the Old Testament—and throughout the Mediterranean world where many Jews were dispersed.[11]

When Our Lord founded His Church and the Apostles began to bring the Gospel to gentiles, there soon arose a need for a new intellectual framework by means of which this new knowledge of God could be expressed. And here Greek philosophy stood ready to be a handmaid to Christian thought, supplying terms, such as *person* and *substance*, that the Hebrew intellectual tradition had not possessed. As theology developed, the Church made increasing use of philosophy both to articulate that theology and to refute the multitude of errors and heresies that arose.

This union of divine revelation and classical Greek and Roman thought gave shape to European or Western culture, which was the first culture to be thoroughly conquered and permeated by the Faith.[12] Then, from this homeland of the Church, Catholics have carried the Gospel throughout the world. It was evidently part of God's plan that the Faith be incarnated first in Europe and the surrounding lands and there achieve a certain intellectual and cultural expression and stability. Although by no means is all of this European expression universal, important parts of it are; for the theology and philosophy of the Church that grew up in Europe can never be replaced or regarded as Western impositions. They are universal because they deal with realities that are the same for all nations, such as the one true God or the essential nature of man. Even the Latin language is rightly seen as more than a European cultural expression and, in the use the Church has made of it, a truly universal means of communication and of theological and philosophical investigation.

Our Lord referred to the period between the establishment of the Church and the last days as "the times of the Gentiles" (Luke 21:24). This is the period we are now in (*CCC*, nos. 672–74). We cannot be certain how much of it remains, but the task of the Church during this time is essentially the same. "The Christian economy, therefore, since it is the new and definitive Covenant, will never pass away; and no new public

---

11. See the interesting example of such a direct interaction in Wisdom 8:7, where the four cardinal virtues of the Greeks are enumerated.

12. Although we speak of European culture, we should always remember that even in its earliest times, Western thought was not confined to Europe. Many of the early Fathers and ecclesiastical writers lived and worked in Africa or Asia, and much later Catholic European life would be carried to Latin America and elsewhere.

revelation is to be expected before the glorious manifestation of Our Lord Jesus Christ" (*CCC*, no. 66). Thus, the Church's mission today is the same one she received from Christ just before His Ascension: "Go therefore and make disciples of all nations, baptizing them in the name of the Father and of the Son and of the Holy Spirit, teaching them to observe all that I have commanded you" (Matthew 28:19–20a).

Unfortunately, as we all know, throughout what was once Christendom apostasy and unbelief are the rule more than the exception. Especially is this the case in Europe, the formative homeland of the Faith. But Catholics should never cease trying to carry out the command of Jesus Christ quoted above from Matthew 28, preaching the whole Gospel to every nation despite unfavorable circumstances and the disdain and hatred of the world. We cannot simply allow ourselves to be ranked, along with the other world religions, as one among many spiritual presences in the world, one more attempt on the part of mankind to grasp and express divine truth; for the Catholic faith is not a human guessing game, but a revelation from God, the Creator of all things. A certain boldness in preaching the Gospel is never unsuitable for the Church of Jesus Christ, a boldness that should characterize her witness until the end of the age.

Sooner or later, however, "the times of the Gentiles [will be] fulfilled" (Luke 21:24). Then we shall have the real end of history, the return of Jesus Christ to judge the living and the dead. This is the point toward which everything has been tending since the Fall of our first parents.

> The kingdom will be fulfilled, then, not by a historic triumph of the Church through a progressive ascendancy, but only by God's victory over the final unleashing of evil, which will cause his Bride to come down from heaven. God's triumph over the revolt of evil will take the form of the Last Judgment after the final cosmic upheaval of this passing world. (*CCC*, no. 677)

As we know, these final days and this final triumph are described mystically and allegorically in the biblical book of the Apocalypse (Revelation).

The course of human history, from the first Adam to the final return of the new Adam, Jesus Christ, is a history with cosmic significance in that the

> creation waits with eager longing for the revealing of the sons of God.... We know that the whole creation has been groaning in travail together until now; and not only the creation, but we ourselves, who have the first fruits of the Spirit, groan inwardly as we wait for adoption as sons, the redemption of our bodies. (Romans 8:19–23)

Although sin and redemption have consequences for all of creation, it is only free beings—angels and men—who can sin. "In the presence of Christ, who is truth itself, the truth of each man's relationship with God will be laid bare. The Last Judgment will reveal even to its furthest consequences the good each person has done or failed to do during his earthly life" (*CCC*, no. 1039). Thus the *end*, the purpose of history, is outside of the present world-system altogether. The destiny of mankind as a whole is eternal life with God; but that, of course, does not guarantee that each and every man will attain to this destiny. "We cannot be united with God unless we freely choose to love him. But we cannot love God if we sin gravely against him, against our neighbor or against ourselves" (*CCC*, no. 1033). Thus, the edifice of human accomplishments which seems so solid on this earth will vanish, and the fate of each individual will be either heaven or hell. Even though the present system continues on with impressive and oppressive regularity, it is held in being only by the will of God. When it ends, all will see that the history of the human race was a journey toward God and that whatever of goodness was accomplished will be preserved and transformed.

> "When we have spread on earth the fruits of our nature and our enterprise ... according to the command of the Lord and in his Spirit, we will find them once again, cleansed this time from the stain of sin, illuminated and transfigured, when Christ presents to this Father an eternal and universal kingdom." God will then be "all in all" in eternal life. (*CCC*, no. 1050)

21

The Apostasy of the Gentiles

The Sea of Faith
Was once, too, at the full, and round earth's shore
Lay like the folds of a bright girdle furled.
But now I only hear
Its melancholy, long, withdrawing roar...
    —Matthew Arnold, "Dover Beach"

THE PHRASE "the apostasy of the gentiles" was coined by two out-standing nineteenth-century converts to the Catholic faith from Juda-ism: the twin brothers Auguste and Joseph Lemann. In response to the general secularization of European thought and life in the decades after the French Revolution and the falling away of so many from the Faith, they recalled the words of St. Paul in 2 Thessalonians that the return of Christ would not occur "unless the apostasy[1] comes first" (2:3) and in Romans that "a hardening has come upon part of Israel, until the full number of the gentiles come in, and so all Israel will be saved" (11:25–26). Thus, if the European world was falling away from the Faith, per-haps "the times of the Gentiles" (Luke 21:24) was coming to an end. The *Roman Catechism* had already told us that "the general judgment will be preceded by these three principal signs: the preaching of the Gospel throughout the world, a falling away from the faith, and the coming of the Antichrist."[2] It is to the second of these three signs that I wish to

---

1. Some translations render this as rebellion. However, the Greek word is *apostasia*, and thus apostasy seems like a fitting translation. The Vulgate uses the word *discessio*, a falling away.

2. *Catechism of the Council of Trent*, trans. John A. McHugh and Charles J. Callan (Rockford, IL: TAN Books and Publishers, 1982), 84. St. Thomas Aquinas, in his *Commentary on the Epistle to the Thessalonians*, caput 2, lectio 1, echoes this same teaching of St. Paul. See also the *Catechism of the Catholic Church*, nos. 674–75.

turn my attention in this essay; for it seems to me, however close we may or may not be to the second coming of Jesus Christ, that the process of the "apostasy of the gentiles" has begun and is well under way. That is, the loss of faith among the peoples who once constituted Christendom is well advanced, and there is reason to think that this is part of the "falling away from the faith" that will precede the return of Christ. This apostasy, however, is gradual and has taken place in stages. It has been going on for nearly half a millennium. It would be rash to predict that we are close to its finish. But the process has definitely begun. We are winding down to the second coming, whether that event will take place one hundred or five hundred years hence. Thus, without committing myself to any particular view of the exact circumstances preceding the end of the world and the return of Jesus Christ, much less to a timetable for these events, I shall describe the gradual secularization of life in what was once Christendom up to our own day, when it seems as if those ominous words of Our Lord can be fully applied, "Nevertheless, when the Son of man comes, will he find faith on earth?" (Luke 18:8).

The apostasy of the gentiles, though it has certainly picked up speed in recent decades, can hardly be dated from any time except the late Middle Ages. Since that time there has been an ongoing process, sometimes gradual, sometimes swift, of apostasy from the Christian faith and social order as established by the Church of Christ, the Catholic Church.

In the first place, in order to understand the genesis of this decline, we must look at what the Church had laboriously brought about in Europe through the work of many centuries. Europe at the height of the Middle Ages consisted not only of many Catholics—persons individually committed to the Catholic Faith and, to one degree or another, living that Faith—but also of a Catholic social order, or Christendom. The societies, laws, institutions, and customs of that social order were, at least in intent, Catholic. Instead of the situation we have today, in which Catholics must attempt to live Catholic lives within the public forms of an anti-Catholic society, Catholics in that age, as is natural, transformed the social order to reflect Catholic truth. Today in Europe, despite the presence of a few vestiges of public Catholicism, the real and active political and social forces, especially those of the European Union, are actively hostile to the Faith; in the United States the political order has always formally prescinded from any concern with religion, while social life has been shaped by Protestantism, and lately by secularism.[3] Both of

---

3. Although in the decades after the American Revolution several of the individual States had Protestant ecclesiastical establishments, the general tenor of American thought

these ways of life are unnatural for Catholics. It is true that in some countries of Latin America there are public manifestations of the Faith, such as laws against divorce or abortion or even laws giving a special place to the Catholic faith in the life of the nation; but all this is being swiftly undermined by hostile forces, both secular and Protestant.

After the Catholic social order had reached its zenith during the twelfth and thirteenth centuries, it curiously and suddenly began to decline. Christopher Dawson wrote of it as follows:

> The fourteenth century was an age of division and strife, the age of the Great Schism, which saw instead of the Crusades the invasion of Europe by the Turks and the devastation of France by England. And at the same time the intellectual resources of Western society which had been so much strengthened by the extension of the university movement no longer assisted the integration of Christian thought but were used negatively and critically to undo the work of the previous century and undermine the intellectual foundations on which the synthesis of the great thinkers of the previous age had been built. It is as though the spiritual tide which had been steadily making for unity for three centuries had suddenly turned, so that everywhere in every aspect of life the forces that made for division and dissolution were predominant.[4]

Thus, the long effort toward building a Christian society quickly began to collapse. We are familiar with many of the landmarks of this collapse: the Great Western Schism; the Protestant revolt; the Thirty Years War; the French Revolution; the seizure of Rome and the Papal States by the Piedmontese in the 1860s; the strange internal situation of the Church since the mid 1960s, a situation brought about almost entirely by self-inflicted wounds; the current acceptance in most countries of the grossest sexual immorality as normal and healthy, with legal abortion as a convenient method of getting rid of the inconvenient results of unchastity. What I wish to call attention to, however, is the way that the apostasy of the gentiles has dechristianized, one at a time, specific sectors of our culture, so that until recent decades many people hardly realized what was going on. Thus, the intellectual, political, and economic sectors or aspects of the Christian world were secularized long before the current crises in Church and society, and these earlier efforts made it all the easier for the anti-Catholic forces to gain their current victories.

---

was that religion was a purely private matter. These State churches, at least by the early decades of the nineteenth century, did not represent serious efforts to create Christian political orders.

4. Christopher Dawson, *Religion and the Rise of Western Culture* (New York: Sheed & Ward, 1950), 238–39.

In the passage I quoted above, Christopher Dawson mentions that

the intellectual resources of Western society which had been so much strengthened by the extension of the university movement no longer assisted the integration of Christian thought but were used negatively and critically to undo the work of the previous century and undermine the intellectual foundations on which the synthesis of the great thinkers of the previous age had been built.

Today, we practically take for granted the notion that most highly educated people and intellectuals will be hostile to the Faith and to Christian morals. But what an abnormal state of affairs this really is! Above all, those who spend their lives in study and investigation of truth should exhibit a love of revealed truths as much as of natural truths. There is no enmity between learning and Christian faith, no hostility between the intellectual life and the spiritual life. In fact, however, this aspect of life and culture was one of the first to show signs of secularization and hostility to Catholicism.

Already, only fifty years after the death of St. Thomas Aquinas, Christendom was beginning to suffer from the failure of its thinkers to rally to his thought, and most of all from their failure to accept its supreme practical achievement, the harmony he discerned between the spheres of knowledge naturally known and of that which we know supernaturally, the true character of the relations between reason and faith. The story of philosophy among Catholics in these fifty years is, in that respect, one of steady deterioration.[5]

The chief cause of this was the rise of nominalism, the philosophical doctrine that restricted our knowledge to individual things. This doctrine eventually led to contemporary unbelief. In the next age, we behold thinkers openly skeptical of the Faith, and by the nineteenth century it can be taken for granted that most of the intellectual life of the Western world is no longer Catholic.

This effective dechristianization of European intellectual life has been chiefly responsible for the myth that religious faith is necessarily an enemy of learning or thinking. Today most people unreflectively assume that someone of high intelligence or learning will not hold orthodox religious doctrines. Although as a matter of fact there are many examples of intelligent and learned persons who are orthodox Catholics, the general impression created by the popular media is that such persons do not exist. The atmosphere in most institutions of higher learning is

5. Philip Hughes, *A History of the Church*, vol. 3 (New York: Sheed & Ward, 1947), 112–13.

unrelentingly irreligious. Hence, many people can simply ignore religion—after all, they might say, no intelligent person could possibly believe all that, so why bother to investigate it?

Until fairly recently many people were sufficiently removed from the intellectual life of their societies that they might ignore, and even be largely unaware of, these pervasive irreligious attitudes. Most people did not attend college or university, nor did they read the books and periodicals in which the intelligentsia discussed their ideas. Nevertheless, they were profoundly influenced by them. As Leo XIII pointed out in his encyclical *Aeterni Patris,*

> Whoever turns his attention to the bitter strifes of these days and seeks a reason for the troubles that vex public and private life must come to the conclusion that a fruitful cause of the evils which now afflict, as well as those which threaten, us lies in this: that false conclusions concerning divine and human things, which originated in the schools of philosophy, have now crept into all the orders of the State, and have been accepted by the common consent of the masses. For, since it is in the very nature of man to follow the guide of reason in his actions, if his intellect sins at all his will soon follows; and thus it happens that false opinions, whose seat is in the understanding, influence human actions and pervert them. (no. 2)

Thus, even those who might never have read a learned book or article were affected. A good example is Freud. Although few people have actually read him, who in ordinary conversation has not talked about complexes, repression, the unconscious, and so on? Who has not heard of "paradigm shifts" though never having read Thomas Kuhn? This situation has existed since the advent in the late eighteenth century of mass literacy and widely diffused reading matter. The secularization of the Western mind began with a segment of the intellectuals but has now gradually conquered the minds of most people. Even in the United States, where belief in God and adherence to religion is more widespread than in Europe, most churchgoers *think* in essentially secular categories. Thus, the rejection of universals by the nominalists in the fourteenth-century universities has led to the rejection of the supernatural in twenty-first-century mass society.

After the beginnings of de-Christianization in the intellectual sector, it was the political sector that next experienced secularization.

> [The] new approach to history was one of the main factors in the secularization of European culture, since the idealization of the ancient state and especially of republican Rome influenced men's attitude to the contemporary state. The Italian city state and the kingdoms of the

West of Europe were no longer regarded as organic members of the Christian community, but as ends in themselves which acknowledged no higher sanction than the will to power. During the Middle Ages the state as an autonomous self-sufficient power structure did not exist.... But from the fifteenth century onwards the history of Europe has been increasingly the history of the development of a limited number of sovereign states as independent power centres and of the ceaseless rivalry and conflict between them. The true nature of this development was disguised by the religious prestige which still surrounded the person of the ruler and which was actually increased during the age of the Reformation by the union of the Church with the state and its subordination to the royal supremacy.[6]

In fact, the increased "religious prestige" associated with the monarch in the sixteenth and seventeenth centuries, as embodied in the largely Protestant doctrine of the Divine Right of Kings, while it did not seem to shake the medieval notion that civil governments ruled in the name of God and by His authority, paradoxically led directly to the downfall of medieval political ideals. The theory of the Divine Right held that God had designated one particular individual or family to rule, in contrast to the more flexible medieval notion that, although there were many ways by which a king could come to power, once legitimately in power, whatever authority he had came from God. Moreover, the Renaissance doctrine of the Divine Right typically excluded the people from all say in government. Thus, medieval assemblies, which had sometimes forced monarchs to temper their power, very often ceased to meet after the sixteenth or early seventeenth centuries; and monarchs held nearly absolute power, something few medieval rulers ever did. When the inevitable reaction to this one-sided doctrine came, as it did in the English Revolution of 1688 and the French Revolution of 1789, it swept away all vestiges of divine kingship, both legitimate and illegitimate, and made governments simply dependent on the will of the people, with no place for God. St. Paul's dictum, "there is no authority except from God, and those that exist have been instituted by God" (Romans 13:1), was now seen as a quaint doctrine of past times. The state was no longer from God and thus not bound by the laws of God. Expediency was king, and to subject the state to the moral law was considered hopelessly naive and weak-minded. As Secretary of War Henry Stimson made clear in his article, "The Decision to Use the

---

6. Christopher Dawson, "The Christian View of History," in *Dynamics of World History*, 245–46.

Atomic Bomb,"[7] moral considerations entered into this decision very little, if at all. The means were chosen to accomplish the end desired. Indeed, how could the means have been blamed by those who had already sanctioned aerial attacks, which, as Stimson said, had

> been more destructive of life and property than the very limited number of atomic raids which we could have executed.... In March 1945 our Air Force had launched its first great incendiary raid on the Tokyo area. In this raid more damage was done and more casualties were inflicted than was the case at Hiroshima.

Of course, this had been done previously in Europe, and the United States was by no means the only guilty country. The point is that this insouciance shows the degree to which the state had come to see itself as divorced from God. Leo XIII in his encyclical *Libertas* (1888) made it clear that states, as much as individuals, are bound by the moral law:

> There are others, somewhat more moderate though not more consistent, who affirm that the morality of individuals is to be guided by the divine law, but not the morality of the State, so that in public affairs the commands of God may be passed over.... But the absurdity of such a position is manifest. (no. 18)

If each human being is bound by the law of God, how could that law cease to bind us when we undertake action in concert? In any case, regardless of the type of government, monarchy or republic, those who rule receive their authority ultimately from God; and since God cannot be the author of sin, they too may never command or authorize sin.

After the political, the next area of human life to become divorced from God and the moral law was the economic realm. Before the sixteenth century, however much individual Catholics may have sinned, the economic order itself was conceived as an expression of divine order in the world. That is, its purpose was to provide mankind with the material goods we obviously need, but the notion of individual enrichment was limited in accordance with the well-known admonitions of Sacred Scripture about the dangers of riches.[8] The medieval attitude can be briefly summed up in this passage from Bede Jarrett's *Social Theories of the Middle Ages, 1200–1500*:

> We can, therefore, lay down as the first principle of mediaeval economics that there was a limit to money-making imposed by the purpose for which the money was made. Each worker had to keep in front

7. *Harper's Magazine*, February 1947.
8. For example, Proverbs 23:4; Micah 6:12a; Matthew 19:24; Luke 1:53b; 1 Timothy 6:6–10; James 5:1–3a.

of himself the aim of his life and consider the acquiring of money as a means only to an end, which at one and the same time justified and limited him. When, therefore, sufficiency had been obtained there could be no reason for continuing further efforts at getting rich, ... except in order to help others. ...[9]

Although the desire for individual gain was held in check by the monarchies of the Baroque era, who sought to orient all economic activity toward royal and national aggrandizement, in the eighteenth century this system too broke down; the way was now open for the frank acceptance of economic motives. What St. Paul had once called "the root of all evils" now became the mainspring of the economy. Thus, in our own day the state of economic life can be summed up in the words of Pius XI's encyclical *Quadragesimo Anno* (1931):

> In the first place, then, it is patent that in our days not alone is wealth accumulated, but immense power and despotic economic domination is concentrated in the hands of a few, and that those few are frequently not the owners, but only the trustees and directors of invested funds, who administer them at their good pleasure. (no. 105)
>
> This power becomes particularly irresistible when exercised by those who, because they hold and control money, are able also to govern credit and determine its allotment, for that reason supplying so to speak, the life-blood to the entire economic body, and grasping, as it were, in their hands the very soul of the economy, so that no one dare breathe against their will. (no. 106)
>
> This accumulation of power, a characteristic note of the modern economic order, is a natural result of unrestrained free competition which permits the survival of those only who are the strongest. This often means those who fight most relentlessly, who pay least heed to the dictates of conscience. (no. 107)

Even though this was written at the height of the 1929 depression, with few changes it can serve nevertheless as a description of our economy today, where principles of restraint are not only rarely adhered to but are usually denied in theory.

In other words, the reason for the existence of external goods is generally forgotten, as is also the fact that the inordinate desire for money, like the inordinate desire for sexual pleasure, is one of the chief means whereby a soul can turn away from God. We no longer ask ourselves whether perhaps our houses or our cars are not already big enough, or

---

9. (Westminster, MD: Newman, 1942), 157–58. The entire chapter on money-making runs from pages 150–180. Numerous similar quotations could be taken from the works of Belloc, Dawson, Tawney, and other historians of medieval economics.

whether we truly need more new clothes or more gadgets. The whole order of production and acquisition of material goods has become divorced from a Christian conscience. Advertising exists to incite us to buy, whether we need something or not; and credit often exists to enable us to buy it, whether we can afford it or not. But the fact is, many Christians are hardly aware that this is a secularized way of looking at things. The attitudes of our medieval fathers are unknown to us. As Fr. John Cronin wrote in 1950, ". . . sermons on greed, avarice, selfishness in business matters, unwarranted ambition, and unsocial conduct are as rare today as they were common in medieval times."[10] Man's economic activity is now conducted as if God did not exist.

The economic development of modernity promoted and accompanied a corresponding technological development, which we are coming to see has not been an unmixed blessing for mankind. The health of our physical environment is not something that a Catholic can blithely ignore, and its present condition in many respects increases our legitimate fear that we are approaching the return of Our Lord.

Lastly, in this age of economic globalization, we should note the character of Babylon as described by St. John in the last book of the New Testament. As Christopher Dawson noted,

> This is the significance of the judgment of Babylon, which appears in the Apocalypse not as a conquering military power as in the earlier prophets, but as the embodiment of material civilization and luxury, the great harlot, whose charms bewitch all the nations of the earth; the world market whose trade enriches the merchants and the shipowners.[11]

Such a world market is now not only the ideal that so many strive for but, to a great degree, is also a reality that already profoundly affects life in almost every country.

The human arts, especially those called the fine arts, have been used in the service of God and for other legitimate human ends for many centuries. But in our time these arts have also, to a great degree, become aspects of mankind's apostasy from God. Art, like economic activity, is now seen as necessarily free from all restraint of morality. In great part this is because the artist no longer works to support a function, such as composing music for use in the Church, but works simply for whatever ends he proposes to himself, supported by private patrons or govern-

---

10. *Catholic Social Principles: the Social Teaching of the Catholic Church Applied to American Economic Life* (Milwaukee: Bruce Publishing, 1950), 45.

11. "History and the Christian Revelation," in *Dynamics of World History*, 254.

ment funds. The arts no longer have a social context. Governments have always supported the arts, but in the past they did so to promote useful works, things to adorn public life. Most importantly, in the past those who paid the bills considered themselves entitled to judge the artist's work. Now, in what has become a process of self-judgment, only the artists themselves and the "arts community" are held to be capable of passing judgment on any piece of art. So, no matter how destructive of public morals works of art may be, or how absurd in themselves, those who are not part of the "arts community" are loudly told to shut up, mind their own business, and hand over the check. But of course this is a real perversion of the function of art and the place of the artist, who ought to work to beautify and adorn human life and civilization, including above all, the worship of God. The eighteenth century saw the beginnings of the emancipation of the artist from all social and religious context and control, so that in our own day obscenity will be defended so long as it can pass itself off as art. Just as sexual activity entirely divorced from its procreative purpose produces perversion, so the arts, removed from their social purpose, likewise produce perversion.

All these secularizing movements—the political, the economic, the artistic—could at one time often be ignored by the average man, because he did not encounter them directly in his own life; but this is no longer the case. Now in our time the process of secularization has progressed to such a point that it is impossible for anyone with a modicum of Christian conscience to ignore it. This is so because it has intruded into the most personal and intimate areas of human life: into marriage and the family, into our very bodies. Already in the nineteenth century, marriage was an issue that set the Church at odds with the world. In the *Syllabus of Errors* of 1864 Blessed Pius IX devoted an entire section (nos. 65 through 74) to marriage questions. Here the Pontiff was concerned chiefly with the indissolubility of marriage and with civil versus Catholic marriage, showing that the attack on the family goes back at least to the nineteenth century. With our time it has taken on a new virulence. Certainly divorce has reached levels that Pius IX could never foresee. In addition, owing to the availability of technology, we have such barbarities as more effective methods of contraception and abortion, freezing of embryos, embryonic stem-cell harvesting, the possibility of human cloning, and the like. We also have the widespread acceptance of homosexual conduct as normal for human beings. It is now clear that mankind's very existence and nature are being threatened. Can human apostasy and rebellion from the divine plan go further than this? It seems that man's apostasy has now invaded every segment of human life and culture: the intellectual (which was a necessary prelude to all the rest), the political, the economic, the artistic, and now the personal. At this point do we await anything more than the further consolidation of Satan's rule over this world before we see the remaining signs of Our Lord's return?

There is one more affliction, however, with which mankind has been visited. This is the internal situation in the Catholic Church since the mid-1960s. Although it is true that the everyday life of Catholics had been growing more secularized since at least the nineteenth century and that Pius XI had lamented the loss to the Church in that century of the working class, intellectually the Church remained firm in her opposition to modernity; and millions of faithful, supported by a reasonably solid liturgical and spiritual life, lived as practical Catholics. Within the Church, bishops, theologians, and intellectuals promoted a vision of life at variance with that of the apostasy from the Christian social order. The Church was even able to renew herself both spiritually and intellectually after the French Revolution and seemed to enter the twentieth century largely intact despite the crisis of modernism at the turn of the century. There were even attempts to create a Catholic life not just for individuals and families but also for whole societies. But the life and discipline of the Church suddenly collapsed. It was as if a grace had been withdrawn, so that men who before had upheld both piety and common sense now began to talk and act both impiously and nonsensically. The confusion and apostasy within the Church allowed civil society itself to degenerate further. In the United States, for example, would the Supreme Court have dared to permit abortion if the Church had maintained her internal discipline and been willing to boldly confront evils, including lukewarm Catholic politicians? Of course one evil always spawns another, and the various cultural sectors that one by one had become secularized since the late Middle Ages all interacted and influenced each other in ways that I do not have space to describe here.

"The preaching of the Gospel throughout the world, a falling away from the faith, and the coming of the Antichrist"—with these words the *Roman Catechism* tells us to look for the end of the world and the return of our Savior. The Gospel has certainly been preached in most of the world. The falling away from the Faith (apostasy) has destroyed not only Christendom as a civilization but also in our time the faith of millions of Catholics. Although I think that both of these two signs will exhibit further development, may we nevertheless think that, as these signs run their course, it is the third sign that we must now expect? As I said, I am setting forth no timetable. It may be hundreds of years. All I am arguing is that the process has begun and that we know what its conclusion will be.

I must deal briefly with an opposing theory, one brought forward by Prof. Philip Jenkins in his book, *The Next Christendom: The Coming of Global Christianity*.[12] Jenkins argues that the locus of Christianity has shifted from the north—Europe and North America—to the south and that we can expect a new Christendom to be built there. But there are several difficulties with Jenkins's thesis. First, many of what he considers hopeful signs must appear to a Catholic as the very opposite, such as the proliferation of sects in Latin America or some Catholic churches having "[m]illet and corn replace wheat in the host, while wine is made from palm or banana" so that "the Eucharist [becomes] a genuine banquet . . . rather than an imported symbolic affair."[13] The flourishing of sects in Africa and Latin America by no means argues for the triumph of the Church of Christ there. Moreover, reports of various sexual scandals among some African priests seem to indicate that they too are beset by difficulties similar to those which afflict the clergy of North America and Europe.[14] And even more to be deplored are examples of heresies and false doctrine in these local churches, such as those of Fr. Tissa Balasuriya of Sri Lanka[15] and the excessive politicization of religion by some varieties of liberation theology in Latin America. Without belittling the achievements of our brethren in those places, we may well ask ourselves if we can really expect a regeneration of the whole Church from the southern continents. Moreover, for a Catholic, Latin America is an old Christian land and can hardly be considered as part of a "new Christendom." In fact, it was part of Christendom well before North America was.

If my argument here is generally sound, we are in the midst of a process foretold long ago by Our Lord, of the gradual loss of the Faith, of that public faith that produced Christian civilization, and now of that private faith that produces Christian families and Christian men and women. Our task, however, is still the same wherever we may be in this process. To preach the Gospel, to do penance and reform our own lives, to create whatever institutions and structures to promote Catholic civilization that God will allow and bless. For the rest, we must simply await Him.

12. (New York: Oxford University Press, 2002).

13. Ibid., 115.

14. For example, see *Guardian Unlimited*, March 21, 2001, "Catholic Priests Abusing Nuns for Sex," http://www.theguardian.com/world/2001/mar/21/philipwillan.

15. He was the subject of a Notification by the Congregation for the Doctrine of the Faith in 1997 for "statements incompatible with the faith of the Church regarding the doctrine of revelation and its transmission, Christology, soteriology and Mariology."

23891899R00124

Made in the USA
San Bernardino, CA
04 September 2015